FROM THE HEARTS OF MEN

FROM THE HEARTS OF MEN

YEVRAH ORNSTEIN

Fawcett Columbine - New York

A Fawcett Columbine Book
Published by Ballantine Books
Copyright © 1991 by Yevrah Ornstein

Previously published material used by permission, sources are listed in the notes at the back of the book. This edition published by arrangement with Harmonia Press.

Library of Congress Catalog Card Number: 92-72932

ISBN: 0-449-90775-9

Cover design by James R. Harris
Cover photograph by Slobodan Dan Paich

Manufactured in the United States of America
First Ballantine Books Edition: September 1992
10 9 8 7 6 5 4 3 2 1

*In loving memory
of my dear Father
David Ornstein*

This book and my life honor the spirit he embodied.

And

to Savannah –
thank you my little bundle of joy
for opening my heart
to the gift of unconditional love

❄ ❄ ❄

May the good Lord be with you
down every road you roam

And may sunshine and happiness
surround you when you're far from home

And may you grow to be
proud, dignified and true

And do unto others
as you'd have done to you

Be courageous and be brave
and in my heart you'll always stay
Forever Young.

May good fortune be with you
may your guiding light be strong

Build a stairway to Heaven
with a prince or a vagabond

And may you never love in vain
and in my heart you will remain
Forever Young.

(continued . . .)

And when you finally fly away
I'll be hoping that I served you well

For all the wisdom of a lifetime
No one can ever tell

But whatever road you chose
I'm right behind you
win or lose.
Forever Young.

Forever Young
Rod Stewart

Acknowledgments

To *all* the writers/contributors who have given from their hearts and guts with courage and generosity. To my parents for their loving support, vulnerability and encouragement for me to tell my story as I have. To Bob Trowbridge for his multidimensional participation, presence and caring. To Colin Ingram; master literary samurai, who helped work these ingredients into a coherent book, with expertise, wisdom and humor. To Robert Bly, for opening the door with passion and honesty. To Susan Pinkerton; for her artistry, perpetual delight, and friendship. To the *Spirit of Men*, the world over . . . and most of all, to my daughter Savannah who has rekindled the flame within, and brought my inner child back to life in ways I could never have imagined.

CONTENTS

CHAPTER XIV THE NEW FATHERS

CHAPTER XV RITES OF PASSAGE

If my heart could do my thinking
and my head begin to feel
I would look upon the world anew
and know what's truly real.

Van Morrison

FROM THE
HEARTS
OF MEN

Preface

"*Today, lonely for my father . . .*" is the exquisite beginning of a poem written by Robert Bly. The poem is a lament for a relationship that never was. I first heard Robert recite this poem at a men's retreat attended by 90 men in 1983. It was the third day of the retreat and we had all gone through a great deal by then. Emotions were raw as we uncovered much that had been buried for so long.

We spoke of the clarion call of male initiation – "Be a man" – that has echoed through our insides from Day One of our lives. How could we know in our tender years, that the voices that cajoled and beckoned us into manhood were all too often pained and damaged themselves. The culmination of generations of individuals divorcing themselves from life's spiritual meaning and value fulfillment had come to rest upon each one of our shores. Rather than a comforting origin where heart and mind enhanced each other, we came into a world where feelings and thoughts are antagonistically poised and pitted, one against the other.

Narrow notions of masculinity are held high while other facets of manhood are laid aside, sometimes with contempt – often in ignorance. We grew up accepting, believing and not knowing differently. We limped into manhood, imprisoned and molded by a feeling-self that grieved for expression and respect. These parts of our being had been conditioned into non-feeling, into "appropriate manliness."

But deep down, we knew better, and that awareness together with the realities and disappointments of our lives, brought us together in this retreat to revive something from our distant past – awakening that which had slumbered for too long.

So Robert recites the words and plays his dulcimer, and 90 men drop into enormous sadness – together – as the inescapable truth confronts us as never before. Our choices were laid bare; we could retreat into numbness and denial once again, or this time, feel the grief and anger we secretly carried within our hearts and souls.

This time, 90 casualties said – *no more!*

There comes a time when the pain of denying feelings becomes so great that another choice has to be made. And I, with many of my brothers that day, chose to feel, and to share, the enormous grief that was upon us.

❊   ❊   ❊

The Men's Journal evolved as a vehicle for sharing feelings. As publisher, I received articles and poetry from men all over the country. The format of the *Journal* was primarily autobiographical; men sharing and revealing their stories in deeply personal and passionately honest ways.

The following statement from the cover of *The Men's Journal* tells our purpose.

It is the hope and desire of *The Men's Journal* to contribute to the empowerment of men; to engender a feeling of confidence as new images of maleness emerge. Such empowerment, we believe, does not come through the external trappings of power but through a deep knowledge and feeling experience of the inner man. We realize there is no "correct" way to be a man in this culture – each man is different; each must find his own way – and we are committed to exploring through our own lives the rich possibilities for being a man in the 1990's and beyond.

The words from the *Journal* flow from the hearts, minds, and souls of its authors. They reflect our uniqueness as well as the common ground we share as human beings.

❊   ❊   ❊

It is in this kindred spirit that this book is written. It was with great honor that I stewarded the *Journal* and tried to cull the best for inclusion in *From The Hearts Of Men*. Although the *Journal* is no longer published, its voice and intent live on within the pages and stories you are about to read.

I believe the true stories in this book will touch you deeply. They cover a wide range of male experience, from the exhilaration and pain of hard, toughened, athletic male bodies competing in team sports to the intense comradeship of war. From the joy of a new dad holding his first-born baby to the moving lament for a father who suddenly died. And from stories of frustrated childhoods to a proposed rite of passage into manhood.

Amidst all the pains and joys of men, I have heard over and over the yearning for a relationship with their dads – a relationship that never was. For this reason, here is where we begin.

CHAPTER I

FATHERS AND SONS

The Grief Of Parenting
Maxwell Reif

I have begun opening to the impending separation – it may be a day, a year, or ten years – from the wonderful being I have called my father in this lifetime.

This piece is cast as an open letter to him. My grief for a future event seems to be opening me to a much deeper joy in our relationship than I have known in a long time, and I feel thankful for the recent literature on "conscious dying," particularly that of Stephen Levine, for helping me to begin deepening my attitude toward everyone and everything, now, while my father's still on earth.

Dear Father,

I remember like it was yesterday the time when I was three and had had a tonsilectomy and then, having gone back home, started bleeding in a deep throat hemorrhage. You and Mother took me to the hospital. Dr. Cutler put me on the table and ran alongside me in the emergency room, yelling, "I've got a bleeder here!" Then he cauterized the wound in my throat, burning it deeply with something like a gun that he stuck down me.

Terrified by the whole situation, I thought I was being burned alive. I thought it would go on forever.

Then he was finished, and you held me in your arms as I continued to spit blood onto your white shirt and cry.

"Daddy!" I cried, like you were my personal Savior, which I long felt you were.

5

The blood continued to stream from my throat and I felt a boundless self-pity. Your shirt was shocking white, but it was getting bloodied. You just held me and hugged me.

Then you gave me your handkerchief, and slowly the substance that came from my mouth turned orangish and then completely colorless. The crisis was over, and I realized I would live. You were my Protector, as always. You had told me to be brave, and I had done my best, and our love affair continued.

Now, thirty-three years later, it is you who might die. Maybe not today or soon. But the transitoriness of our, and all, relationships, was brought home dramatically to me by your bypass operation, and I feel I am being prepared by forces greater than myself for the initiations of grief, wherein I believe true manhood and womanhood may be found.

Today I allowed myself, finally, to feel what my world would be like without you. My girlfriend had a dream years ago that you had died and I had cried like a baby, and today I did just that.

I have not cried about our relationship for many years. You cried once when I came home at twenty-one, damaged from LSD, but I have not.

I found today that I entered exactly the same place within myself that I went to when I was three and crying in your arms, bleeding and crying onto your white shirt.

I understood why I have never allowed myself to enter that zone for so many years: the feelings are too powerful.

Indeed, at a certain point when I began to grow spiritually, and opened to the love of God, it was exactly the same as the love I had known from you as a child.

Had I not been learning slowly that there is a Love that transcends but does not diminish the love of persons, I believe it would take me many years to get over my grief when you finally drop your body. It will still be difficult, I am certain.

By opening to my grief now, which I have realized is really the loss we experience at the separation from our divine source, I am somehow opening to a deeper and deeper true joy which comes in the understanding and acquiescence in things as they are, including the transitoriness of earthly relationships. This kind of talk has long been just words with me, but it is becoming a bit more.

I realize that you have the same kind of relationship with me as I have with you: a human love relationship with all its poignancy.

Stephen Levine says in one of his books that the contract of every earthly relationship includes its ending. Somehow I have never realized that, though it is so simple. I feel much better having taken it in. It is a basic truth of the universe.

I have come to realize the grief of parenting, and of all deep human relationships; that you raise or love this person whom you cannot control, and you may see them go through sickness, foolishness, and even death that you can do nothing about. And if I have children I will go through it exactly the same.

But nothing else is worthy of the name love.

So now that I know that we may have anywhere from a minute to more than a decade left on this earth together, let me say a prayer that this time, however much it is, may be filled with deepening richness and joy, and that when you do go, or I, we will both know that we will never, ever really say goodbye.

Your loving son,
Max [1]

To Know That He Was Proud

Yevrah Ornstein

Learning didn't make it to the upper echelon of my agenda of meaningful things to do while I did my time in public school. My interests were pretty simple: drawing, surfing, playing with friends, sports, math, being active with my body and creative with my hands. These were the main ingredients of my contentment. I was a very average student; my grades said that.

There weren't many subjects that turned me on – very few in fact – and no teacher in that time ever inspired in me a zeal or passion for learning per se – education's primary purpose as I view it today.

My love for drawing began early in my life and later moved on into four years of mechanical drawing pursued throughout my high school years. My oldest brother was away at college and I redesigned his bedroom into a drafting room, enhanced by his stereo and made precious by its total privacy. After finishing other homework, I would go into my "sanctuary," close the door, put a record on the phonograph and draw for hours and hours, often late into the night. I was free to be the fanatical perfectionist I really was. It was one of those activities in which I was totally and delightfully absorbed. The internal chatter ceased, and the hurts and the conflicts of my life were put to rest, at least for a while. It was an idyllic interlude for me – creative and free – and mine to do with as I pleased.

I was also in a program certified by the American Institute of Architects (A.I.A.) where we were required to enter a national contest. We had three months to complete the project which consisted of multiple drawings done on large sheets of vellum (which is similar to ultra-sturdy tracing paper), math computations, and a written report.

Unlike the other students who worked on their drawings in class, I'd use class time for problem solving and rough sketches. Class was only 45 minutes long – roughly equivalent to my ritualistic preparation time at home – cleaning my equipment, sharping my pencils so they were up to surgical exactitude, lining up the Beach Boys, the Beatles, Harry Belafonte ("Daaay-O"), etc.

The equipment at school was pretty schlocky and the thought, the possibility of someone bumping into my drafting table in class, which wasn't all that uncommon, would have been grounds for murder. It was safest and the best of all possible worlds for me to work at home, uninterrupted, for as long as I liked, secluded in my sanctuary.

After three months of intense, joyful concentration, the day came to wrap it all up. Do you remember when Mohammed Ali used to scream "I am the greatest!" into the camera? I, like Ali, was absolutely convinced that no one could have done better, technically or artistically.

The deadline arrived and I handed my teacher all my work, securely entombed in a disaster-proof cardboard cylinder. Without the slightest reservation or timidity, I simply said; "I've won." (I wish I had that kind of confidence today).

Now my teacher knew I was good but he clearly saw the possibility of a major letdown looming on the horizon. He told me he had several honorable mentions over the years but none of his students had ever won or placed in this contest. We were one of only eight high schools in the country that were eligible to enter, with the majority of the entries coming from architectural and engineering colleges.

A few weeks later, returning home from being with friends, my mom and her three bridge partners were waiting for me at the door. This was not the run-of-the-mill welcome home; I knew something unusual was about to happen. Mom was radiant, and the instant before she broke the news, I realized I had won the contest!

Then there was Dad's reaction.

My father worked in the real estate business in New York City, and the most fulfilled I had ever seen him was when he was putting up a new building. He'd work closely with the architect, the engineers, the bank, etc., being intimately involved with all phases of such a prodigious project. One of my proudest memories of my dad is when he showed me an elegant brass plate he placed with reverence on the front of one his buildings. It was an expensive touch for an address marker and although I was young at the time, I knew it was unique and unlike most plaques of its kind. My father said that the city had given so much to both him and his family that this was a small way of saying "thank you" to New York, the city of his childhood and the place where he spent his entire working life.

One of Dad's dreams was to have been an architect. So what he saw in me as a draftsman was both a natural ability coupled with an obvious fervency and passion. What he projected upon me was his own unfulfilled desire.

The evening the news came of my having won the national drafting contest, my father told me he was proud of me! For the first time, in the first eighteen years of my life, my father told me he was proud of me!

I know many men who have never, ever heard these words spoken by their fathers, and they endure and often mask a wound of profound depths and ramifications. Pride goes beyond a simple word or nod of approval. It speaks of a quality of relationship, a tone of relating, an ongoing presence and sense of self in relation to one's own son. Many of these sons are wounded and driven by an invisible scar that is tragic – tragic in the sense that they live a life of nondirected search. Pursuit of the American dream as we know it is usually an unholy and misplaced grail; look at the faces of "successful" men in their 40s, 50s and beyond. Their eyes say it all. Study the look of never finding fulfillment that these faces and lives reveal.

To have the simple recognition of fatherly pride, to be assured and feel secure within this essential need, is crucial in the life of a child and adolescent who all too often becomes an emotionally stunted adult, pretending to be whole, but knowing the truth to be otherwise.

I suppose I should be grateful, and I am – to have at least heard it once in the first eighteen years of my life. At least, on that day, my father told me he was proud of me. But our time together had gone, and with my leaving for college soon, I was for all intents and purposes coming into my own, taking over the reins of my own destiny. And having waited eighteen years for an expression of recognition from my dad felt like . . . well . . . too late in coming. The damage had already been done.

It would be many years before I would know my father saw me with such eyes once again. There were battles yet to be fought and a significant leaving before we would reunite, not only as father and son, but as friends.

There are the other dads who need not verbalize their obvious pride in their sons. They feel and radiate this in special and perhaps private ways and those sons know in a soulful way how their fathers truly feel about them. It's not questioned nor longed for and if this visceral comfort and support is present then perhaps the words aren't necessary after all.

But for the remainder, there's an emptiness within when these needs aren't nourished through recognition, involvement, presence, and pride from the omnipotent parent/s. As a friend is fond of saying, when holes appear, demons rush in.

One of the greatest gifts a parent can bestow upon a child is in guiding him or her to discover and befriend that wellspring within; the inner river of strength and tranquility we all possess, in spite of whatever damage has been done.

But sadly, so many of us are needlessly damaged in this way . . . so many.

❊   ❊   ❊

On Children
Kahlil Gibran

And a woman who held a babe against
her bosom said, Speak to us of children
And he said:
Your children are not your children.
They are the sons and daughters of Life's
longing for itself.

They come through you but not from
you,
And though they are with you yet they
belong not to you.

You may give them your love but not
your thoughts,
For they have their own thoughts.
You may house their bodies but not
their souls,
For their souls dwell in the house of tomorrow,
which you cannot visit, not even in your
dreams.
You may strive to be like them, but seek
not to make them like you.
For life goes not backward nor tarries
with yesterday.

*The archer sees the mark upon the path
of the infinite, and He bends you with His
might that His arrows may go swift and far.
Let your bending in the archer's hand
be for gladness;
For even as He loves the arrow that flies,
so He loves also the bow that is stable.* [2]

❉   ❉   ❉

*Treat the earth well.
It was not given to you by your parents.
It was loaned to you by your child.*

Kenyan Proverb

The Next Step
Yevrah Ornstein

At a time when the earth was preparing for its seasonal slumber and the fallen leaves were serving as fertilizer, making way for new beginnings, men too were emerging from that which had lain dormant. Out of the collective silence and the stoic posture so many of us have learned so well, men were coming forward with stories that needed to be told . . . shared . . . and listened to.

I wrote two articles for the premier issue of *The Men's Journal*, one of which was entitled "The Wimp Conspiracy or Where's the Beef?" The following paragraph is excerpted from that story.

". . . and with my father, I've come to be much more compassionate and feeling for the male role model that he inherited, passed down from father to son, born out of an authoritative European heritage. My father came to visit with me — three days — just father and son. One evening I invited eight men friends for dinner. In their company I paid homage to my father, to honor and celebrate him and our relationship. We toasted one another that evening; raised glasses and expressed our deep love and respect for one another." [3]

What I didn't include in that article was something that happened later in the evening – it just felt too personal to include at the time.

The dinner was a pot luck and we had spread all the food out on the dining room table. I think my dad was surprised to see a group of men put out a spread the likes of which awaited us. It truly was a gourmet dinner; appetizers, entrees, great desserts, and no duplications.

As eight men of varying professional backgrounds and ages moved from the living room to the dining room, my dad stayed back to allow the other men to go before him – it was a polite and kind gesture. I too waited, to be at his side. As I began to go into the dining room, I felt a strong surge of affection for him and turned to hug him and whisper in his ear, "I love you, Dad." I didn't know until later that one of my friends saw and heard what I had said to him.

Around 1:00 a.m., half of the guys got up to leave and said their good-byes. After they left, Dad said it was time for him to turn in and he, too, said good night.

Four of us stayed up for a couple of more hours, talking, joking, enjoying being together. Not long after Dad went to sleep, I put my hand on Jack's knee sensing that something was troubling him. He looked at me and then scanned the other men in the room. He told me later that he was looking into those present to see, to feel, if it was okay, safe to reveal a mournful memory that had come back to him, challenging his surface composure.

Jack is a middle-aged man with three teenage girls – an educator by profession. He is what I privately call a Boddisattva – someone who is highly developed spiritually, and has returned to the world to be of service to others. This describes Jack well. He is one of the most caring, giving people I know.

Jack turned to me and said that he had heard what I had whispered to my father. Then he began to cry. After a few minutes, when he was able to talk again, he said that he had never told his father that he loved him and now that his father was dead, it was one of his greatest regrets and one of his deepest wounds. He thanked me for the gift *I* had given *him*, simply by virtue of his having been witness to what happened between my dad and me. A few days later I wrote Jack, to say some personal things and to thank him for the gift *he* had unwittingly given *me* in return. For what had transpired between Dad and me was indeed very special. But the added realization that Jack, like so many men, never get to tell their fathers that they love them until it's too late, enhanced the specialness of my words enormously. Thank you, Jack.

As I travel through that time once again, I am recalling three pieces from the *Journal* that belong here. I welcomed them because it reminded men that their dads are not going to be around forever.

Letter To A Dead Dad
Richard Shelton

Five years since you died and I am
better than I was when you were living.
The years have not been wasted.
I have heard the harsh voices
of desert birds who cannot sing.
Sometimes I touched the membrane
between violence and desire
and watched it vibrate.

I learned that a man
who travels in circles
never arrives at exactly the same place.

If you could see me now
side-stepping triumph and disaster,
still waiting for you to say my son
my beloved son. If you could see
me now, you would know I am stronger.

> *Death was the poorest subterfuge*
> *you ever managed, but it was permanent.*
> *Do you see now that fathers*
> *who cannot love their sons*
> *have sons who cannot love?*
> *It was not your fault*
> *and it was not mine. I needed*
> *your love but I recovered without it.*
> *Now I no longer need anything.* **[4]**

❉   ❉   ❉

The following letter, from a father to his son, made me yearn in retrospect for a kind of guidance I never received. I'm sure you, too, will be impressed.

Letter To A 16-Year-Old
William Harrison

January 31, 1985

Dear Tim,

Today you are 16 years old. I wish I could tell you all that means to me and how I feel when I realize you are now 16. My father used to tell me, "You'll never understand how I love you, how I feel about you, until you have a son of your own." How true! This is an attempt to tell you about some of that, even though you may not fully comprehend it all.

You are at an age that, in our society, signifies the threshold of becoming a man. Why sixteen? In other societies, historically, this "threshold" was usually at a younger age, and it was celebrated in much more specific, ritualistic ways. It used to be a very clear, very special event when these "rites of passage" occurred for young teenage boys. Today, we rarely have such celebrations of this transition, and so you will not have this kind of experience. Today, "growing up" is a very fuzzy and confusing process.

So perhaps the best we have is to notice what's going on at 16. It's not very significant, compared to the entire process of "growing up," but I think we notice this birthday as special because at 16 you can earn the real and symbolic adult privilege and responsibility of driving a car, where you have the freedom to move about on your own, to be able to create your own life in more flexible and independent ways than ever before. And it's also when you are entrusted with the risks of operating a machine that can be a deadly weapon, creating destruction, pain, loss and crippling guilt because of a few seconds of inattention or poor judgement. Becoming 16, then, creates perhaps the most significant single, practical change in your life that denotes moving from a child to an adult, from a boy to a man.

You are a very capable, responsible person. You are sensitive to other people and their feelings. I enjoy so much your emerging openness, your sense of humor, your creativity, and your alertness to your world around you. I am very proud and grateful, and I enjoy seeing these qualities expressed in you.

What I want to especially encourage now is both simple and crucial, and it is difficult to state clearly; most of us – certainly including me – have struggled to discover this much later in our lives than 16, and we wish we could have learned it sooner:

Know and honor your self as a separate, autonomous, perfect human being. Have no apologies or doubts about yourself compared to anybody, and especially compared to your own ideal of what you think you "should" be.

I'm sure it will be many years before you get a real grasp on what that means. But at your age, you will go through many changes very quickly. In a competitive, confusing society, everybody is taught, it seems, to pass judgement on everybody else, and especially on him or herself. You will have many confusing, frustrating moments when you may not feel very good about yourself at all.

Be gentle and patient with yourself. You will have conflicting urges, desires, cravings of all sorts that may not seem to make sense. You are soon going to be dealing with new decisions that spring from sexual feelings, about schooling and career decisions and about earning money versus spending your time in other ways. You will find yourself confronted with mixed feelings about relating to girls, to boys, to me and your mom, to your friends and to people you don't know. Guess what? *Everyone* has gone through that before, and we all still do! You are not alone or different in that regard at all.

In times of confusion, know that you have an inner voice that, if you will listen to it, will guide you at these times. And it will not be a voice necessarily reminding you of all of society's rules, or your parents' "words of wisdom," or any other knowledge acquired outside of you. Rather, it is that deep core of your Being which is connected with the cores of all the rest of us in the universe who share that essence of human existence, which is love.

So how do you live with this in mind? It isn't always easy. Notice your own feelings, confusion, changes, insights, accomplishments, joys and pains both physical and emotional. Consider them all as opportunities to learn more about yourself. Never put yourself down or judge yourself harshly. Instead, know that inside you is the essence of perfection as a human being. You needn't always be "perfect!" Just work on being aware of yourself, your feelings and your reactions.

Most importantly, perhaps: trust yourself. So many times, especially when I was much younger, I felt I had an idea, an answer, an observation or a feeling response to what was going on in class, or among my friends, between your mom and me, or whatever. But I decided that it wasn't worth mentioning. If my feeling was "different," then I thought it was probably wrong. I often wouldn't let anyone, including my parents, know of these thoughts or feelings, because they might be judged silly or wrong or, worst of all, dumb. Now as I look back on many such occasions, I wish I'd believed in my feelings. Trust yourself.

Try to get in the habit of mentally standing aside and looking at yourself as though part of you is a separate observer. Then let your inner voice tell you how to love and support that guy, Tim Harrison. *How to watch yourself with detached awareness and give yourself loving support may be the most important thing you ever learn to do!*

Feel okay to express any of your thoughts and feelings to others around you, including your friends – boys and girls – your teachers, your grandpa, your mom and me. Doubts, fears and confusion are real, valid and okay. So are your questions you want to ask about things you think "everyone else already knows" (Guess what? Everyone doesn't know!). Also, feel really free to express your *good* feelings, your caring, your concern, and your love to those people, too. It's as hard today for young men in this society to feel okay to say positive, caring things to people, including to their friends and parents, as it is to talk about fears, confusion and emotional pain.

At the same time, know that it's fine to keep some feelings and thoughts to yourself if they are incomplete, simply "private," or for whatever reason. But always be totally honest with *yourself* no matter how much you care to reveal or withhold from others!

Always try to feel and see yourself as absolutely connected to the Universe, its people, its energy, and at the same time allow yourself to be separate and distinct, neither better nor worse than anyone else in the world; simply and wonderfully unique. Your task in life is to find out who you are and to learn how to express all your essence and your potential in loving ways – that's all! That's *everything* that's important!!

In a way, I feel like you and I will be learning these things together. My comments may sound strange or unclear to you now. That's fine. Just know that I want so much to share with you, as most fathers want to do with their sons, the things that I have decided are important and which, in many cases, have taken me a long and painful time to figure out.

I hope you will keep this letter and read it every so often over the years, for each year as you get older there may be some new meaning here for you.

Tim, I indeed celebrated that birth day when you came into our lives in Ithaca, New York, in 1969. And I celebrate now who you are and who you're becoming with a great deal of joy each day. Happy Birthday!

Love,
Dad [5]

Mine Died
Warner Jepson

"I want every last leaf raked up," he warned. I'd apparently
not done enough. That was often the case. I was often not good
enough for him. Isn't that the problem fathers have with sons?
They aren't good enough.

I hated the humiliation he gave me. I would hate him and
laugh inside, superiorly, at his blind, "puerile," (that's when I
discovered that word; first used it on my grown – President of the
Bethlehem National Bank – father) temper. I even at times wished
him out of the way.

Then he died – suddenly. I was 16 and had no idea what that
meant. Not for a long time to come. Not until I saw how much I
became . . . no, was, yes – wow! – like him. Not until I noticed
how much emptier the house was, how much it didn't move the
same anymore. The force was gone. Not until I realized that it was
possible that the rest of my life might be different if he'd been there
to talk to, listen to, learn from. There was no more of him to get.

I dream of him often. Oh, so happily. He'd just been away
with another woman and was back now. Those days, I didn't even
know what an "another woman" was; there weren't any.

Then I'd wake up. Oh, so sad.

What would he have been like at 80? I've met other men
who are 80, got to know them and like them. But not dad – I didn't
know him at 60, not even at 52. I'm older than that now; that's
younger than me.

Would he be like the way he had been to me? Or would he
be like the way he really was? Father's don't treat their *sons* like
they treat the *rest of the world*.

For their sons are themselves, and as hard as they are on
themselves, so they are hard on their sons. They try to make them
into their own image, as they try to improve their own. Which can
be bad if they aren't satisfied. They may forgive and tolerate the
rest of the world, but if they aren't so with themselves, then, son,
you get it. And the poor kid doesn't know this is why his father is
yelling at him. And the poor father doesn't even know it himself.

But one day that part of the journey, childhood, child-rearing and parent-rearing, is over and the father can relax and quit his testing. The son's a man now, can't be formed anymore – can't comb the hairs on a butterfly. So father may leave his son – and himself – alone.

Now that father and son are alone and separate, they can come together; grown men, equals, and friends, able to need each other, because they belong to each other, being a part of each other.

Except mine died when I was 16. [6]

❋   ❋   ❋

"Sometimes a Man . . ."
by Rainer Maria Rilke
translated by Robert Bly

Sometimes a Man stands up during supper
and walks outside, and keeps on walking,
because of a church that stands somewhere
in the East.

And his children say blessings on him as if
he were dead.

And another man, remains in his own house,
stays there, inside the dishes and the glasses,
so that his children have to go far out into
the world
toward that same church, which he forgot. [7]

Once I Heard My Real Dad
Yevrah Ornstein

Dad's reaction to my leaving for the Peace Corps was dramatically different from Mom's. He immediately – and I mean immediately – went from listener to rage, from calm to hurricane, in the blink of an eye.

Conjuring up every disaster scenario possible, he was screaming; "What if you get there and there's no job?" "What if you get there and nobody wants to work . . .?" "What if you get there and . . . blah, blah, blah." I think you get the idea. It was the first, real, knock-down, drag-out fight we ever had. It went on for hours – two bulls standing face to face, snorting, spitting, veins popping, mom in the corner quietly freaking out. The works! Neither one of us was about to back down.

This guy definitely had a knack for pissing me off, big time!

I thought his scenarios were ludicrous and I told him so. I countered each one as they came my way. Towards the end I yelled back, "If it doesn't work out, I'll come home; so what's the big fucking deal?"

The low, hurtful blows came when he said, "You're wasting your life . . . when are you going to grow up? . . . Is this what I put you through college for?"

I had come for his blessing, for I knew my father to be a man of deep altruism and generosity, and here was something I thought he'd be genuinely proud of. I was off to spend two years of my life to work with others in need; or as the Peace Corps credo goes, to help others help themselves.

Instead of pride in his son, all I got was flack and bullshit and fury. Halfway through this battle, he took a swing at me. I pulled my head back narrowly avoiding getting punched in the face. I grabbed him by the collar, squeezed it shut, pulled my fist back and cocked my arm to hit him. For as much as I wanted to – and I had the desire of years standing there with me – I simply could not punch out my own father. I held him like that for a few seconds, then released him, feeling totally deflated and disgusted by the whole scene. Hitting one's own father instinctually felt like a biological and spiritual violation – something I just couldn't bring myself to do.

Today, looking back, I'm real glad I didn't.

It was obvious that he'd never give me his blessings and that any hopes or expectations along those lines were a total waste of time.

I look back on that episode with no regrets. I had years of stuffed, stored up anger and resentment towards him. I had been intimidated by him my whole life and hadn't had the balls to stand up to him before. This confrontation triggered the venting of so much pent up stuff, it was a therapeutic blessing in disguise. A lot came out in those three hours. Much of the bile and puss and crap of living in his castle, a lot of the resentment and fury I felt towards him was for the first time cut loose, and I matched his rage.

When it was all over, we were both exhausted and emotionally spent.

Then, he said an incredible thing to me; it was the bottom line, the truth finally came out. He told me I would be thousands of miles away and if anything happened to me, he wouldn't be able to help me, I'd be on my own.

I was stunned, shocked into speechlessness. What more could I say? My father had just admitted that he was frightened for me. This was his distorted, tragic way of saying, by default, I love you and I want to protect you. *INCREDIBLE!* The fight was out of me, as well as him too. The argument was history, and sadly, even with the truth out in the open, we both felt like losers.

And as I said, in retrospect, I'm glad it happened. There were 24 years of shit to begin unloading.

Gratitude
Colin Ingram

I grew up in Chicago during the years of World War II. Lots of things were scarce then, and food was rationed. But in the midst of these scarcities, our family was well off because my father had a wholesale food business and we were able to get just about everything edible (including the greatest of rarities during WWII – bubble gum!). Everyone liked my dad – he had friends everywhere, and he knew how to treat them. I got a good glimpse of that one day, as well as how the city of Chicago worked.

I was riding in my dad's truck, helping to deliver some wheels of hard-to-get Wisconsin cheddar cheese to restaurants. Have you ever seen a "wheel" of cheese? It's a solid chunk, about the size and shape of an auto tire, and weighs 50-80 lbs. We were delivering them to a posh restaurant in the downtown section of Chicago known as "The Loop." Even in the 40's, the Loop was a very crowded area, and it was almost impossible to find a parking place. At that time, all of the downtown traffic police rode horses, and they spent most of their time handing out parking tickets to the many illegally parked cars and trucks.

We double-parked our truck in front of a restaurant and before making the delivery my dad took a big knife, cut a wedge out of one of the cheese wheels, and wrapped it up (in waxed paper – there was no plastic then). That single wedge was about a foot and one half long and, by itself, weighed almost 20 lbs. My dad told me it was for one of the cops (that's what they called themselves – never "policemen" or "peace officers") who was having a hard time making ends meet. This particular cop – an Irishman, like most of the Chicago cops – had a big family to feed, and 20 lbs. of Wisconsin cheddar was a treasure.

A moment later I heard the sharp clip-clop of hooves on pavement, and a burly, middle-aged cop came up to our truck and leaned over into the cab. He called out, "Hi, Carl, hawaya? That your sonny boy with you?" I waved to the cop and, after the mutual inquiries about families were over, my dad said, "Mike, I'm overloaded with too much stuff this week, and it's only going to waste. Could you help me by taking it off my hands?" and he handed over that big wedge of cheese. You should have seen that cop's eyes light up when he saw it. He grinned, and stuck the cheese into his saddlebag, two-thirds of it sticking out like a bright orange tower. After thanking my dad, the cop asked, "Delivering today, Carl?" my dad told him yes, and the cop said, "Just double-park here and I'll watch things for you." I helped my dad carry in two cheese wheels to the restaurant, and when we came back outside, there was the cop, seated on his tall, brown horse, holding up a line of traffic until my dad could move our truck out of the way.

That was how Chicago worked in those days. It wasn't exactly bribery or payoff – I sensed the cop would have helped my dad even without the gift of cheese – it was a way of greasing the wheels of society, and of ordinary folks looking after each other whenever they could. But even as a boy, I was impressed by my father's thoughtfulness, not only in giving, but in the way he had given so that the cop lost no dignity in receiving.

My dad was a quiet man. He never talked much – never about himself or his feelings and, as far as I can recall, he never asked me about mine. In many ways we were strangers who never did get to know each other. But in terms of all his dealings with the world, he was a wonderful role model. Kindness, loyalty and respect for others flowed from him like water from a spring. And where most of us count ourselves fortunate to have a few really close friends, my dad had them by the dozens – persons who would do anything for him, and he for them. I've tried to be like that for my own friends and associates, and for my own son and daughter.

I could list the things I would have changed about my dad, and it would be a long list. I would have liked someone to whom I could bare my soul; and I would have loved it if my dad and I could have discussed life, death, the subtle hues of a spectacular sunset, or even how to act with girls (My sex education consisted of my dad asking me, one day, if I knew about "men and women" – I don't think he could have brought himself to say "sex" – and I replied, "yes." That was it.). But he wasn't like that; it couldn't be.

I prefer to look at all of the good things my dad was, rather than blame him for the things he wasn't. Now that I am a parent, and I understand the absolutely enormous amounts of energy, care and sacrifice that parents must give to their children – year after year – I can't help but appreciate what my own dad did.

Acknowledging and releasing pent up resentments toward parents is a necessary, healthy step toward wholeness. But in the process of maturing, there must come a time when the individual ceases to blame his parents for his problems.

I, for one, want to thank my dad for the untold thousands of things he put up with for me; my youthful brattiness; my tendency to disobey and to do whatever I wanted; my breaking, misusing and losing so many things that were valuable to him; all of the worry, the strife and the frustration I no doubt caused him while I went about the process of growing up; and for doing his best to feed, clothe and shelter me for eighteen long years.

No, Dad, you weren't perfect, but I owe you one hell of a lot.

*If it doesn't matter
who wins
how come they keep score?*

Vince Lombardi

*The great thing about
being a football player is,
you don't have to take
a shower to go to work.*

Jay Hilgenberg
Chicago Bears

CHAPTER II

SPORTS

The Contemporary Initiation To Manhood
Yevrah Ornstein

There was a time when I was obsessed with one focus – surfing. I took to the sport with a passion in my early teens, surfed every chance I got, and after one summer, my love of it coerced me into buying a wet suit so I could do it year round.

In those days, surfboards were enormous klunkers. Nonetheless, I was in hog heaven in the ocean (my second home) – speed, thrills, sun, and pure exuberance. Growing up by and in the ocean turns your blood into part sea water, and it never, ever, gets out of your system.

The second winter came and Lewis (my surfing soulmate) and I bought wetsuits. Back then, what we used for protection against the frigid waters and 10-40 degree air temperatures were diving suits. They were of a similar ilk as the first fiberglass boards – thick and clumsy – but they worked. Paddling was like having some clown on your back pulling your arms back as you paddled forward, gleefully, cynically hissing, "You sure you want to be doing this?" ("That's right you son-of-a-bitch, I *do* want to be doing this!") The compensation was, the extra work generated lots of body heat.

I remember the first time Lewis and I suited up. We lugged our boards and suits down to the beach and stripped down to our bathing suits to begin the arduous task of putting these things on; these were pre-nylon-lined days. About a third of the way into this ritual, I turned around and saw a handful of people on the boardwalk, staring at us incredulously. "Hey, Lewis, turn around ..." We laughed, knowing we must have looked really strange; part-human, part-seal – echoes of Kafka's metamorphosis. No doubt this weird sight was heightened by the snow on the beach, and the imminent prospect of more to come.

Now surfing was heaven for me. Unlike the more "masculine" sports, there were no human adversaries; no one to beat up on and no one to beat up on you, other than the waves. So, in many ways, surfing is a solitary sport and the challenge is a private contest and a personal joy and feeling of accomplishment.

I have two older brothers, both of whom were superlative athletes. My mom was a "tom boy" and Dad played handball, rode horses like an expert, and played lacrosse at City College of New York.

In time, I began to realize that surfing wasn't quite gladiatorial enough – I was expected to do battle with humans. You see, competitive, *contact* sports were where the Golden Fleece lay, and although I was mostly content, feelings of inadequacy and "wimphood" began to creep into my little haven. The pressure was unspoken, often transmitted by way of example; one brother was a wrestler and the other was a football player.

I loved to play touch football – which to this day I still maintain requires greater agility and is a whole lot more fun than tackle football. It's more difficult to avoid simply being touched than to dodge being jumped on (usually with the intent to do you bodily harm).

I suited up one day in junior high school – tackle football – it was time to "play" a *man's sport*.

So there I am, out there sweating my ass off with a group of, for the most part, equally freaked out kids who have also caved in to the pressure. I don't think there were many of us out there for the love of the game. Probably three-quarters of the kids were likewise putting their bodies and their future on the line to get Dad's approval, or brother's, or friend's.

I hated it! It totally sucked! If you've ever been on a JV (junior varsity) team you know what total chaos it is. The name of the game is definitely not about skill, for that hasn't yet been developed. That leaves brute force to compensate for the lack of ability, grace and teamwork, which hopefully begin to mature with practice and experience. What also reigns supreme is confusion from leader-of-the-pack jockeying, which begins to make itself known early on.

I remember this neanderthal on the sidelines – known as *Coach* – screaming his brains out at us. "Hit the deck, I want 50 push-ups, then I want 75 sit-ups and then we're (hah!!! *we're?!*) going to run wind sprints and then we're going to do it again, then again and again." Do you know what a drag it is to do this stuff with helmet, shoulder pads, hip pads, those "sexy" football pants with thigh pads, shin pads and a cup on? It shits!!! The theory is that intimidation, along with the workout, would whip us right into shape; shades of pre-military training. Back then, there were lots of torn muscles in the beginning of the season. Stretching and gradually working our way into shape was not part of the game plan – I guess that was the coach's way of weeding out the boys from the men.

I remember standing in a row on the goal line and one of the kids pissing in his pants, out of fear, nervousness or whatever; urine running down his leg, and him just standing there, staring straight ahead. While many of us saw what happened, we turned away in embarrassment. You can bet your ass that's one hell of a humiliating memory to live with.

Well, all it took was one day of this crap and I was history. Back in the locker room, after one of the more unpleasant days of my life, I was thinking, "Hey, I really love to play football, but this sure as hell ain't my idea of a good time. It's back to touch football for me." I hated being encumbered by all that equipment, the jock mentality of the whole scene, and the coach being the asshole he was . . . *adios tackle football!*

I did enjoy playing tackle football with my friends, but only in two ways, both of which left us intact. One was in the snow and the other was on the beach. In the beach version, if you were on the sand it was touch, but as soon as you went into the water there were no out-of-bounds and anything went, which usually meant flying tackles. It was great fun, the water cushioned the fall and I don't think any of us ever got hurt doing this. It really was a blast; plus there was no armor to slow you down.

My next encounter with contact sports came a couple of years later in high school when I went out for the JV lacrosse team.

The bedlam of first year lacrosse is a sight to behold. Lacrosse is not a well known game, so I'll say a few words in case you've never seen it.

The game is played on a football field with ten players on a team: three mid-fielders, three defensemen, three attack and the goalie. The equipment consists of a lightweight helmet, hockey gloves, high-density foam shoulder pads, and pads to protect your arms and elbows. These, as well as the shoulder pads, are optional. The game is a hybrid between hockey, football, and basketball. The stick is (used to be) made of wood, leather and cat gut and the ball is the size of a hardball and made of hard rubber. The ball is thrown and caught with the stick; players are not allowed to touch it with their hands. The goal is six feet wide by six feet high and has a circle around it called a crease, as in hockey, which offensive players can't cross over.

It's a very fast game, lots of contact. You can hit with your stick or your body. It was invented by the American Indians, who still play and are among the best players around. Interestingly, lacrosse, not hockey, is the national sport of Canada. The Indians would play for days at a time and the field would span miles. It's said that there were fatalities back then in the good old days.

Strategies resemble those used in basketball in that many of the plays make use of pics, and the movement and use of players is similar to both basketball and hockey.

It's illegal to hit someone in the head/helmet, although it happens fairly often, sometimes on purpose and sometimes inadvertently. Sometimes the refs see it, sometimes they don't. Penalties are similar to hockey in that some penalties are spent in the penalty box and the offense and defense go into one-man or two-man up or down set-ups. There are fast breaks as in hockey and basketball, and the individual positions have specialized kinds of functions as in soccer.

One of the things that distinguishes lacrosse from other contact sports is that it is legal to hit someone with your stick; it's very much a part of the game. There are legal hits and illegal hits.

Now, when you have a group of kids who don't know squat about stick handling and setting up plays – *teamwork* – it's insane out there.

I was tall and skinny the first year I played, and I hated the game intensely. *Coach* was really – well, let me put it this way – the man was not well. He would literally stand on the sideline during a game and scream "KILL!!!" I kid you not. He was also the wrestling coach and a stocky little son-of-a-bitch. Most of us were totally intimidated by this little dictator. I remember when he would yell my name out during a game: "Get in there Ornstein," and my stomach would start doing flip-flops. Butterflies in the gut? Hell, there were bats in there!

The first year, I, like just about everyone else out there, didn't have the slightest idea what I was doing. The game was a free-for-all and very violent; almost all hitting and tackling and no teamwork or finesse. And I think that *Coach* sadistically bathed in the glory of it all.

As I said, I was skinny, had no stick skill, got my ass kicked around – a lot – hated it immensely. So why in the world did I do it?

There was something about doing a sport my brothers hadn't done. There was the violent contact aspect to satiate the pressure I felt to prove my manhood. Dad had been a lacrosse player in college. One uncle was an All-American lacrosse player and his two sons were both fine players. I think one of them made All-American. Getting the picture now?

Although I loathed the game the first year, believe it or not, I went out for the team again the following year. I felt driven by invisible forces and although I was having intense back pains at the time, the pressure to play plus the shame of not going out for the team drove me to it once again.

I had filled out some over the summer, and Dad and I worked out once in a while together. Actually, it was great. He'd have me run around him in a circle and quick-stick with him. It was excellent for sharpening up my reflexes and good stick-work practice, and he was a damn good teacher. I could see how much Dad enjoyed working with me in this way and he was obviously pleased with my progress. For a kid who was starved for recognition from his father, this was a rare and welcome gift. I also used to play against a wall on my own, practicing for hours on end, determined to get better.

By the time lacrosse season came around again, I had gained some confidence along with some weight, but I was still very scared of the game. About half way through the season, I ended up in a cast from torn cartilage and ligaments in my knee.

I went out for the team again the following year, my senior and final year of high school. But this time things were different. The caliber of play was dramatically different and the coach was an honorable, decent human being. His name was Tony Piazza and he soon became one of the strongest influences of my life up until that time.

Tony's emphasis was on ethics, finesse, stick ability and teamwork. The team took precedence over the individual. Lacrosse was still a dirty game at high school level, and a lot of teams relied on brute force to win.

Defensemen are the big boys in lacrosse, most of whom were football linemen staying in shape during off-season. These, for the most part, were not nice people – on the field, that is.

So, like most teams, we had our mix of small and quick, averaged size endurance players, and the big boys. During practice and workouts, Tony drilled and honed our skills. He would not tolerate dirty playing and made his ways known in a gentlemanly manner; none of the temper tantrums of *Coach* from two years before. He spoke softly and engendered a tremendous amount of respect from his players. A good parallel is the contrast between Bill Walsh of the 49'ers and Mike Ditka of the Chicago Bears: brains, control, and finesse versus vulgarity. There were occasional times when he'd pull one of our own players for a cheap or dirty shot on the field.

Because we were good with our sticks, we often intimidated and riled other teams, and when players are flustered, they blow whatever sense of timing they may have and their game deteriorates quickly. It's easy to sucker someone who's pissed off at you.

So, we were good, and as the game went on, most teams became more enraged and blew off whatever skills they had while they focused on trying to beat us up.

I remember at half time, Tony saying to us, "Listen guys, I know what's going on out there, but I don't want you stooping to their level," and if we did, we got taken out. That's pretty incredible coaching and modeling.

I learned a great deal that year, playing for Tony. More than anything else, I learned not to quit. There was something about him and the whole experience that instilled in me an attitude of refusing to give up, to want to push on.

The other gift from that season was the meaning and experience of working together as a team: The whistle blows. Two strong men wrestle for possession of the ball. Our man wins out and starts working the ball downfield to set up a play with the three attackmen. I am point attackman, in front of the goal. One of the midfielders passes the ball to another attackman; back it goes to the midfield, then back and forth in the midfield. Our midfielders know I'm suckering my defenseman, and they're stalling, waiting for me to break into the clear.

I run to my left to get the guy who is guarding me moving in that direction. It doesn't work. He doesn't fall for my feint. I plant my cleats into the grass and cut back sharply to the opposite direction. My defenseman isn't snookered; the other attackman rushes in to set up a block. We run toward each other at top speed, my defenseman alongside me. Wham! My defender is down. The midfielders have been watching closely and the ball is driven to me as soon as I'm clear. I spin around. Now I'm one-on-one with the goalie. I deliberately stare at the upper right-hand corner of the goal, and the goalie's eyes follow mine as he tries to anticipate the direction of my shot. Two quick steps toward him and, using the momentum of my body, I fire into the dirt at the lower, left-hand corner.

Suddenly, he knows what's happening and his foot shoots out – a fraction of a second too late. The ball is moving too fast to see, but the net reacts from the impact. It's in! The adrenalin explodes inside of me and I am oblivious to having been struck hard by another defenseman rushing in to block my shot.

The play worked perfectly. We had practiced it countless times until it was automatic . . . until we were a synchronized pattern of motion and intention, playing together as a single entity. When I had scored, we had all scored.

These guys, these strong-willed young men, had willingly bowed to a collective effort that surpassed any individual talent.

Knowing your teammates' movements inside-out becomes a transcendental experience of a sort – exhilarating, fulfilling, much more so than if you'd done it all yourself. Great!

A coach occupies a high place in a boy's life. It is the one grand component of my arguably useless vocation. If they are lucky, good coaches can become the perfect unobtainable fathers that young men dream about and rarely find in their own homes. Good coaches shape and exhort and urge. There is something beautiful about watching the process of sport. I have spent almost all the autumns of my life moving crowds of young boys across acres of divided grass. Beneath the sun of late August, I have listened to the chants of calisthenics, watched the initial clumsiness of overgrown boys and the eyes of small boys conquering their fear and I have monitored the violence of blocking sleds and gang tackling. I can measure my life by the teams I have fielded and I remember by name every player I ever coached. Patiently, I have waited each year for that moment when I had merged all the skills and weaknesses of the boys placed in my care. I have watched for that miraculous synthesis. When it comes I look around my field, I look at my boys, and in a rush of creative omnipotence I want to shout to the sun: "By God, I have created a team." [8]

❄   ❄   ❄

I played lacrosse in college and the game then was a very different experience. I enjoyed it – even though it still frightened me. Going into a game is a scary experience. The atmosphere in a locker room is intense before a game and there is definitely a feeling of an impending battle. Once you're out there, your adrenalin takes over and you're in the flow.

My second year, I suffered a hyperextension of my other knee and ended up in a cast for two or three months. Nevertheless, I went back and played again during the third and fourth years.

I was playing attack, and the coach had designed a couple of plays to take advantage of my height. It was a kamikaze play that often worked. One of the other attackmen would come behind the goal with the ball and I'd come across the crease line right in front of the goalie who would be facing the attackman with the ball and he'd have his back to me. The idea was to throw the ball over the net, over the goalie's stick and I'd jump up and quick-stick it in while I was on my way down, hopefully. The strategy was that by the time the goalie turned around, the ball was already in the net; he'd never even see it. It worked pretty well but it left me totally exposed (like football receivers who jump up for a pass – they're sitting ducks) to be nailed by one or two defensemen, which is usually what happened.

Ah, what we do for points.

We were back from spring break early – the lacrosse players, that is – to work double practices; one in the morning and one in the afternoon. This was excruciating stuff.

We had a new player on the team. He looked old enough to be a coach, himself. He was big and mean and very fucked up in the head. He had just come out of the Marines and was out to prove himself and out to impress the coach at my expense. This guy was a real dirty player, often stabbing me in the back with the end of his stick; illegal hits, the works. To get to the point, he beat me up every practice. The only satisfaction I ever got was, one day in practice I snapped after he hit me late, and I spun around and smashed him in the head as hard as I could with my stick. Other players jumped in and separated us.

After a few weeks of this, I was pretty badly racked up from the double workouts, strained muscles, Mr. Marines, etc. I was sitting down for lunch one day and the only way I could sit was to use my arms to lower myself slowly; my legs, knees and ankles were hurting me so badly.

Finally, the day came when, after one of these slow, painful, ridiculous descents, the total insanity of what was happening forced me back into sanity. I decided right then and there: that's it – I quit. I'm not doing this anymore, this is totally nuts!

I handed in my equipment that afternoon. The coach never even asked me why.

It's not easy to quit – at least it's not easy for me. There's pride, and peer pressure. But my decision was so quick, strong and final, that I didn't feel any embarrassment about it. I was going to miss the guys and the fun and the exhilarating aspects of the game, but the pain and damage were just too damn much.

I have two regrets about playing lacrosse. One, I went into it for the wrong reasons. Several years ago I had one of those realizations that stops you in your tracks. All of a sudden I flashed on the symbolism of the name of the game – lacrosse – and saw how I had put myself on "the cross" to impress my father and my brothers, and how I had "sacrificed" myself/my body "for them." Today I am still troubled by knee problems, vestiges of a violent sport that has taken its toll on me. For all the good I derived from the game, I'm sorry I did it. It's simply not worth the pain I live with, and I'm concerned about the pain that will be there tomorrow. If I could do it again, I wouldn't.

The other regret has to do with asking my dad not to come to our championship game in high school. I was afraid that I might not have a good game. I was afraid I'd try too hard with him there and blow it. As it happened, I had one of the best games of my career and my dad never got to see me on the field. He never even saw me in a game.

Dad would have been proud of his son. We could have bonded in a way that would have enriched our time together. And now that he's gone and I am a father, I recall my stupidity and its resulting sadness.

I won't repeat this mistake with my daughter.

❊ ❊ ❊

Men's Bodies – An Intimate View
Patrick Reilly

Over the years I've worked with roughly a thousand different people, doing Rolfing.

Ron, compared to most athletic men, possesses a great amount of sensitivity in his body. This particular kind of sensitivity can be represented most vividly by a great cheetah, bounding over the plains of Africa, his sinews in evidence with every move as he strides gracefully, yet with abandon, seeking his prey. Never for a moment do you believe that he will fall in a hole, twist an ankle or seek the wrong trail. He is invincible.

It is as if his program is preordained, controlled genetically. This is the kind of body sensitivity to which I refer: discriminating selectivity, athletic prowess and innate information that enables you to use your body more suitably. Many men, even those involved in serious athletics, do not possess it. Most often it seems that they have developed and used their bodies in machine-like fashion. Their bodies will carry them forth in battle until they expire or are injured; then they will seek someone to patch them up in hopes of being able to continue in their usual fashion.

The cheetah is able to proceed at high speeds in relentless pursuit of his prey. At the end of his quest he will literally throw his body into the fracas, much like a football player. Yet he maintains a sense of his position in space at all times, so as to not subject himself to unnecessary injury. Certainly it is a quirk of our culture that often more adoration is given to the injured hero than to the athlete who is still in action. The injured cheetah is not of great assistance to his family's survival.

During Ron's second session, tears, and then great sobbing began to emanate as I worked on his ankle. Before committing himself totally to running, Ron was also a soccer player. After college he played on a semi-pro team where he was the youngest and fastest man on the team. In order to keep their competitive edge over him, many of the older team members would kick or step on his ankles in order to slow him down. As we worked on his ankles, memories of these painful experiences flooded into his awareness, permitting him to see why his ankles now felt weak and unstable and why he was constantly worried that they would give out.

Machismo often takes precedence over good common sense. The thrill of the game at seventeen is a faint memory, compared to the ever present pain in the right knee at forty. Generally, the joy of using one's body vigorously and naturally is lost in the repeated efforts of pushing one's body to produce an exceptional result. With many people, running has been a way of regaining that cheetah-like freedom in the body; take a look at the faces of the people crossing the finish line at a marathon. Notice the agony. It is rare to see a smiling face. There is a line of productive usage, and when that line is crossed, constant pain and bodily degradation replaces natural athletic prowess as the operating mode. [9]

Face To Face
Frank Cardelle

"Did you win?" I could not move. His thundering voice coming from his six foot frame made my whole body tremble. I turned, and his penetrating eyes met mine. He was looking right through me. Caught within his steel-like stare, I felt numb, motionless. My throat was parched, trickles of urine ran down my leg. I felt dizzy in the presence of this master of interrogation. My legs became rubbery. I wanted to run but was immobilized. He waited, then his voice rolled out again, "What is the matter? The cat got your tongue?" This sent a chill down my spin; my gut was tied in knots and I finally could not hold back. My body began to shake and the urine burst from my groin, streaming down my legs. My chest heaved, my voice cracked, the ache inside exploded, and my emotions rushed through my body like jolts of electricity. My eyes welled with tears and I began to sob uncontrollably. The urine continued to stream down my leg, forming a pool at my feet, and I stood completely vulnerable, broken, the hardness of my body armour dissolved.

The emotions oozing from my heart's cavity were the accumulation of the many times I had been hurt and had tried to hide it for fear of being called a "cry baby." Now I was my real self: scared, confused and open to the deep hungering pain of needing to be supported – most of all by my father. I wanted to reach out to him and be held.

"Stop that crying!" he bellowed, "You're a big boy now!"

Another chance for father and son to touch was destroyed by the destructive messages that are passed down through the masculine fraternity. Another chance, an opening, a new beginning, was turned into another wound and barrier to a natural, healthy connection between father and son. "Close your heart's door, this is not how men touch and that is how it is, so live with it." [10]

Along with our "war stories" (wounded passages from boyhood to questionable manhood) I welcomed and championed in *The Men's Journal*, the good fathers, who are out there, and deserve due recognition. In Stephen's story, we have such a one.

Thank you, Stephen, for sharing and praising the natural father.

Lessons My Father Taught Me
Stephen Barlas

On those weekend afternoons in 1967 when everyone else's father was locked inside the "9 to 5" prison, my dad made regular jailbreaks to the cracking asphalt tennis courts at Long Island's Carle Place High School.

I could not relax until he arrived. My nerves felt more tightly strung than the gut in my wooden, autographed, Wilson Kramer racquet. During warm-ups, the white tennis balls shooting off my racquet sprayed around my opponent's court like water drops from a rotary lawn sprinkler. The guy on the other side of the net drooled in anticipation. My thoughts were elsewhere, looking over my shoulder, straining to see the family Pontiac Catalina with black-wall tires lumber into the school parking lot.

Spectators rarely came to our tennis matches. At Carle Place High, like every other school, football was Zeus. Parents – even the mothers and fathers of my tennis teammates – jammed the football stadium stands on Saturday, as excitement and popping shoulder pads echoed around town. In those years before Connors and McEnroe, high school tennis drew sneers, not cheers.

Tennis's stigma never stopped Dad from attending both my home and away matches. Though the hour and the day were always inconvenient, he broke away from his civil engineering business in Queens. He never said why he came so religiously to my matches. I never asked for a reason.

As he dodged the field hockey players on his way from the parking lot, it was hard to tell what was shorter, his crewcut or their freshly-mowed playing field. Other fathers were letting their hair grow long. Being "mod" was not important to Dad, not any more than following the fad of white-walled tires. "Being there" – lugging a crumpled grocery bag filled with Hershey bars for our team – was.

When my father finally reached the 25-foot-high mesh fence that ran around the four courts that were veined with cracks, he crammed three fingers of his right hand through one of the tight, square wire openings.

That was what passed for a pre-match handshake. On those Fall afternoons, 17 years ago, excitement and confidence jumped through his fingers like electricity through a power line.

Remembrances of those three-fingered handshakes surfaced last year with the birth of my first child, Veronica. I work out of my house in Arlington as a freelance journalist. My wife, Margie, is at home caring for our daughter. Like everyone else, I am trying to get ahead. But there are numerous times during the day when I drop what I am doing and, sometimes eagerly and sometimes begrudgingly, skip downstairs from my second-floor office to help out or just to play. Veronica is a magnet. I am beginning to realize what drew my father to my high school tennis matches.

When my mother became pregnant with my brother early in 1951, the year after I was born, Dad was working for a construction company in the Bronx. In early December, on Sunday morning, Mom went into labor. That night Dad called his boss. He was taking paternity leave and he would not be in for two weeks, he said. Dad might as well have told him he was a communist.

Family also came between Dad and Lizza Brothers, another big construction company in New York in the 1950's and 60's. Lizza wanted Dad to work Saturdays, which he did. But when those weekends began to pile up like railroad cars in a wreck, Dad objected. Weekends were for the family. Pretty soon, he was spending whole weeks with us while he looked for a new job.

In my boyhood, almost every dad took his sons to Madison Square Garden, Yankee Stadium and later Shea Stadium to watch the New York professional teams. Few fathers, though, led their kids to the door outside the "home" dressing room to gawk at our heroes as they filed out. Dad not only led us to Olympus, he also tried to get photographs of us and our gods. Once he nearly became the object of a Sophoclean tragedy. In his enthusiasm, he popped a flash bulb in the face of Gump Worsley, the gruff New York Ranger hockey team goalie. The Gumper did not care about Dad's good intentions. What he cared about was being able to pull speeding hockey pucks out of the air. That rifled rubber disk would now have to compete with flash bulb spots for the attention of Gump's eyes once the game began. Clearly annoyed, Gump took his goalie stick, an imposing wooden scythe, and whipped it against the cement wall just outside the dressing room. It narrowly missed Dad's head.

There were a few times, though, when I wished the Gumper's aim had been better. My father's refusal to allow me to get my driver's license at age 17, when my friends were obtaining theirs, was one of them. He thought I would be better able to handle the responsibility at 18. This despite my life being as harmless as any Benedictine monk's.

The "no-drive" edict put a damper on a social life that was burning as well as damp logs. Practically the only dates that had ever brushed my lips were the ones in boxes in the fruit section of the A & P. When I started to go out as a high school senior, my dad had to drive me and the girl back and forth to wherever we were going. Mostly, we sat in the back seat as Dad piloted the Pontiac to movies in the area. It was then that I learned to squeeze every drop of meaning from the word "humiliation."

For me these days, "being there" means keeping enough diapers and wipes stacked on the dictionaries in my second-floor office. Sometimes it is inconvenient to help out with the baby sitting during my working hours. But on my way upstairs at 8 a.m., I pass our bedroom and hear Veronica's gleeful chattering. Out of the darkness, Margie's eyes catch mine. They say silently what her voice quickly confirms. She has been up three times during the night, feeding an avidly-nursing baby. She can get some much needed sleep if I take Veronica.

So up we go to my aerie; me, my daughter and her red sassy seat that I anchor onto the side of my desk. Work invariably beckons. And for a while, as madly-teething Veronica gnaws on a corner of my appointment book, progress is mine. But she eventually insists on my full attention.

Not much work gets done during those hours. That worries me. It is not always easy to sort out my priorities so that Veronica comes out on top. Yet Dad always seemed relaxed and content at my high school tennis matches. Work could not give him the satisfaction that I think he got from seeing my forehands and backhands starting to dive deep into my opponent's court.

He taught me the importance of "being there." It is a lesson I keep trying to remember. [11]

When Andrew's article came to the *Journal*, I felt like I was hanging out with one of the guys. Yeah, I remember that distinctive *fragrance* that wafts through your typical locker room, the by-product of good old honest sweat and crotches and Right Guard deodorant. Those were the good old days before those strangely suspect, innocuous little beige boxes mounted in the corner of the john were silently misting some de-people-izing, sanitizing chemical into the air – mute musak of a bacteria-free universe. If there's a sweet piece of male Americana for many men today, you'll reminisce with this one.

Locker Room Memories
Andrew Hidas

I went out and played a woefully rusty game of basketball the other day. Next week – God and my musculature willing – I think I'll play again.

Oh no, I'm not looking to get serious about it. As a young boy, there was never a time, it seemed, when I wasn't a basketball player. It was a given, like my name, my left-handedness, or my skin. *Ballplayer*.

But sixteen years of organized ball as a player and coach were finally enough to satiate my appetite for whistles and scoreboards and conference standings. There's no more glory to be had, no more fiery dreams to be stoked. Nothing unfinished in my – dare I say it? – "relationship" with the game.

When I left basketball to pursue graduate study, I sensed a kind of myopia in the world of sports. The vision of T.S. Eliot seemed more acute than that of Dean Smith, the "Four Quartets" infinitely superior to the "Four Corners" offense. I dismissed basketball as an arcane, self-limiting diversion as I explored the experiential smorgasbord of my 20's. There was a smug pride in dropping it from my life like an outworn relic, useless as an old shoe.

My world soon changed: credit card statements were rife with billings from "Moe's Used Books," while "Mitchell's Sporting Goods" dropped off into consumer limbo. Drilling the

18-footer from the baseline became passe; my new quest was for out-of-print books on William Blake.

As a boy, weekends always meant following my big brother down to the gym, baloney sandwiches and bananas in hand, like a regular 9-to-5 brownbagger job. Lunch was whenever our team lost and had to vacate the court. But suddenly, my Saturdays were spent pursuing Blake through the musty stacks at Moe's. It faintly reminded me of the gym, any gym, how all gyms smell. The used bookstore and the gymnasium are olfactory cousins, sharing a particular bond.

As for old man Mitchell, I was glad to see him survive the loss of my patronage. My leather hi-tops had become ripped, brittle, and stained with old sweat, my socks yellowed with time. (Actually, my books seem to degenerate in much the same way.) I saw no reason to replace them.

But now it's 1985, I'm much closer to 40 than 20, and I wonder about this urge to play again.

There is, I would speculate, the matter of roots, of returning to what I know and have done well. There is the beautiful concreteness of a game with rules and boundaries, a beginning and end. Basketball can be a well-defined anchor in a shifting and relative age.

There is the desire to piece together the whole of my life, to feel its expanse. Some months ago I looked in the mirror and found gray hairs, along with a sudden sense of history. There is also a desire to tread lightly towards middle-age with a well rounded exercise program, after several years (and several thousand miles) of single-minded, single muscle-group obsession with roadrunning. My knees easily survived the million jumps and cuts of my basketball career, but eight marathons seemed to age them 80 years.

On the court, there are those exquisite details of the low-post cut, the backdoor pass, the carefully timed tap. There is the occasional competitive flicker, the flailing elbow or grunting rebound. And oh, that flying dipsy-doo bank shot, the muttering opponent, a familiar glow of satisfaction rising in your chest, warming your veins!

Afterwards, there is laughter and relaxed beer-drinking, which have (thankfully) replaced the cokes and bumbling post-game romantic maneuverings of more tormented adolescent years. While I may have lost the elegance of my hook shot, so too have I lost the awkwardness of my kiss, and I pronounce myself pleased with the trade.

All the foregoing has to do with reasons for again picking up a ball. But as Pascal said in "Pensees" ($1.95, used, Penguin edition at Moe's, unmarked), "The heart has its reasons that reason knows not of."

And the heart knows about the locker room.

Probably no symbol is more universal, more readily understood, more evocative of what is deepest and most indelible in an athlete's memory than the locker room. Mention it to an athlete and there is an immediate nod of recognition; locker rooms are everywhere one and the same.

Every athlete *knows* the locker room in a way that he (or *she;* something that has changed dramatically since I last laced up sneakers) knows few other things. He knows it in his gut, with his nose, in the way he sits on its benches and stands in its showers, in the way he walks through the locker room door. It is a knowledge born of elementals: sweat and tiredness, exhaustion and injury, pungent smells, bitter tears, jubilation and victory, regret and defeat. Within that barren stone room, the athlete learns both the purity and the passing of all his accomplishments, and the renewed intention that lifts him from failure.

I remember sitting in locker rooms, my head on drawn-up knees, weeping, tears warming the cold concrete floor. There was a crucial, missed free throw or misdirected pass; whether it was against Lincoln or Belmont or perhaps in college against Whittier hardly matters now. The particularities fade. Yet they were losses of a heart wrenching totality, when the promised rewards ("Work hard, be a team, give your all, and the championship is yours") were not forthcoming, and youthful hope stood betrayed. Everyone then sought his own refuge in the locker room, there to sit and grieve, dumbfounded. They felt like tragedies at the time, and they were.

Yet there are thousands of joyful hours and showers and joshing, jiving conversations that also comprise one's locker room past. And for an athlete there is always a future: the next practice, the next game, the next year ("Next season starts *Tomorrow*" is a favorite scrawl on locker room blackboards of all those whose seasons end short of that final salvific championship).

For me, "next season" began just the other day, 12 seasons after my last one, as I stood in yet another locker room rummaging around for two pairs of socks and a jock. As I slipped into an old cotton shirt and shorts and stooped over a gym bag to unpack my new shoes, I had to pause. Another collision with the power of memory was upon me, and I did well to sit, to bow, and to be washed by its waves. [12]

> *. . . then the day came*
> *when the risk to remain*
> *tight in a bud*
> *was more painful*
> *then the risk it took*
> *to blossom . . .*

Anais Nin

CHAPTER III

MEN SUPPORTING MEN

A Men's Group? Me?

Yevrah Ornstein

There comes a time when change becomes imperative. I believe we are at such a juncture, individually and collectively.

As Jim Croce said in one of his songs:

> . . . *cause I've had my share of good intentions*
> *and I made my share of mistakes*
> *and I've learned at times it's best to bend*
> *because if you don't*
> *well, those are the breaks.*

Perhaps there have been moments in your life when you too have felt up against a wall, at an impasse, truly stuck. We've all known crises such as these where if something didn't give, then it surely felt as though something was going to break.

One such impasse came to me at the end of a six-year relationship with a woman. After repeated endings, the grand finale finally came, digging its heels in one day with the proclamation: *"That's it, no more!"* Too much damage, too much pain and too much loss of self-respect – for both of us.

Not long afterwards I saw an ad for a "men's group." Living in the San Francisco Bay Area you get to see every type of therapy, every type of supplement, every type of anything imaginable, and then some – *ad nauseum.*

This was a new one for me though: a "men's group." The woman I had lived with had been in a women's group for several years and although I had certain fears and concerns about the privacy of our inner relationship being discussed with a group of outsiders, I saw clearly and dramatically the benefits she gathered

47

from their weekly get-togethers. Perhaps one of the most attractive and obvious pluses was the quality of the friendships that evolved amongst these women, most of whom I liked and respected a great deal.

I called the phone number in the ad and was greeted by a guy named Larry. He was one of the two facilitators leading the men's group (both of whom were psychologists), and they were putting out the word for their third such group. The two things that grabbed my interest were the weekly topics and the immediate comfort and ease I felt with this stranger. The topics were intriguing, and the prospect of delving into – really exploring – such potent topics with a group of other interested men was enticing and fascinating. Larry was a man who sounded genuine and real and fun to be with; the kind of guy you could really get down with – trust, really trust with your innermost thoughts and feelings and then go out and throw a football with. I also liked the fact that both he and his partner Randy had done other men's groups; we weren't going to be their guinea pigs.

Fifteen men showed up that first evening, most of whom stayed for the full eight weeks. We met one evening a week, and Randy and/or Larry would present a topic: intimacy, anger, sexuality or competition, etc. Information was given in a lecture style, but it was made real, alive, and three dimensional because they spoke freely of themselves, their relationships, their joys as well as their frustrations – past and present. They personalized the material in such a way that made both them and the topics accessible and circumvented the podium style lecture, the kind where you often feel like you're being talked down to – "I know this stuff and you don't" – a style that leaves me irritated, cynical and usually disinterested. Anything other than "we're in this together" would have been contrary to the spirit of the group. Whether they intended it or not, there was a feeling that translated into, "Hey guys, we're all bozos on this bus." I think we were all pretty much dazed and mystified by this wild creature called *relationships*. That feeling of shared disorientation and confusion wasn't one of embarassment but, interestingly enough, it felt comforting to know that these other men were in the same boat, or perhaps I should say, bus.

So this was why these things were called support groups.

The rest of the evening we spent talking about our lives as they related to the topic for the evening.

As the weeks passed by, I looked forward with growing excitement to each gathering. I found it fascinating to hear other men speak openly and honestly about themselves, how they *really* felt about women, their jobs, sex, their dads, so forth and so on. The barriers were coming down, male posturing atrophied as we became more comfortable speaking and sharing from our hearts.

The group was entitled, "Men in Relationships," and I was the only one without one, being freshly and painfully separated and sorely in need of a deeper understanding of what went wrong and what not to do next time.

Most of the men were older than me, which was a surprise. I was 32 at the time, about half were in their 50's and 60's, and one was in his early 20's (looked upon with much respect and envy – to be getting a jump on this material so early), with the rest of us being in our 30's and 40's. About half the guys were married and, all in all, the mix was excellent.

It felt healing to be with these men. The group served as an antidote to the way I had become in the last couple of years. I felt free to talk of things without fear of attack or an ensuing argument. I felt trusting of the men there and I felt like I was being heard in ways that I hadn't experienced in too long.

And perhaps most welcome of all, I felt accepted – not judged.

I came to see that most of us, most men, feel very alone and unique with our problems. The idealized version of the male we've inherited paints a picture of perfection: steady, self-assured, confident, able to get it up and keep it up at a moment's notice, athletically superior, fearless, all knowing, stoic . . . Most men today can verify that, from early on, these are but a few of the messages, images and models we've been bombarded with.

How can a man be nurturing and empathetic when one of the central and earliest of instructions in masculinity is, *big boys don't cry?*

How could we not feel grossly inadequate by way of comparison? Our true feelings run head long into the abstract, culturally sanctioned, idealized man. Imagine the conflict between these underground feelings of inadequacy, not cutting the mustard, not making the grade, while believing deep down that other men are together, other men know what it means to be a man – it's just me and a few others that don't seem to have the program down. If no one's talking about it, I guess there isn't (or shouldn't be) a problem, right? These ambivalent feelings, way down there, are felt to be "inappropriate," "unmanly," because of our intense, relentless and heretofore unexamined training. We are thereby urged to sweep this seething cauldron of conflicting feelings under the rug, and if they do surface and if they are felt at all, they are to be stoically endured in solitude, lest we be seen as weak and inferior, a sissy or a fag.

All of this crap, these intensely contradictory messages, compound and feed the dilemma of knowing oneself as a man.

❀   ❀   ❀

It is immensely healing and comforting for men to hear other men reveal their true selves; their pains, disappointments, inadequacies, as well as their triumphs and joys. It's as if the weight of a life falsely lived begins to be taken off of one's shoulders and looked at honestly and realistically for the sham and the burden that it really is.

Here's a fine story by Keith along these lines.

The Way Of The Lodge
Keith Thompson

Opening the door is easier than Roxanne imagined it would be, as is walking out into the humid morning air. Gary sits there, says nothing, watches her go. Both know she won't be living in that house again. He knows their ten year marriage has been getting "weird" (his word), but he didn't believe Roxanne would ever just . . . leave. Now she's gone. He folds his clenched hands onto the kitchen table and stares, numbed, through streaked glass at the neighbor's vacant back yard. "Oh great," he finally says aloud, to which the house responds with intimidating apathy. He places his head in his hands and tries gain: "Oh, this is just great." Still nothing. Thought: So this is how it will be. Thought: I hate that thought. Pause. Thought: God, I hate my life.

Weeks pass. Roxanne files for divorce. Gary gets stoned. Gary stays stoned. His friend Bob tells him about a group of men who get together one night each week to talk about problems with work, tensions with women, hassles with their kids, doubts about living, and, occasionally, fears of dying. Bob suggests he join.

"You gotta be kidding," Gary responds. "I wouldn't be caught dead at something so trite and precious and self-important as a men's therapy group." Gary is angry and hurt, and being angry and hurt with no male friends is every bit as good as being angry and hurt with no female friends. Bob assures him it's "just a regular gathering of men who talk about real things," and repeats his invitation. Gary again declines. Bob says, "It may help." Gary looks at him, thinks for a moment, and then says, "Okay, I'll try it."

At first Gary listens to other men's stories. "I assumed from the start that my own problems were stupid and trivial, so I just shut up." By the second meeting he's talking. To his surprise, the men listen; so he continues talking. About Roxanne. About *all* women. About "how women are." His voice fills with an anger he tries to control. Bob says: "You don't have to swallow your anger. Not here." Gary pauses, and then thinks to himself: "Right." He stops swallowing it long enough to let out a bellowing roar, one that lifts him off his chair and onto trembling legs.

Looking around the room, expecting rejection, he's surprised to see smiles. Sinking back into his seat, he feels warm energy running up his spine. "That's all for now," he says, finally laughing at himself. The men laugh with him and then, a rich silence fills the room. For the rest of the evening he listens to others talk about what's going on in their lives. By the end of the meeting, he has made a striking realization: his personal fears, doubts, and anxieties aren't as sickeningly subjective as they seem in the enforced solitude of what he calls "that desperately empty house." *Other* men have similar problems!

After Gary became a regular member of the group, we spent a morning down at our regular breakfast haunt talking about what he feels he's been learning.

"All through college in the 70's, my best friends were feminist women," he told me. "The few male friends I had were involved in questioning the idea that men must always be strong, silent, unflinching, disciplined, invulnerable, and largely unresponsive to women. It was the first wave of the age of the sensitive male. We placed a huge premium on a kind of openness to women's feelings that I now realize was a hybrid of sensitivity, uncertainty, and a fear of being deemed ideologically impure by feminist friends and lovers who were setting the standards."

"Not a bad deal," I said. "In terms of getting approval from strong women, being perceived as a sensitive, caring man has its payoffs."

"That's part of it," he said. "The process also allowed me to see myself as superior to other men, who *obviously* weren't as finely-tuned, politically or spiritually. The pay-off lay in our right to interpret the approval of politically correct, independent women as evidence that my few friends and I, along with Phil Donahue and Alan Alda, were among a handful of prototypical 'transformed American men.'" He paused for a moment. "If you ever want to feel really alienated from every other male alive today or at any time in history, just start telling feminist women you agree with Susan Brownmiller that all men are latent rapists – all men except *me*, of course."

We sat together silently in the restaurant as a waiter refilled our coffee cups. "I'm interested," I continued, "in something you've said twice: that you had only a few male friends during this period."

"A very few," he said. "My pattern was always to go to one of my assertive women friends everytime I felt wounded or some sense of failure. I always assumed most other men didn't want to hear about my weakness, whereas a woman will usually be sympathetic. Like most men I know, I've always found it easier to talk about 'the deep stuff' with women . . . " (Gary paused to find the right words) . . . "but since I joined this men's group, the exclusivity of this feels off-base."

"More than that, it took me a while to see that expecting women to find any of my stuff interesting was a naive and a doomed expectation. Lately, I've begun to sense that male feelings and female feelings are just different – different modes altogether. I can't prove that, or even explain it, really. I simply no longer believe that entering my feelings is synonymous with entering my so-called feminine side, or checking out of what I consider to be essentially male within me."

In the weeks after I talked with Gary, I began to think about the way two or more male friends talking about things they value is related to something ancient, something sacred: The Male Lodge.

In nearly every culture, the lodge – as a mythic image, a metaphor, and often a physical place – has been associated with certain feeling-qualities of men being men together. In traditional cultures, the sweat lodge is where songs and prayers are offered all through the night. Other lodges, like my father's, feature the sounds of billiard balls and poker chips as background songs. When Ralph Cramden and Ed Norton and Stan Laurel and Oliver Hardy needed time to get themselves out of trouble, especially with their wives, they invariable headed for the lodge.

Although sweat lodges, Elks and Rotary gatherings and men's rap groups don't serve precisely the same functions, they do tend to share some rather enduring ideas: Refuge. Sanctuary. Privacy. Friendship. Comraderie. Brotherhood. As a physical location, the lodge provides retreat from concerns about money and work, family pressures, and responsibility to roles prescribed by what Jung called "the collective."

And, a place to get away from women. *Not because women are wrong, or the enemy, but because they are, in fact, women, and men are men, and men and women need time away from one another.*

As Gary discovered, when the male lodge takes the form of a men's talk-group, it can become a context for the naming of male wounds, often beginning with blame. Though blame itself can't heal wounds, the act of blaming a person or situation signals that at least *some* degree of emotion has returned to a man's numbed, overly-apologetic psyche.

Blame can even be courageous if it leads beyond itself, down into feelings of guilt and rage, and even deeper into old sorrows whose connections aren't clear; toward ancient feelings of loss and abandonment, near the naked sense of inferiority which Rambo's firepower cannot mask, but makes only more obvious – and more pathetic.

Inferiority – Alfred Adler said to be human means to be inferior; perhaps inferiority is the deepest wound of all. And yet men, myself included, find it easier to discuss feelings of inferiority with women – perhaps because patriarchal Western culture has objectified women *as* inferior. At the very least, men are generally reticent to discuss "the wound" in the presence of other men. One power of the male lodge – whether as an actual physical place or as the simple pleasures of long term friendship – is that it allows men to develop feeling judgments and values of their own, unconstrained by the notion that women are the rightful arbiters of feelings. Because intimacy, and feeling in general, is defined in our culture as "a feminine mode," male intimacy is seen not as *different* from women's, but *as inferior when compared with women's*. In this sense, feeling in our culture tends to be over-determined by women. As Jungian psychologist James Hillman puts it: "First of all mothers, next sisters and aunts, grandmothers and teachers, and then childhood lovers exert their influence over the development of the feeling function in men and women."

Men's therapy groups, poker clubs, fishing cabins, pool halls, ski condos, rain-or-shine running partnerships, men working together on an extended project: all are lodge archetypes. Perhaps a lodge exists when any group of men are allowed to *be real* together; sometimes in silence, other times through words – especially words that help work through some of the gnarled stuff and which keep old wounds from healing.

In ancient Greece, men would take important questions to the oracles; questions like: "To which God must I make an offering or sacrifice so I can come to terms with my suffering and understand its connections to the rest of my life?" One mode of woundedness belonged to Apollo, another to Dionysius, others to Hermes and Hephaistos. Greek Gods were not merely idols of worship, statues in parks, or centerpieces of city pools into which coins were tossed for good luck. They were, rather, archetypal symbols and psychic patterns; profound images for styles of living; distinct constellations of inner energies which resonated with similar patterns in the soul of the world.

Each Greek God was, in a sense, also a place – a lodge, if you will – enabling a specific way of *treating* the wound. A particular kind of wound was understood to belong to a particular

God, or mythic structure, or metaphoric "location." "Taking the wound to Apollo" was in some way connected with bringing clarity to suffering, with delivering the wound to consciousness. Hermes the Messenger held the place for ambiguity, multiple meanings, and irreverence.

Ecstatic Dionysius helped to dismember the wound, to differentiate it into discrete parts – the task of psychotherapist and shaman alike. Hephaistos, the lame-footed blacksmith scorned by Zeus for his deformity, personified the skilled and sensitive artist who experiences *through* the perspective of a crippling wound, rather than transcending (denying) his inferiority in the hope of some higher glory.

When what first appears as personal suffering steeped in shame or guilt begins to recognize itself in the motifs of myth, fairy tales and other teaching stories, something changes. New questions become possible: "What story have I been living, and whose story is it?" And new insights: "This is not my story alone." Crisis may convert to koan, emptiness to openness. No less pain, perhaps. But finally *the wound speaks to us.*

Make no mistake: your average Moose Lodge is seldom a place where men can be found sitting around exploring their woundedness. (Not even in California). One of the factors in "making a lodge" is the stipulation that, at least for this time, in this place, we gather together apart from every other identity; we gather as provider, father, husband, and lover; in this place, now, we gather *as men.*

This shared understanding is in itself a way of getting on speaking terms with wounds specific to being male, a process quite different from the subtle, heroic rationalizations of defeat and failure ("It was all for the good – I've learned many lessons as a result").

Where then is the lodge? How does one get there? The path is so overgrown that it is hard to recognize the need to begin asking ourselves difficult questions: "To which *place* must I carry my anguish that I may understand and live with it? What is the meaning of this deep loneliness?" Questions like these seldom point the way to quick or soothing answers. They don't provide peace of mind. But asked regularly, and intently, they can begin to point the way beyond whining and blame, beyond projecting long-denied griefs onto women, onto our families, and onto the world at large.

The lodge door opens wherever and whenever men walk this path, which is also the path of *living* our wounds. Living them, as in seeking their purpose, learning why they are present. As in not refusing their dark energies, their veiled gifts, the opaque depressions that somehow open to new depths of soul. As in Dr. Freud's remark about the equally modest and ambitious goal of psychoanalysis: to transform hysterical misery into ordinary unhappiness.

I'm not suggesting we shift from Rambo's denial of pain to Sartre's romanticising and idealizing it. (Rambo's lodge and Sartre's have one thing in common: by definition, they can have only one member.) Rather, I'm reaching for words and images to confide and entrust to fellow men, the knowledge of not-so-private wounds.

Trust, a Zen master once said, is a continent with an infinite coastline and an endless interior.

If this is so, where do we begin?

Here, where we are. So far, I know one thing: the task doesn't require us to stop talking to women, only that we start talking to each other: "Man to man," as my father, and every father, has at one time said. This is the way of the lodge. [13]

CHAPTER IV

THE ILLS OF THE MACHO MAN

As Keith so aptly writes, ". . . the task doesn't require us to stop talking to women, only that we start talking to each other." Yes, this was what some of the power and value of that first men's group was about, talking to one another, for the first time. There was something new and different for me with those men that had to do with extending boundaries of intimacy. I have always had close male friends. Boys and men with whom I have had the closeness and comfort of being somewhat emotionally open.

It's common to hear men speak of their inability to get beyond sports, politics and business in their conversations with friends and co-workers. I've been fortunate to know men who have felt comfortable with varying degrees of vulnerability, but it was almost always when it was just the two of us, when we were in private, alone. In that men's group I was beginning to explore quality, heart-felt communication and caring with a large group of men, and as the weeks progressed and the level of trust matured for all of us, it became easier and easier and very rewarding to reveal ourselves to one another.

Being honest about oneself and one's feeling is truly a liberating experience. To be in the company of another who is doing so, feels like a gift.

In our time together, I often reflected upon my powerful man-woman relationship that had crashed. It had been the most significant friend/lover relationship of my life. Although drained and exhausted by the struggles and the hurts that had become the norm in the last couple of years that we were together, I wasn't bitter. Very much to the contrary, I had never before felt so grief-stricken.

The men's group had opened my heart to the deep pain that resided within. It was there that I felt supported and encouraged to feel my true feelings – all of them. With this newly found clarity, I wrote the following piece a year or so after our separation.

Beyond The Place Where There Is Time
Yevrah Ornstein

The place is Delphi, Greece, the home of the Oracle and the Temple of Apollo. And as the days and the weeks unravel, I am discovering why I was drawn there one day in the month of April.

The official portion of the ruins is swarming and overrun with tourists from all corners of the globe. This twentieth century dance of nasal "Hey Harry, come get a look at this" struck me as strange and paradoxical to the intent and solemnity of Delphi.

I needed to get away from this scene and do some exploring; this is my preferred way. I came upon a path that, in the way of a gesture, was partitioned off by a broken down little gate. Often that's all that's needed to dissuade most tourists – but for me, it usually reads as a flashing neon sign that says, "Yes you, come on in."

Passing through, I found more remnants of an ancient glory, relics of an engineering masterpiece scattered about and a solitary man totally absorbed in measuring, drawing, and recording sculptured stones. He was wonderful in his total absorption, concentration, complete oneness with his work and obliviousness to the rest of the world. I couldn't help but wonder if he was one of the original builders of Delphi, returning to build once again, this time from another perspective.

Wandering further down this path, out of view and away from the din of the tourists, I came upon something that surprised me, initially; then I felt intrigued, as it beckoned and finally captured me. Carved into the mountain, was – I'm not quite sure what to call it – a cavern. On the outside were bench-like areas worn thin with the passing of centuries. I felt a deep sense of reverence and awe, and found myself reflexively and instinctively bowing before slowly entering. It felt like a very special and holy sanctuary. Inside were three bath-like coffins recessed beneath arches, at right angles to one another. How strange and fascinating that my first impression conveyed such seemingly disparate images: not knowing if I was looking at bathing pools or open coffins.

At the zenith of its glory, as has been passed down through the annals of time, Delphi was laced with hugging, volcanic, gaseous clouds, slivering up through crevice and rock, creating what must have been a truly awe inspiring, mystical feeling. As I found out later, this was indeed one of the reasons this site was chosen for the Oracle of Greece. As I thought about the relationship between a place to bathe, to rejuvenate, rest, and be revived – juxtaposed with the strong image of coffins and death, – my thoughts went to the inextricable relationship between life and death, endings and beginnings, decay and renewal. Rather than deferring to official or scholarly records to discover the purpose and history of this cavern, I decided to be as open as possible to the energies of what struck me as a sanctuary – to feel into and follow their beckoning whispers.

The positioning of the baths/coffins reminded me of the body – the left and right symmetries, the center being the heart. It seemed to me that conflicts in one's life may be resolved in the center, in the heart. *"As a man thinketh in his heart . . ."* Perhaps this is the path of balance, of harmony, of peace and of resolution.

As my thoughts and feelings drifted, I realized how difficult it had been for me to let myself be nurtured and cared for by lovers, by friends, and even by myself; to be taken care of emotionally, physically, sexually . . . to allow myself to receive. And the presence, the spirit of this sanctuary was comforting to the deep sadness that was upon me. And with that comfort, I came, at last, to say goodbye to a deep relationship of many years. She was to marry another.

And so I saw the connection to my impression of death; the coffins of this place. They symbolized allowing a part of myself, a macho way of being, to die. I realized that to nurture myself means acceptance – accepting the way things are, accepting the pain when it's there, and accepting the struggles I've known, as well as the joys; and to cease trying to change them, deny them, or make them go away. For me, this was a different kind of warrior than I've been before.

My tears, like the springs that fed those baths, came from within the flesh of the earth – from the core of my being, bringing healing, nurturance, and new beginnings. [14]

❆   ❆   ❆

What one society prizes and respects as desirable is often frowned upon or ridiculed by another. There are primitive tribes where men are lavishly pampered through a "male pregnancy" while the pregnant wives continue working in the fields. Greek and Italian men hold hands in the street, while their American counterparts are viewed with revulsion. Can any of these behaviors be called innate, or normal or abnormal?

When we look closely at behavior patterns and compare our outward actions to our inner feelings, we know something is wrong. Each one of us knows that we do some things because they have been imposed on us by our culture. And the more we examine our own feelings, the more we sense that many of these cultural impositions don't fit. Much of the material in this book is meant to help us examine our own, real feelings and, by so doing, discover what we are – not what society thinks we should be.

Of all the poems I received in my time with the *Journal*, the following is my all time favorite and now it is my privilege to share it with you.

No One Told Me
Robert F. Anderson

*They don't tell you
what it's like
to hold the naked body
of your child
fresh from the bath.
There's no "Father's School"
to instruct you*

in the joy of a wet and squirming,
then dry and
incredibly soft
little bottom.
Only mothers
pass on the folklore
surrounding that joy
Fathers are merely told
of pride
when the kid gets to school or
Eagle Scouts or
the football team or
the roll call of dead veterans.

I can only anguish at
all the joy I missed
all the closeness I avoided
because of the embarrassment
at touching the nakedness
of my infant sons.
No one taught me one could be
intimate
without being sexual.

And now suddenly
my babies are grown men,
knowing how to be a father
only from me.

I'm sorry boys.
So sorry.

But no one told me. **[15]**

❊   ❊   ❊

Many of us have a place inside of us that is empty, yet
consists of deep, pent-up and bruised emotions that are due to

hidden societal expectations. These emotions are also composed of longing for the loving, close contact we desire from our fathers. We learned that being close to our fathers wasn't supposed to be part of growing into a man. We were taught to mimic our fathers. They taught us the best they knew how, modeling the men we were to become. The ache we once felt, that urge to embrace our fathers, diminished in time because eventually we accepted that "that's the way it is." Fathers and sons were taught not to be close, at least in the physical sense, and eventually, in every way. By cutting off one aspect of human contact, we eventually cut off the rest. For most of us, this learned pattern of becoming a man was more of a rule than not. It was the acceptable norm, and most father and son relationships model this kind of non-intimacy. Then the sons carry this kind of relationship into their adult and family lives and continue it with their own sons. It is no wonder that men are scared to death of close, intimate contact with other men. From the beginning we are taught that men do not become intimate with one another. Our fathers, brothers, playmates and the whole community continually remind us of this script. We learn that if the majority conforms to this conduct and practice, it must be right. To have differing feelings is wrong. So, our nation has produced men who are practicing the "right way" of interacting with other men and this continues to leave an emotional wound. [16]

❀　　　　❀　　　　❀

Why, Dad?
Yevrah Ornstein

My father was a very physical, playful man in our early years. He was the only father I knew who would spend time with me and my friends; trips down to Mary's Carvel stand for soft ice cream, weekends on the boat, organizing baseball games for my birthday, swims in the ocean, wrestling, being pinned down and tickled to the edge of near-suffocation (a bittersweet experience). This was some of the great stuff of having a dad. I still remember how it felt to fall asleep on the couch and to have Dad carry me up to bed in what felt like the most secure place in the world to be – his arms. These are sweet remembrances.

Then something happened. A physical distancing came into our lives. I somehow knew, intuitively, that it was no longer appropriate for us to have this touching kind of relationship – it was indeed time to "be a man."

I could see Dad reach out to me as he always did, uninhibitedly, and then stop mid-motion and pull his arm back. The physical contact had always felt natural, unquestioned, taken for granted. What happened, Dad?

There have been times when I've met childhood friends many years later and compared stories – our recollection of times gone by, but more importantly, what we were thinking and feeling inside; the stuff we never talked about. Children don't have the means, the verbal skills to articulate many of these feelings, those currents that are coursing through so sharply. How could I, without the words, tell my dad I was confused and upset about this change? And besides, we never had conversations, anyway. I don't ever remember him asking me how I felt or what I thought about.

His own uncertainty no doubt contributed to my confusion as to what was happening. I remember sensing, feeling the ways in which he was torn internally. I could feel him at cross currents with his desires, his natural impulses to be close to me and my brothers in this way; and yet there was that foreign messenger, pulling him away from us. It's no mystery to me today who that intruder was – it was the ghost of his father, and his father's father and so on for who knows how many generations. The ghosts of the past carried with them the memories and the hurts and the weight of many, many years of blindly accepted customs.

It has been enlightening and comforting to hear many other men speak of similar experiences and memories, and as is so often the case, we had quietly wondered as children: *Did I do something wrong?*

The issue of lineage, the passing along from father to son that which was inherited, is seen here through the eyes of another son:

Your Fathers
Maxwell Reif

Your fathers enjoyed things,
Your fathers got their hearts broken too.
They were young, they were small,
They were cared for by their parents,
They saw the snow in the city for the first time and wondered,
They found themselves suddenly big and wondered where
childhood
had gone like clothes outgrown,
They found the world suddenly difficult and wondered
where Magic had gone,
And the shock was so painful they decided
To forget there ever was such a thing as Magic,
In their hearts now are horses and carts and snowy streets
from fifty years ago,
Things Chagall expressed but few else ever could.
Your fathers lingered in a small world just like you
Fifteen years to find it gone like water left in the sun.
They sipped and dawdled the morning
Only to find all at once the harsh light of the afternoon.
Your fathers' fathers were a world of mist and green,
A primeval world rising out of non-being for them,
A world they kissed goodbye
As you will kiss your father goodbye
And your son will kiss you.

Fathers who ride on one horizon and set on another,
That is all we ever have,
And we are forever saying goodbye,
And hello. [17]

As I said before, I am convinced that much of what we call masculine and feminine do not exist as <u>innate</u> attributes. I think we are composites of a far vaster range of expression than we presently understand.

Our yearning, our need for touch as human beings, is vital to our survival and wellbeing. The father does not simply lose his natural desire to be in physical contact with his son, it doesn't simply evaporate. The impulse, the need and the pleasure go elsewhere as they are sublimated and all too often redirected into business or other "appropriately" defined pursuits. As these impulses are channeled elsewhere, distortions occur.

In a world in which yearnings and impulses are boxed in, constricted by narrow definitions of male and female, we solidify the process through our judgements and need for conformity.

It's okay for a father to touch his son but only up to a certain age (if at all), at least on this side of the Atlantic.

Our denial is related in part to Jung's view of "shadow" creation. The denied "feminine" is disenfranchised, repressed, and sublimated, and its unwanted traits are distorted and placed elsewhere; i.e., on the feared and hated homosexual, or on Reagan's casting of the Soviet Union as the "Evil Empire," etc.

Robert Bly addresses this dynamic within the family when he writes:

> *Then what? If a man, cautious*
> *hides his limp, Somebody has to limp it! Things*
> *do it; the surroundings limp.*
> *House walls get scars*
> *the car breaks down; matter in drudgery, takes it up.*

Continuing the plight of the son-father relationship, Shepherd Bliss discusses its psychological and socio-political ramifications for society. In the following article, Shepherd raises the question: In light of the son's longing for the father and its prevalence amongst men today, is it any wonder there is a crisis in masculinity?

Fathers And Sons
Shepherd Bliss

What I'm going to do now is tell you some stories. I'm not going to draw too many conclusions from these stories. I suggest that you draw your own conclusions. I'll draw a few of my conclusions. Your conclusions may be very different. But I'm going to tell you some stories about some men in my life.

But first I want to frame this by talking about three elements of our historical moment that I think are really important as we think about ourselves as men, individually and collectively. First of all, it is crucial that we think about our international moment; a key characteristic of our international moment as U.S. men is that the United States lost the war in Viet Nam – the first war that we lost. Then we were humiliated in Iran, and finally, to try to get it up, the United States went into tiny Grenada. Think about that. Think about what that means. That's where we went to try to resurrect that soldier image, which is one of the places men have historically gone to find their masculinity.

A second place is economics. What's happening economically? I can tell by the looks on your faces that you know what I'm talking about. We're under-employed. We're unemployed, and we're not as often employed with our hands as we were. We're employed in service sectors, using our minds. This changes how we feel about ourselves. Many women are demanding access to our jobs. This changes it. The traditional breadwinner image of what it means to be a man has changed.

The third thing is our domestic situation. Think about what's happening, domestically, to men today. I spoke to a couple of men immediately before this talk and I was struck by the new demands on men, domestically – to help with the children, to do dishes. Basically legitimate demands, but what it means is that we're no longer king of the castle. So the soldier image, the breadwinner image, the king of the castle – these have all changed.

Is it any wonder that there's a crisis in masculinity? Is it any wonder that many men are confused and some go into violence? They go into self-abuse, child abuse, spouse abuse or other-abuse. Or they go into passivity. They go into that soft man that's just so passive.

So the issues of masculinity are not only individual issues, as we each work toward being the best possible man. They have to do with our nation and our world. I want to bring these two – the personal and the political – together here from the beginning . . .

So now let me take a leap from the personal metaphor that I've been using to talk about our society as a whole, and what's happening with respect to fathers in our society. Our disconnectedness from our wounded fathers has a lot to do with the problems in the world today; we need to work on them not only politically in an electoral way, but politically in a personal way in terms of what's inside us as men.

The male longing for the father has an intimate biological basis and a social-political basis. This is a time – it has been for a while now – that sons are longing for fathers. So these sons explore different options, often destructive, turning to certain kinds of leaders: gurus, spiritual leaders, that may lead them astray. I'm not saying that all spiritual leaders do that, because they don't. Many of them are beautiful. Many political leaders, also, will lead us astray. Many figures emerge in this vacuum, and people will give up their own common sense in order to follow that leader, because this is a time of great longing. The return to the father is a torturous return, and the path is unclear.

The issues surrounding men and masculinity take on a much greater importance during this Nuclear Age, when the planet is threatened by destruction. The preservation of this planet and this endangered species of humans is dependent in great extent, now, upon men getting back in contact with some of our ancient values of bravery, courage, preservation of family and that which we love – including the land which gives us survival. We men, as men (in addition to as humans and as citizens), need to get back to being men as life-preserving agents. At the Ninth National Conference on Men and Masculinity in Washington, D.C., Joseph Pleck spoke to this when he gave the keynote. He said that the bomb has transformed the importance of masculinity today by transforming its consequences. [18]

In this next piece, Stan Dale provides further insights into the schizophrenic consequenses of our limited notions of "appropriate" gender.

Why Men Are So "Crazy"
Stan Dale

Women give birth to and raise little girls/young women. Women give birth to and raise little boys/young men. Therewith starts the cycle which produces "crazy" men. Because boys don't usually have in their fathers a role model for tenderness, warmth, intimacy, and sensuality, all their ideas about these things come from women – specifically, their mothers. As a result, we men are forever at war with ourselves, and with everyone else as well. In our society, men who exhibit qualities of tenderness, compassion, intimacy, and warmth (mother's qualities) are reviled and castigated by both men and women. Yet is there a woman alive who hasn't longed for a tender man? And, secretly, don't most men yearn to drop the tough-guy act?

A steelworker friend of mine who lives in Chicago epitomizes the typical macho man. One day, tears in his eyes, he confided that he writes poetry, and that it is his greatest wish to feel, before he dies, the softness of a bird with his hands. In actuality these man's hands are rougher than scouring pads. They are the hands a "manly" man is supposed to have. They are the hands that support him and his family by doing work he secretly hates, the same hands of his steelworker father before him. Nevertheless, this man is a sensitive person and his desire is to be able to express himself sensitively.

The instant a male baby is born, the delivery room becomes a metaphor for the rest of his life. With rare exceptions, the male baby is touched briefly by the male doctor before being thrust into the care of the female nurse and then into the waiting arms of his mother. The father gets to hold the newborn infant for a few minutes and then immediately hands it back to the mother, who, for the next eighteen years or so, is the sole guardian of the child's life. Except for a few brief moments, the male child is suckled, reared, and nurtured by women.

I'm not blaming women for men's craziness. They, too, are victims of cruel social programming.

Scared Silly

As a man, I believe there is no way I can fully know what a woman wants, feel what a woman feels, act as a woman acts, or understand psychologically and physiologically what a woman is. I can try to intellectualize about it, but that's the best I can do. Realizing my own limitations in understanding women, how can I expect a woman to know any more about men than I do about her?

Hell, we men don't even know ourselves. We're scared silly of other men. We don't trust them and we sure as hell don't want to get intimate with one. What "real" man would ever cuddle or kiss another man – let alone engage in sex with one?

But it's "natural" for a woman to suck a man's cock, right? We want women to do to us what we'd never do to ourselves. Then we call them "cunts," "nymphomaniacs," and "whores."

We don't treat ourselves much better. We call each other "cocksuckers" and "motherfuckers" and everything else in between. Ever wonder why so many put-downs are sexual?

I think it's because men are still at war with the femaleness inside themselves and with all it represents. We're not merely angry with women, we're angry with those like ourselves – other inorganic, gyandromorphic ("exhibiting characteristics of both sexes") males.

As boys we needed our fathers to nurture us and provide us with our identities, but even if father was around, nurturing wasn't his job. Our fathers were inorganic too, and we've just become their carbon copies. (The trusty dictionary also tells us that "inorganic" means "not arising from natural growth.")

From early childhood, the "crazy" boy is fed confusing information. "Girls are made of sugar and spice and everything nice. Boys are made of snips and snails and puppy dogs' tails." "Take care of Mommy." "Never talk nasty in front of women." "Women are beautiful and sexy." "Respect women." Then those "respected" women – but not mom – got stared and whistled at even by Dad. But Dad never stared or whistled at other men. What must the boy think?

He got the message, over and over, that women are desirable. He quickly learned – frequently from his own mother – that men (and boys) are brutes, nerds, incompetents, and klutzes.

Boys and men love looking at and touching women. They want women to do what they won't do for themselves. We want women to touch, admire, and love something we loathe. I call it the Groucho Marx Syndrome, because Groucho said "I'd never belong to any club that would have me for a member."

Is it any wonder why thousands of men become transvestites, cross-dressers, or even transsexuals? I've counseled and have been intimately involved with several transvestites and transsexuals. Most of them come from families where the female members were loved, admired, and respected, and the male figures were autocratic, hated, or absent. In one case the father was admired, but he loved only women and wouldn't even touch his son. When the son grew up, he had a sex change operation and entered a beauty contest hoping that now his father would admire him/her.

I have a close friend who is a cross-dresser. He loves to tell about the treatment he gets from men when he becomes a "woman." Besides loving the way soft, "feminine" clothing feels on his body, his drinks, food, and taxi fares are all paid for by the men to whom he gives his attention. This man is strictly heterosexual and he isn't – by any means – the prettiest "woman" you've ever seen.

One rainy night in San Francisco, he accidentally locked his keys inside his car. He was dressed in female attire and a couple of men nearly broke their necks jimmying the lock. A month later he did it again, only this time he was dressed as a man. Not only did no one offer to come to his aid, but when he called his motor club to ask for help, one of the men angrily said, "This ain't a garage, Mac."

Who's To Blame?

The popular book *My Mother, My Self* clearly bears out the female-female connection. A similar book for men would have a more fractured title, like *My Mother Is Me, But I Ain't Her. My Father, My Self* wouldn't have the same meaning. Although most men's lives are influenced by their fathers, it isn't the same kind of experience.

Women share a sisterhood that men never experience . . . Men simply are not conditioned to relate to each other's experience.

Little girls spend the first few years of their lives in the company of their mothers; learning what they do, how they think, and how to be a woman. Little boys spend the same early years with Mother, also learning how to be a woman, but at the same time getting lots of directives on how to be a man. They shouldn't show their hurt feelings, shouldn't cry, should stick up for their sisters, and learn how to conquer the universe. In general they shouldn't be anything less than John Wayne. Then after they've successfully absorbed all this information, they're suddenly supposed to be warm, sensitive lovers and husbands. How?

Over the years, the majority of women I've interviewed on my radio programs and met in lectures, workshops, and counseling have admitted they feel they need men in order to be complete. And they don't hesitate to use their "femininity" in whatever way is necessary to get the man.

A man needs a woman, too. He wants to attract her, to feel accepted, and loved by her. But in addition to using his physical self or his emotions to win her, he uses money. He has to pay for it. The going rate for a Las Vegas call girl is a thousand dollars a night. Wives and live-in-lovers don't really cost much less.

I say to women, "Don't get me wrong. We need you. We need your love and your acceptance. Since childhood we've been trying to get your love any way we can because, deep inside, we don't honestly believe we're lovable or sexy.

"That's why *we* call *you*, why we ask, and even beg for your attentions. But we pay and pay and pay." Very early on a man gets the message, "All she wants is your money."

Women get destructive messages too. "All he wants is your body." Well, men do want women's bodies. But most want more than that; they want love. But the only acceptable way for men to express wants and desires is through sex. Since we're not free to touch out of affection, the only way to get the stroking and attention we crave is through sex.

A lot of men are saying, "To hell with it! Who needs the bitches?" They're buying girlie magazines and blow-up dolls. And very often they're staying home alone, masturbating.

It's Time For A Truce

Where are we headed? I don't know. There's been a resurgence of interest in the "good old days" when sexual roles (stereotypes) were clearly defined. That accounts for the current craze for cowboys and macho men and women abandoning their hard-won liberties and looking for guys who will "take care of them."

I'm only an observer and chronicler of psycho-socio-sexual phenomena, but I do know that sexual education combined with awareness and experience can give us the tools to change what needs to be changed.

I know that men are going to have to throw out the John Wayne image and dare to become caring, sensitive people. We must dare to be loving fathers and husbands. I know we can't hide behind our jobs and let women raise the children alone. We've got to stop being the "head" of the household and realize that marriage and parenting are shared responsibilities. But it must be reciprocal. Women cannot play the role of helpless victim, relying upon men to support them and add meaning to their lives.

As humans, we must destroy our outdated programming, our poisonous "family heirloom" of male and female stereotypes. We must bond together for common goals and stop being adversaries.

You alone are responsible for your own life. You are your own authority. Don't say social change can't be made until you've tried changing yourself. Realize what you want, and know it can be done. Dream the not-so-impossible dream. [19]

CHAPTER V

COMPETITION

Competition/Cooperation – The Male Dilemma
Yevrah Ornstein

The Peace Corps advertisement goes: "It's the toughest job you'll ever love." After I returned from Ecuador, I saw one of these ads on TV again. It was instantaneous time crunch, as I recalled so vividly how I felt seeing it before I had gone.

I had a naive, romantic notion about what the Peace Corps would be like, and now that I had done it, it was interesting to compare the vision with the reality. The fairest way to advertise the Peace Corps would be to include, "It's the toughest job you'll ever love and hate."

In all honesty, I don't think I knew a single American down there who didn't go through his or her periodic bout of loathing the country, its people and the Latino culture. Then there were scores of experiences, and more times than I could remember, when these people were even more delicious than New York cheesecake – and that's a tall order.

The clash between idealistic, highly motivated, dedicated volunteers and the Ecuadorian culture and bureaucracy was very intense. It is a mixture that is inevitably, inherently, fraught with difficulties and static, and results in lots of Americans packing their bags. In many ways, it was as if we or they were raised on a distant planet, from the far reaches of another galaxy; one that barely resembled earth as we know it.

After I had been in-country for a year and a half, a friend from the States came down to visit. By that time I had worked on two schools, one in the mountains, (the Andes run down the central portion of the country), and one in the jungle. I was then living and working on the coast, visiting communities, doing evaluations and choosing sites for future schools. My time was my own to arrange, and with my being considerably ahead of schedule, I decided to take a few weeks off, show her my favorite sites and then fly out to the Galapagos Islands, which I hadn't yet seen.

Half of the beauty of the Galapagos is under the water. It's the clearest ocean and the most varied and abundant sea life I've ever seen anywhere. The water temperature is ideal, warm enough so that you can stay in for hours and cool enough to be refreshing. Often you'll be accompanied by as many as 15 to 20 seals who are a curious, playful bunch, and who love to swim at you and then veer off at the last second. It's their version of tag, and they're so quick and graceful that it was rare indeed that I could touch them as they accelerated past me. Like all animals in the Galapagos, they're completely harmless and intend no malice towards humans.

The most magical aspect of the Galapagos is that the animals have no fear of man. Perhaps this is because they are no longer hunted – I don't know. But what I do know is that these islands have the most balanced, harmonious feeling of any place I've ever been to. There's a quality to this feeling that is palpable, tangible and extraordinarily soothing.

You can sit next to Blue or Red Footed Boobies and they don't fly away. You can sit next to seals and they'll go back to sleep or their beloved sun-bathing, or you can perch atop a cliff alongside a bizarre looking iguana and share a splendid sunset. Do you have any idea how amazing this is?

One of my most precious memories is walking on a pure white sand beach, polka dotted by hundreds of seals. The entire sand-bar was blanketed with sun-bathing seals. I sat down next to a pup and her mother. The mother was fast asleep and the pup was totally open and curious about this visitor, this creature, that had sat down next to it.

As the pup fearlessly rose to its front flippers, I got on all fours. We were now on eye level and about three feet from one another. I slowly began to lean towards him or her and he/she, to my surprise, began to do the same. After a minute or so of slowly inching towards one another – get a load of this – we were actually touching noses. There I was, eye to eye, touching noses with a baby seal, looking straight into those wonderful big brown eyes, thinking to myself, I can't believe this is happening. And then, all of a sudden, mom woke up.

Mom reacted to the news the way my dad did to my going into the Peace Corps: major upset, instantaneously . . . honking and squawking and mobilized to defend her baby. She scared the piss out of me as I jumped back several feet. When it came to fight or flight, my adrenalin went right to my legs. I translated seal-speak real fast and moved away begrudgingly, thinking what a mood-destroyer she turned out to be.

And yeah, I understood. Nonetheless . . .

My Galapagos experience showed me something so new and special that it changed some beliefs I had held, for as far back as I can remember. Perhaps seven or eight years before my visit to the islands, I had read something I found quite fascinating and very different from my own perspective.

I used to wonder why nature was cruel in the ways in which life was perpetuated. It seemed to me that for all its extraordinary brilliance and intelligence, it was possible and preferable to sustain life in other ways. Why did life have to be predicated upon the killing and eating of other life forms? It seemed totally plausible and within the vast realm of alternate possibilities that nature/life could be put together in other ways. I thought this way of life sustaining itself to be inherently cruel. I felt sorry for animals that were the victims of the hunt, the losers in the struggle for life.

Cats stalking mice – apparently for the sheer fun of it, not necessarily for the food of it – seemed like a malicious way to get one's kicks.

I have always had a very strong feeling of kinship and appreciation for animals and I just couldn't fathom or accept this aspect of the natural order of things.

What I read radically challenged my views on the subject. The author spoke of the animals' innate wisdom and awareness of immortality; the animals' understanding of "natural guilt," as manifested in not being gluttonous; their innate memory of having been both prey and hunter; and their natural sense of fairness and balance. The idea of a mother eating her young as a supreme act of love was certainly a radical perspective. The author went on to say, in regards to this, that the mother is totally aware, intuitively of what the environment is capable of supporting in terms of value fulfillment, and if the environment isn't capable of supporting a life of quality, the mother will, as an act of love and letting go, eat her offspring.

To put it mildly, this was an entirely different world view than the one I had known, been taught, accepted and believed in. I must say that when I read this, on a gut level I recognized, sensed in some vague yet distinct and familiar way, something that said yes, this is true, this is the way it is.

Although there was nothing in my experience to confirm these ideas, there was nothing within my experience that said they weren't true, either. So I let them sit there simply maintaining a position of openness to the possibility of these ideas being so.

The essence of what I was reading spoke of the cooperative nature of life in contrast to the competitive/survival of the species version handed down to us by Darwin.

Ironically, my feelings occurred in the Galapagos, where Darwin had done his research and had formulated his survival of the species theory of evolution. It was amazing to me that our experiences were so vastly divergent, for it was here that I came to know, first hand, directly, in a total kind of way that transcends knowing something mentally, that nature truly is predicated upon cooperation and not competition, as Darwin believed.

I had a profound sense and experience of the interconnectedness of the abundant life that surrounded me. As I watched enormous pelicans plummet down from the skies to feed their voracious appetites, I was struck with the knowingness that life is eternal and that what I was witnessing was a transformation of form from one animal to another; and yet the basic essence, the soul-ness of life is inviolate and indestructable. I knew intuitively that all the life forms living on these islands partake, willfully, of this dance. They contribute to the sustaining of all life by giving of themselves to benefit the life of others. I understood and felt, viscerally, that the animals know far more than we do in this way. This is an ancient wisdom buried deep within our body, mind and spirit, but we have forgotten that, which at some other level we know to be so.

I watched an iguana and a snake fight to the death. In the past I would have been saddened by the conquest, the seeming destruction and loss of life. As I watched this battle I knew that life is circular, which freed me up to watch this contest with total fascination and no pity. In the end, the snake had a paralyzing grip on the iguana and I watched mesmerized as it unhinged its jaw and slowly began to eat it. Some 20 or 30 minutes later it was gone: now you see it, now you don't. Iguana undergoing transition into snake-hood, while its soul-essence was now independent of its union with matter, physical form.

I thought about the struggle, or more appropriately, the desire and valuing of life which is innate to all beings and realized that there was no contradiction. Obviously all life has a basic instinct to survive; and yet beyond this most basic of drives there are other dimensions of awareness and consciousness. Value fulfillment, quality of life, the immortality of the soul, innate wisdom and love are realities that extend beyond the apparent illusion of survival of the fittest. That which had been an abstract concept was now something I knew viscerally.

The quality, the vibes, I really don't know the words to describe it; the feeling that permeates the Galapagos is tangible in its own way. I had never experienced this ambience anywhere else in all my travels. I knew a door had opened into the true nature of the vastness of life supporting life; an opening that radically changed previously held attitudes and ideas.

This is the magic of the Galapagos.

I have dwelled on this subject because competition is a major theme in male acculturation and male conditioning. It is woven in and through. It permeates and colors our concepts of manhood. It is one of the predominant themes we have to deal with in our development as men.

Many of the articles, stories and excerpts in this book touch upon competition in one way or another.

We do accept in too many unquestioning ways, the necessity, inevitability and reality of competition. This is part of our orthodox way of thinking. We accept that competition is an innate aspect of nature, rather than question whether it is a screen of human invention that we have placed upon the world and ourselves.

❄   ❄   ❄

The following is an excerpt from an interview by Beth Ashley, published by *The Independent Journal*, a Marin County,

California newspaper, August 21, 1984. In this interview I applied some of the things I learned from my time in the Galapagos to men's issues and men's lives.

On Manhood . . .

"Men see themselves as aggressive and competitive by nature. We subscribe to the Darwinian theory of the survival of the fittest (I don't know about you, but it sure as hell didn't come across as a theory to me – it was more like scientific gospel). Darwin left us a tragic legacy that equates evolution and human nature with murderous intent/competition in the way the species advances itself. This is the antithesis of viewing nature and ourselves as embarked upon a vast and intricate journey towards greater fulfillment whose flowering is intimately tied to social, political and ecological balance, harmony, interdependence, global community and cooperation. This latter, alternate view moves us to a change of perception and feeling about the purpose and meaning of life from survival to value fulfillment, quality and beauty. Darwin's theory is a reworking of Judeo-Christian dogma into a scientific lexicon; a translation of his own religious and cultural heritage. Science emerged as the new religion and the new priesthood . . . the same old oppressive baggage in new clothing. Darwin's social, political and religious heritage defined, shaped and molded his perspective. This was his filter, his lens, and it was this selective awareness that focused upon, picked out the outermost appearances and "confirmed" what he already believed and had been trained to accept as the reality of nature.

The consequences of this, of our cultural view of ourselves and our world, are tragic and life threatening in many ways.

Masculine energy is concentrated on and coupled to that aggressive mentality which, on the dark side, gives us the license to dominate women and rape the environment." [20]

❊ ❊ ❊

The following excerpts come from a philosophy that has been of singular significance in my life. I've excerpted material that profoundly addresses and challenges our conventionally held ideas about competition, cooperation and nature. I hope you, too, find it provocative and stirring.

On The Limitations Of The Self
Seth

The beliefs of Darwin and Freud alike have formed together to create a screen, and experience is accepted and perceived only as it is sieved through that screen. If Christendom saw Man as blighted by original sin, Darwinian and Freudian views see him as part of a flawed species in which individual life rests precariously, ever at the beck and call of the species' needs, and with survival as the prime goal – a survival, however, without meaning. The psyche's grandeur is ignored, and the individual's sense of belonging with nature is eroded, for it is at nature's expense, it seems, that he must survive. One's greatest dreams and worst fears alike become the result of glandular imbalance, or of neuroses from childhood traumas. [21]

Survival of the human species, as it has developed, is a matter of belief far more than is understood – for certain beliefs are now built in. They become biologically pertinent and transmitted. I mean here the transmission of beliefs into physical codes that then become biological clues.

If women have felt their biological survival depended upon the cultivation of certain attributes over others, for instance, then this information becomes chromosome data, as vital to the development of the new organism as any other physical data involving cellular structure. *(In other words, conscious attitudes eventually manifest as genetic alterations. – Ed.)*

The mother also provides the same kind of information to a male offspring. The father contributes his share in each case. Over the generations, then, certain characteristics appear to be quite naturally male or female, and these will vary to some extent according to the civilizations and world conditions. Each individual is highly unique, however, so these models for behavior will vary. They can indeed be changed in a generation, for the experience of each person alters the original information. This provides leeway that is important. [**22**]

In your terms, the psyche is a repository of characteristics that operate in union, composed of female and male elements. The human psyche contains such patterns that can be put together in multitudinous ways. You have categorized human abilities so that it seems that you are men or women, or women and men primarily, and persons secondarily. Your personhood exists first, however. Your individuality gives meaning to your sex, and not the other way around.

In direct opposition to current theories about the past, there was far less sexual specialization, say, in the time of the caveman than now. The family was a cooperative unit. The basis of early society was cooperation, not competition. Families grouped together. There were children of various ages in such a band all the time. When women were near birth, they performed those chores that could be done in the cave dwellings, or nearby, and also watched over other young children; while the women who were not pregnant were off with the males, hunting or gathering food.

If a mother died, the father took over her responsibilities, the qualities of love and affection being quite as alive in him as in the female. After a woman bore, she nursed the child, taking it with her on food-gathering excursions, or sometimes letting other women in the group nurse the child. Often after childbirth, women soon joined the hunting expeditions, and the fathers made clothing from animals' hides at home. This allowed the male to rest after prolonged hunting activity, and meant that no adult member of a family became overexhausted. The work, then, was interchangeable.

Children began food gathering and hunting as soon as they were able to – females as well as males – led by the older children, going farther away as they progressed in strength. Qualities of inventiveness, curiosity, ingenuity, could not be delegated to one sex alone. The species could not have survived such a division. [**23**]

He [Darwin] spent his last years proving it [his theory of evolution], and yet it has no real validity. It has a validity within very limited perspectives only; for consciousness does, indeed, evolve form. Form does not evolve consciousness. All consciousness does, indeed, exist at once, and therefore it did not evolve in those terms. It is according to when you come into the picture, and what you choose to observe, and what part of the play you decide to observe. It is more the other way around, in that evolved consciousness forms itself into many different patterns and rains down on reality. Consciousness did not come from atoms and molecules scattered by chance through the universe, or scattered by chance through many universes. Consciousness did not arrive because inert matter suddenly soared into activity and song. The consciousness existed first, and evolved the form into which it then began to manifest itself.

Now, if you had all been really paying attention to what I have been saying for some time about the simultaneous nature of time and existence, then you would have known that the theory of evolution is as beautiful a tale as the theory of Biblical creation. Both are quite handy, and both are methods of telling stories, and both might seem to agree within their own systems, and yet, in larger respects they cannot be realities . . . No – no form of matter, however potent, will be self-evolved into consciousness, no matter what other bits of matter are added to it. Without the consciousness, the matter would not be there in the universe, floating around, waiting for another component to give it reality, consciousness, existence, or song. [24]

I have told you often that you do yourselves a grave injustice by limiting your conception of the Self. Your sense of identity, freedom, power, and love would be immeasurably enhanced if you could understand that what you are does not end at the boundaries of your skin, but continues outward through the physical environment that seems to be impersonal, or not-self.

Biologically it should be easy to understand that you are physically a part of earth and everything within it. You are made of the same elements, you breathe the same air. You cannot hold the air that you take within you and then say, "This is myself, filled with this air. I will not let it go," or you would find out very quickly that you were not nearly so independent.

You are biologically connected, chemically connected with the earth that you know; but since it is also formed naturally and spontaneously from your own (collective) projected psychic energy, since you and the seasons even have a psychic interaction, then the Self must be understood in a far greater context. Such a context would allow you to share in life experiences of many other forms, to follow patterns of energy and emotion of which you barely conceive, and to sense a world-consciousness in which you have your own independent part. [25]

For now think of it [evolution] as you usually do, in a time context. It has been fashionable in the past to believe that each species was oriented selfishly toward its own survival. Each was seen in competition with all other species. In that framework cooperation was simply a by-product of a primary drive toward survival. One species might use another, for instance. Species were thought to change, and "mutants" form, because of a previous alteration in the environment, to which any given species had to adjust or disappear. The motivating power was always projected outside.

All of this presented a quite erroneous picture. Physically speaking, earth itself has its own kind of gestalt consciousness. If you must, then think of that earth consciousness as grading upward in great slopes of awareness from relatively "inert" particles of dust and stone through the mineral, vegetable, and animal kingdoms. Even then, remember that those kingdoms are not so separate after all. Each one is highly related to each of the others. Nothing happens in one such kingdom that does not affect the others. A great, gracious cooperation exists between those seemingly separate systems, however. If you will remember that even atoms and molecules have consciousness, then it will be easier for you to understand that there is indeed a certain kind of awareness that unites these kingdoms.

In your terms, consciousness of self did not develop because of any exterior circumstances in which your species won out, so to speak. In fact, that consciousness of self in any person is dependent upon the constant, miraculous cooperations that exist between the mineral, vegetable, and animal worlds. The inner intent always forms any exterior alteration. This applies on any scale you use. Consciousness forms the environment. The environment itself is conscious. Atoms and molecules themselves operate in their own fields of probabilities. In their own ways, they "yearn" toward all probable developments. When they form living creatures they become a physical basis for species alteration. The body's adaptability is not simply an adjusting mechanism or quality. The cells have inner capabilities that you have not discovered. They contain within themselves, memory of all the "previous" forms they have been a part of.

The fact is that the so-called process of evolution is highly dependent upon the cooperative tendencies inherent in all properties of life and in all species. [26]

If we must speak in terms of continuity, which I regret, then in those terms you could say that life in the physical universe, on your planet, "began" spontaneously in a given number of species at the same time. In those terms, there was a point where consciousness, through intent, impressed itself into matter. That "breakthrough" cannot be logically explained, but only compared to, say, an illumination – that is, a light occurring everywhere at once, that became a medium for life as you define it. It had nothing to do with the propensity of certain kinds of cells to reproduce – [all cells are] imbued with the "drive" for value fulfillment – but with an overall illumination that set the conditions in which life was possible as you think of it; and at that imaginary, hypothetical point, all species became latent. The inner pulsations of the invisible universe reached certain intensities that "impregnated" the entire physical system simultaneously. That illumination was everywhere, then, at every point aware of itself, and the conditions formed by its presence.

[However, as] you begin to question the nature of time itself, then the "when" of the universe is beside the point. The motion and energy of the universe still come from within. I certainly realize this is hardly a scientific statement – yet the moment All That Is conceived of a physical system, it was invisibly created, endowed with creativity, and bound to emerge [into physical reality].

There is a design and a designer, but they are so combined, the one within the other, the one within and the one without, that it is impossible to separate them. The creator is within it's creations, and the creations themselves are gifted with creativity. The world comes to know itself, to discover itself, for the planner left room for divine surprise, and the plan [is] nowhere foreordained. Nor is there anywhere within it anything that corresponds to your "survival of the fittest" theories. [27]

I have an intense desire
to return to the womb.
Anybody's.

Woody Allen

CHAPTER VI

BONDING, LOVING, TOUCHING, SEX

More Of The Peace Corps

Yevrah Ornstein

Picking up my story about the Peace Corps in Ecuador, inevitably, living and working in another country and culture is going to work some changes on you.

Today, my ideas about poverty are different than before going to Ecuador. Ecuador is rated as one of the poorest countries in South America, based upon per capita income statistics, GNP, etc. In time, a number of us Americans began to joke with one another about, "Save any Indians lately?" There was a recognition of concepts and attitudes we had before we arrived that were blindly elitist and condescending. There was an assumption that we could "save" these poor, exploited people.

Now, there is an enormous amount of exploitation on the part of the West – us – towards the Third World. But many of us began to see that these people had a richness and a wealth and a security that by way of contrast with back home, radically changed many of our attitudes on a number of subjects. I got to see so clearly that Americans are amongst the most impoverished peoples in the world. The paradox is so enormous. We enjoy one of the highest material standards of living in the world today and yet we are the world's most insecure and lonely people. I have come to see our "defense" situation as a reflection of the fear we hold inside. Our display of military might is in direct proportion to the degree to which we feel impotent and frightened; and to the grotesque way in which we deny what we feel, and the ways in which we distort it and project it outward onto an enemy. I don't say this as an outsider, pontificating as one who is above and beyond doing this.

Probably the single greatest difference between the Ecuadorians and ourselves that I came to see during my time with these people had to do with a fundamental human need. Simply put, Ecuadorian children never, ever question whether their parents love them. Absolutely, regardless of the size of the family, and regardless of the hardships imposed by feeding so many, the children are totally secure in their feelings of being loved, of place and belonging.

In contrast, I think this is the number one doubt that plagues most Americans.

I know I was haunted with this question after the age of five. Most people I know have their own version of this deepest of wounds. The impact upon self-image, our building of psychological and emotional walls is epidemic in our society. The majority of the articles received by *The Men's Journal* echoed the underlying hurt and damage done to the fabric of the inner family, its being torn apart, and these most fundamental of doubts and insecurities left as residue.

So many of us grew up wondering: *Am I loved?*

So here we visited another way, where the "poor Indians" had a sense of belonging and an unquestioned knowingness of being loved that rendered our feeling sorry for them ludicrous. How can you feel sorry for a people, or consider them downtrodden when they are so much more secure, happy and at peace with themselves and their neighbors than yourself and just about everyone you know back home. It may behoove us to invite Ecuadorian Peace Corps Volunteers to the United States to teach Americans how to love their children.

Perhaps it's needless to say, but most Ecuadorians endure substantial physical hardships and material poverty. The abundance we enjoy is hard to believe in comparison. Many Americans, even at the poverty level, have amenities most Ecuadorians can't even begin to afford.

Emotional grief versus material poverty. Many Americans know starvation of another kind.

It was your typical day in the jungle – warm, pleasant, with the sounds of children being themselves at the nearby school providing the background music. It was time to break for lunch and half a dozen of us were relaxing, shooting the breeze.

Somehow the topic of birth control came up. I had been curious about their ideas on the subject in light of it being a strict, Catholic society. I mentioned birth control and got back six blank stares. I was amazed; they had no idea it even existed, and this was in 1975/76!

It was like the first time one of your friends shows you a rubber; when he knows what it is (sort of) and you don't. "What the hell is that?!" (I thought it was the ultimate state-of-the-art design in water balloons).

I ran down the basics of birth control and some of the various methods available. Their faces were like those of innocent children, enraptured and fascinated with what I was saying. It was a strange experience to be sitting with this group of men, all of whom were fathers with as many as ten kids, and me a single man of 25, telling them about birth control.

After "the lecture," the juicy, burning question for me was: would you use it if you could, if you had them? Every one of them said, *"Si, claro!* – yes, of course!" There were some giggles, some shyness, but the response was unanimous.

Many of the men spoke uninhibitedly of the difficulties of feeding so many mouths and keeping so many children in clothing. None of them wanted to have so many children, and none of them talked about this with an air of self-pity, victimhood or regret. They all spoke of their intense love for all their children and the gratitude they felt towards God for the blessing bestowed upon them through them; but given the choice . . . That was one of the more interesting lunch breaks we had.

In the brief six months I lived there, several deaths occurred, some of which were children. I witnessed the grief the parents endured and knew and felt their love, loyality and commitment to their children. This was in no way affected by the number they had or the hardships endured.

❊   ❊   ❊

As I've traveled extensively through Third World countries, I've always appreciated the comfort and joy people take in touching one another. It always seems so natural and easy. What a contrast to the uptight American mode.

Our attitudes and reservations about touch are strongly and prominently contrasted in our ways of relating to one another, especially for men.

In Ecuador, as in probably most Indian, supposed primitive cultures, infants are in constant contact with the mother, wrapped in blankets and carried on her back. The mother's constant, intimate contact with the baby provides her with a direct awareness of the baby's needs which are attended to by an immediate response. There seems to be a much healthier and calmer relationship between parent and child.

One of the things I noticed is that infants and children cry far less often than back home in Western societies. The cacophony of screaming children seems to be accepted and viewed as somewhat "normal" in industrialized countries, whereas in countries like Ecuador, screaming, whining children are definitely the exception rather than the rule.

Temper tantrums were rare, and I didn't see the classic power struggles and their concommitant expressions of rebellion.

At a very young age the Ecuadorian child is a contributing member of the family. The children obviously enjoy sharing in the household duties and chores and I'm sure they feel a sense of worth and satisfaction from being an involved member of the family. There was so much less bickering and fighting amongst the siblings. I don't mean to paint a totally inflated picture; I'm sure Ecuadorian kids cry and fight with one another and act like jerks, but to tell you the truth, I didn't see it, and I lived with these people for two years in the three distinct topographies of the country. The differences between our kids and theirs are indeed dramatic.

I have a friend who gave birth to her son in a hospital in Sydney, Australia. I spoke with her on the fifth day of her stay and she told me the nurses were very surprised with her getting up several times in the middle of the night to see her newborn son in the nursery.

I'm amazed that today, still, mothers, fathers and children are separated at such a crucial time and for so long.

Both my brothers and I were fed "formula," as that was considered the enlightened, modern, scientific choice over mothers' milk.

Can you imagine that breast feeding was viewed with such disdain? Amazing!

Baby In A Pouch
Leah Wallach

A frail baby girl, born in a Michigan hospital 12 weeks prematurely, grew fat and feisty when removed from the isolette and carried around in a kangaroo-like pouch.

Ciji, 1 pound, 12 ounces at birth, had to be separated from her mother and placed in a neonatal intensive-care unit. Premature babies like Ciji often have to be taken from their mothers and sustained by machines until they develop sufficiently to handle life beyond the womb. These procedures save infants who might otherwise die but also disrupt the normal process of infant-mother bonding. In Ciji's case, as in many births by young mothers, this mother – just sixteen – wasn't very interested in her newborn child. The postbirth separation had prevented the mother from bonding with Ciji. "I would say, 'Pick her up, hold her, touch her,' " Dr. Marta Airala, a pediatrician at Albion Community Hospital, says of Ciji's young mother. "She would do it for a few minutes, but then she would stop."

Dr. Airala had been thinking of using a pouch to help mothers of preemies reestablish intimacy with their infants by constant physical contact. Ciji seemed the ideal candidate to test the idea.

Dr. Airala prepared a cotton gown with a preemie-size pocket positioned over the chest so the baby would rest on the left side, near the beating heart. Ciji's mother began carrying her baby in the pouch whenever she was in the hospital.

Ciji thrived on the human contact. Her emotional, physical, and neurological improvement was dramatic. Her appetite increased; she gained weight; and she became alert and demanding. After ten days of the pouch treatment, she was plump enough to go home.

Dr. Airala, a native of South America, got the idea for the pouch by observing women in traditional cultures, who often carry their babies next to their bodies. "Human mothers have been carrying their infants close to themselves in a variety of positions for thousands of years," she says. "The pouch is just another application of the same principle." [28]

❊ ❊ ❊

"Homo"
Yevrah Ornstein

I don't know what effect not having that close, intimate contact with my mother at birth had on me as a child and what, if any, effects it has upon my life today. It just strikes me, intellectually and intuitively, that our "scientific" approach is sheer idiocy.

Although Ecuador is not as "touchy" as other countries I've visited, there certainly is not the stigma we attach to men touching one another. In the States, the specter, the fear of implied homosexuality is very intense. Natural yearnings, natural impulses in this area often conjure up internal consternation of latent homosexuality, while society frowns upon anything outside the narrow range of acceptable, proper physical expression.

In countries like Italy and Greece, men walking down the street hand in hand are a common sight. Men are not maligned with jeers of "faggot," "homo," or any of the other injurious labels we use to ostracize and hurt people.

One of the most painful changes I had to endure as a child had to do with the assassination of my natural impulses and needs for physical contact and touch.

I have always been a very physically oriented person – I still am. The acceptable, condoned channel for this trait is, of course, sports. It's ironic that the macho male is directed towards *contact* sports. But beyond that, as a child, I liked to express my affection for friends, male and female, physically. Walking down the street with an arm around a friend, plain and simple, felt natural and good. Slaps on the shoulder, pats on the butt, as well as wrestling, were innate impulses – uninhibited expressions of play and affection.

This was all okay stuff until the seventh grade. We had gone from elementary school to junior high school, and what once was an extended family of kids, principaled by an elegant, loving, elderly woman, was transformed into a prison-type environment, ruled by an extremely severe and ancient witch and her fascist sidekick disciplinarian, who was a Korean Marine Corps war veteran. I still vividly remember that shithead and the perverted joy he seemed to derive from frightening "little men." Even then, I thought him a pathetic, comic caricature of himself . . . as he busted me several times for wrestling in the hall with friends.

In seventh grade, the word "homo" entered our vocabulary. The kids I went to school with had never heard this word before. It was a new one for me as well. But it didn't take long to figure it out.

One day I put my arm around a friend, and began to hear tauntings of "homo!" Before long, my own friends would be mimicking the insult. It didn't take long for me to stop, as the discomfort of being called "homo" was really unsettling and hurtful.

I remember being very confused at the time. All I knew was that something I had been doing as long as I could remember, a part of me that felt friendly and natural, was now bad/wrong.

This was the beginning of my socialization into hetero/homosexual training, and it really stunk.

In addition to the confusion and the feelings of rejection, there was a lot of hurt inflicted. It's a very unpleasant experience when the pressures to stifle a part of yourself that you've always felt to be normal, natural, and pleasurable are now branded as deviant and defiling. What a shame.

It took many, many years before I got back to that natural part of myself, and today I enjoy a physical closeness with my closest male (and female) friends that is an integral, valued and unquestioned part of our being together. We know the pleasure and comfort and distinction of how touch can be intimate without being sexual.

I went through this experience alone. I never told anyone about it when it was happening, nor did I turn to anyone for advice. I simply accepted it as – this is the way it is. As Robin Williams says, "Reality – what a concept!"

Here's a beautiful letter sent to *The Men's Journal,* written on this very topic. It was sent to me personally. I was very much touched by this wonderful man's honesty, and I felt for his dilemma.

Dear Yevrah/MJ,

I tend to fall in love with things and I've fallen in love with your publication. You've hit me in a deep place. The articles, poems and letters talked of concerns that were mine also. I'd like to share some with the magazine, and so give a little to people I'm getting so much from.

I have this real yearning for touch and communication with other men. Touch is the hardest. It scares the hell out of me. I'd like to put my arm around another man, maybe kiss another man. But instead I'm scared. Scared that such desires might be sexual. So scared that it's hard to give myself any space to find out. All I feel is fear. Some of the poems in *The Men's Journal* have been very helpful to me in regard to this.

Another thing I like about many of the articles in *The Men's Journal* is the way they are not anti-male. The writers affirm that there is something naturally positive about being a man. For example, I loved the cover photo of the Fall '85 issue of the Warrior's basketball player, sitting back with a grin on his face. It was somehow an affirmation to me of the goodness in the traditional male value of strength, whether it be physical, emotional, or something else. I sense that there are qualities and reserves we can draw from inside ourselves and that we shouldn't merely imitate women to become more complete as men.

But I don't know. I sense that I've only taken baby steps towards my goals, and that the men's movement is just born, open and tentative. But that's good! It's the most creative time, before we get too sure of ourselves. I know we're all people, men and women, and I'd like to be able to recognize that. I'd also like to know and feel the differences between men and women. And I'd like to love both sexes as fully as I can, in whatever way is appropriate for me.

Lets keep in touch.

Warmly,
Alex Marshall [29]

The Way I Felt In Fiji
Yevrah Ornstein

This letter from Alex takes me to a very special experience in Fiji.

I was staying on one of Fiji's smaller islands, a "puddle-jumper" flight from the main island. There's a six-seater plane that gets you there in about 10-15 minutes. The plane takes off and flies absolutely straight on, no banking at all, up to a certain altitude, and then descends for a landing.

I've seen much prettier islands than Fiji, but what makes Fiji so special are the native Fijians, who make up about half of the population. The other half are from India, and are equally kind. But it was the native Fijians that are really special. They are the happiest people I've ever met anywhere. Have you ever heard the expression *bulla bulla?* Well, it comes from Fiji, and it's their way of saying hello. One "*bulla*" is your ordinary run-of-the-mill happy, friendly hello. *Bulla bulla* means they're really happy, really jazzed. Most of the time, what you'd hear is *bulla bulla*. Eye contact was almost always met with the most beautiful, open smile you can imagine and an enthusiastic wave of the hand. This place absolutely knocked me out. If you ever want to get rid of your walls, hang out with these people for a while, but be prepared for a shock when you return home.

This particular island is actually two islands, separated by a fairly narrow and shallow channel. The distance between the islands is about 150 yards or so. When the tide is low, the water is about two to three feet deep and at high tide, it's about five feet deep. On the island with the landing strip, there are two hotels while the other island is populated solely by Fijians, wooden huts, grass roofs, fishing nets, small boats pin-striping the beach . . . your run-of-the-mill idyllic setting.

The majority of the people who work at the hotels live on the other island, and with all property communally owned in Fiji, it truly is their island. There was an open grass hut set up by the beach on the other side of the channel and I wanted to see the wood carvings for sale there and to do some exploring and hiking.

I got up early one morning and headed over before any of the other tourists would be making their guided tours to the "native village."

The tide was about half way in and the water was up to my waist at mid-channel when I met a man who was going in the other direction. We stopped and talked for a while, and in true Fijian fashion, he was happy and as pleasant as can be.

He asked me where I was from, where I was going, etc. I knew my own story inside out and was much more interested in him and his story.

He had grown up on the island and had recently returned to be with his children and grandchildren (this guy didn't look a day over forty-five). He had recently returned from living in Australia where he had lived and worked for a number of years. He said he enjoyed Australia but the pace of life was too hectic for him and he wanted to live out his remaining years with his family in a more sane, serene and natural environment.

Having lived in Australia for five months, one of the biggest differences I appreciated is their tempo. They are definitely, a whole lot more laid back than we are, so if this guy from Fiji found Australia hectic, well, you can imagine what Fiji's like. Now all this sounds pretty uneventful, but what made this encounter particularly unusual was that we were holding hands the entire conversation. There we were, standing in water up to our waists, in the middle of a channel, carrying on a warm casual conversation, holding hands. After we shook hands upon our first meeting, we unconsciously continued to do so.

This man was extremely well built. It was obvious he had made his living by using his body, and he exuded an incredibly beautiful muted power that felt very masculine to me. In his presence and within this shared moment, I had one of the profoundest and most pleasant experiences of feeling my own deep masculinity that I have ever felt in my life. It's a feeling that's difficult to describe with words.

When I look back upon that time, I realize I encountered a rhythm and current within myself that speaks the name, Manhood. I have occasionally felt it drumming with other men, and when heartful sharing in a men's group is happening. I've felt it in the presence of certain kinds of women, particularly those who have a strong and beautiful sense and relationship, ease, and peace with their feminine side, their womanhood.

By way of example, this man engaged those parts of myself, gave them permission, voice, elevation and song. He was simply being himself, his natural and beautiful self, and he gave me the gift of meeting him on equal footing and the gift of me being myself. We stood on common ground, and it was an exquisite encounter.

We said good-bye, went our separate ways, and I was left bathing in a quiet glow of powerful peacefulness. There was something about him; our holding hands, our chemistries that allowed me to feel something very wonderful – what I knew to be primal male energy.

And how sad that holding hands is seen and feared with such disdain at home. Imagine the reactions we would have fielded had we been standing on a street corner in Anywhere, USA.

And how ironic that so many years ago I was shamed away from my natural impulses, needs, joys and desires into self-judgement, repression, embarassment and guilt; and then, some 25 years later, some 10,000 miles from home, I had one of the strongest feeling experiences of true and balanced, life-affirming moments of "being a man" I've ever known.

❄   ❄   ❄

Leo Buscaglia has interesting things to say about touch in his book entitled, *Love*.

Love touches, fondles. Physical love is necessary for happiness, growth and development. We have mentioned earlier that the infant needs to be fondled or he will die even if all his biological needs are met. Freud's statement that at the base of all mental illness is the lack of sensual gratification has had many and varied interpretations, even to labeling him a "dirty old man." What he meant by sensual gratification extended from the mother nursing her child and changing his diapers to the most passionate of sexual experiences, and all physical gradations in between. Even a handshake may be classified as sensual gratification. No matter the degree, and we will hope all men will take the opportunty to experience the entire gamut of experience, Man needs to be touched. The power of the sexual drive attests to this. In some people it becomes so powerful that it directs their entire lives. Kingdoms have been known to rise and fall, wars have been declared, murders have been committed just so that someone could have that moment of sexual union; often without love in the real sense, strictly in passion.

Love is not sex, though sensual gratification in varying degrees is always a part of love. To attempt to write a book on love without the consideration of the import of love would be absurd. It is impossible to realize a situation where one loves deeply and sincerely without a desire for some form of sensual gratification. Our mores against the most superficial human contact are so great, even to laws which prohibit it, that many have moved almost completely away from any form of physical love except on a purely animalistic level. Even the choice of shaking hands, man with woman, is, according to Emily Post, at the discretion of the woman. If she extends her hand, the male accepts it. But she is also "right" not to extend it. And so we distance ourselves from each other, through manners as well as laws.

There is no doubt that someone is real when you touch them, when you feel their flesh on yours, even for a brief moment. I continually breach etiquette in that I always extend my hand to men and women alike; I cause looks of horror when I hold their hand longer than is accepted and cover it warmly with my free hand. It frightens some – who look at me quizzically wondering, "What is he after?" – but it affirms to us both that we are two human beings relating on a very real level. It might present a new philosophical statement: "We touch, therefore we are." Surely there are few people who do not find being touched or touching others pleasurable. There are some, of course, who find it, in a pathological way, unpleasant. I have known occasions when people have said, "Please don't touch me. I prefer not being touched." Of course it is their right, which must be respected. Nevertheless, love is physical, it touches. [**30**]

※　　　　　　※　　　　　　※

Men And Massage
Dave Mueller

Although the similarities between males and females are numerous, the considerable differences in child-raising and training for each of the sexes shape the lives and the bodies of men and women in different ways. On the surface these differences would seem to be in appearance, dress, mannerisms and interests. On a deeper level, the expectations and beliefs of parents and society contribute to structuring the very reality of the way each sex perceives itself, its role and acceptable behavior.

For men, this difference in training has been reflected in alarming statistics. Men on an average live eight years less than women. Higher rates of lung cancer (6 to 1), heart disease (2 to 1), suicide (2.7 to 1), and greater job hazards such as industrial contaminants, physical risks and highly competitive working environments are aspects of the male role in our society. The very definition of "manliness" is that of being strong and brave, and ignoring pain and fatigue. This leads to a lack of knowledge, and denial concerning their bodies, nutrition and ways of building support systems. These and many other dynamics make stress and men's ability to cope with it a major factor in their lives and deaths.

An awareness of how stress influences men would seem to make massage therapy an obvious source of help. Yet there are factors which tend to deter men from seeking help in general and massage therapy specifically. The first aspect is that of touch. For many men, experiencing touch is limited to contact sports and sexual experiences. This on the one hand can lead to associating touch with pain, fear and anxiety involved in sports such as football and hockey. This expectation that touch is rough or dangerous can contribute greatly to men isolating themselves. On the other hand, when touch is limited to sexual experience the perception can be that sexual experiences are the only way to give and receive the nurturing and caring aspects of touch. This can cause confusion when experiencing nonsexual touch – leading to embarrassment, doubt and fear, resulting in the avoidance of all forms of touch that are not sexual.

This is further confused by misconceptions about men's sexuality, such as the perception that an erection is an aggressive, sexually overt act, rather than a natural physiological occurrence with many causes such as temperature, relaxation and the unconscious association of touch with sexuality. This ignorance concerning men's bodies can lead to doubts concerning sexual preference, inappropriate choices in acting out sexual feelings and feelings of shame. Aspects of sexuality and touch have been further confused by our society's practice of inappropriately referring to sexual service as massage.

Through experiencing the warm, nurturing, work of a sensitive massage therapist, a man can realize the enjoyment of safe, low risk, physical contact with people. The body awareness encouraged in massage can enable a man to experience himself athletically through caring for his body rather than using himself as a machine. Massage can help foster a flexible, dynamic strength which can outperform mere brute strength. Therapeutic massage also offers men a space and time to experience and enjoy the pleasure to their bodies. The nonsexual quality frees the individual to focus on the other aspects of touch which would otherwise be clouded by sexual activity. By seeking out responsible and respectful massage therapists, men can find the physical support they need.

A second aspect concerning men and massage is their perception of relaxation. The "work ethic," which has been a strong influence in men's training, views relaxation with suspicion. The message is that relaxing is being lazy, a sign of failure and nonproductive. This belief encourages men to work and play to the point of exhaustion in order to maintain a feeling of success and accomplishment. This leaves men able to rest only when they're sick or disabled. This may cause men to be prone to injury and illness because it is the only "legitimate" way in which to get rest.

The body reflects the belief systems we hold. This can be seen in the way that some men have a tendency to immediately fall asleep when they engage in activities such as reading or watching television. In this sense, the mind and body have been conditioned to respond in only two ways: they are on (working), or they are off (sleeping). There is no middle ground in which to experience slower, calmer activities.

Habitual restrictive thinking can limit the body's ability to respond in healthy ways. This can be seen in the way a man's image of his body affects the way he holds himself. Continually swelling the chest in order to appear large and powerful can lead to rigidity of musculature, which inhibits both breathing and movement. Body building for cosmetic purposes, such as to develop strong flat stomachs, can interfere with a man's ability to release and express emotions and "gut feelings." Yet, even though holding the body tense affects men so dramatically, strong, rigid bodies are still held as an ideal. (A sign of the changing times may be the fact that both Arnold Schwartzenegger and Mr. T receive massage therapy.)

Massage therapy offers new opportunities for men to experience relaxation and rejuvenation. This can lead to learning new responses and can provide new ways with which to cope with stress and fatigue. After a massage, it is possible for muscles to have a new "frame of reference" which encourages them to release tension and express their full range of motion and emotion. Flexibility and openness allow greater adaptability in both body and mind.

A third aspect of men and massage is that of wounds and injuries. Since many men are trained and encouraged to pursue sports and other activities which put them at risk physically, the likelihood of injury and damage is heightened. This occurs partly from a mentality of "no pain, no gain," a way of thinking in which success is measured by how much damage one receives. Wounds become "badges of courage" to be bragged about and shared. The need to ignore pain in order to appear manly requires a detachment from the body and the emotions. This can impact men in different ways, ranging from decreasing their ability to experience pleasure to causing them to ignore serious health conditions. This detachment from their bodies and denial of its signals can have fatal consequences which are confirmed by the percentage of men who are unaware of their own heart attacks as they occur.

With its ability to assist the internal healing process and increase self-knowledge, massage therapy gives men tools to cope with wounds and prevent injuries. The nurturing, relaxing pleasure experienced in massage builds a self awareness which begins to find pain and injury intolerable. This leads to men being more caring and careful concerning themselves and others.

Massage therapy offers many opportunities for men. It can allow them to go through life without the rigid armor which blocks feelings and new experiences, by building an inner strength which provides them with safety. It can allow them to better know themselves and their bodies, releasing greater creativity, performance and success. It can allow them to practice being vulnerable with a caring professional, and encourage them to trust the help of others. Massage can touch and nurture that special strength and sensitivity that lies within the body, mind and spirit of each man. [31]

These past few years we have seen a significant rise in public awareness about sexual, physical abuse and molestation violated upon adults as well as children. We have been horrified by its pervasiveness and the degree to which these acts have been hidden from view. Much good has and is coming about through these disclosures. Hotlines are in place, counseling centers are available for many, there are homes to shelter battered women and there are counseling programs for batterers, etc.

But in redressing problems, or attempting to do so, we sometimes swing too far in the other direction in response to our outrage.

Has the pendulum swung back too far? The following examples may help you decide.

The Myth Of The Dangerous Dad
Jed Diamond

As a psychotherapist specializing in family relationships, I was pleased to see the issue of child sexual abuse getting public attention. When I thought of my own children I couldn't remain professionally detached. I felt a blind rage toward the male childcare workers I read about who were accused of abusing small children.

Three weeks later I was stunned when it was me being accused of "touching the girls inappropriately" at my 10-year-old daughter's elementary school where I volunteered as a teacher's helper once a week.

What for me was an innocent gesture, putting my arm around a shoulder as I knelt to help a student, was seen as suspect by the classroom teacher. I wanted to run away and hide. I knew I hadn't done anything improper, yet I felt soiled. I said nothing.

Weeks later, I finally was able to bring up the incident in my men's group. There were eight of us who had been meeting weekly for six years to discuss our feelings and become closer friends. Was I the only one who had been touched by this feeling, I asked? I found that most of the men had their own horror stories to tell. A number of men had friends who had actually had their children taken away on the basis of someone's accusation of child molesting. "I'm afraid to even touch my friends' children anymore," Dick, a 42-year-old father of three children from Berkeley, said with real sadness. "I used to wrestle with them and throw them up in the air. I played with them like I would my own daughter. Now I worry that I'll be thought of as a 'dirty old man' or even worse."

"My daughter Laurie just turned nine," said Les, a 45-year-old father from San Francisco, married for the second time. "Lately when I give her a pat on the bottom, like I've always done, I get a look from my wife which says I've done something wrong. I don't get it."

I had joined the men's group, like the other men, to learn to be more feeling, especially with my wife and children. Now that we were taking the first tentative steps to be more open, we felt the doors being closed in our faces. It didn't seem fair.

This unwarranted fear of men has become so widespread that *Nurturing News*, the longest continually-published national quarterly addressing the nurturing characteristics of men and boys, devoted a special issue to child molestation (*Nurturing News*, March 1985.)

While deploring child sexual abuse, the journal also warned about the negative backlash against men. According to editor David Giveans who lives in San Francisco, "Child molesting is not a male-only club. Children need nurturing touch from both males and females that is intimate without being sexual."

At present only 1% of childcare workers are male, according to the magazine. Many experts are concerned that this tiny number may soon become zero if the fear of men is not checked. Almost all believe that this would be a tragedy for men, women and especially for children.

Sandy Ruben, president of the Boston Association for the Education of Young Children, and Lee Block, an early childhood educator, spoke to the frustration many men feel in an article titled "Male Child Care Workers Speak Out On Child Sexual Abuse" (in the same special issue of *Nurturing News*). "When we were hired, we were asked questions like, 'Could we change diapers?' 'Could we comfort a child whose parent just ran out the door late for work?' But now the undercurrent seems to be, 'Should we even be allowed to work in childcare at all?' "

How is it, I thought, that we find it so easy to assume men are "dangerous?" Dr. Warren Farrell, clinical psychologist and author of the internationally acclaimed book *Why Men Are The Way They Are,* suggests it is a result of what he calls the "New Sexism." He says, "In the past quarter century we exposed biases against other races and called it racism, and we exposed biases against women and called it sexism. Biases against men we call humor." He cites numerous examples of "funny" cartoons and stories in various women's magazines which portray men as dogs, wolves, turkeys, sharks, worms, and guppies.

Objectification of a group is a prerequisite for rejecting, hurting or even killing them. Objectification of women as sex objects is a prerequisite for the rapist. Objectification of Vietnamese as "gooks" was a prerequisite for dropping bombs on them.

We have not yet raised our awareness to see that objectifying men as "potential child-molesters" is a prerequisite for depriving men of their place in the family and their connection with their children.

John, a 38-year-old Bay Area businessman, had gone through hell in the last three years. He was given custody of his two children after a lengthy divorce and custody battle. His wife, June, had mistreated the children on a number of occasions when she had been drinking, but was allowed visitation rights. On one of the visits she failed to return the children. "I went out of my mind with worry," John said with tears in his eyes. His voice began to rise with anger as he continued. "When I finally found them, she accused me of molesting my 3-year-old daughter. I spent two years and $25,000 proving the accusations were false. I was completely cleared of all child molesting charges, but the stigma of being accused carried into the civil case, and in the end, I lost custody and now see the children only once a month."

Unfortunately, John's experience is becoming increasingly common. In the highly charged atmosphere now surrounding child abuse, being male and being accused is often all that is needed for people to assume guilt.

An attorney with a San Francisco law firm, Fred Butler, understands what divorced men feel when they seek to maintain contact with their children. Butler, 44, who specializes in family law, went through a difficult court battle to get shared custody of his 2 1/2-year-old daughter. He now volunteers for "Equal Rights For Fathers," a Northern California nonprofit organization concerned with the rights of children, parents, and second families. "I believe in shared custody," says Butler. "Children need the opportunity to have continued care from *both* parents."

Traditionally, both men and women believed that parenting was really mother's job. When mom and dad separated, it was assumed that children would be better off staying with her.

"All that has changed," Butler says. "As more and more women are getting involved in the work world, men are more deeply involved with their children. Men are now beginning to fight for their rights to continue to be fathers even after divorce."

Recently, Jerry Johnson, host of KCBS radio's weekly program, "Man to Man," raised the question on his Sunday show of whether more men were being falsely accused of molesting. His guest, David L. Corwin, M.D., president of California Professionals on the Abuse of Children, had some startling things to say. "There is an increased awareness of child sexual abuse," said Dr. Corwin, "but along with it there is an increase in the number of men being falsely accused. And this can be absolutely devastating for a man."

All would agree that we must protect children from "inappropriate touching" by men and women. However, experts in the area of sexuality are worried that in our zeal to protect children from abuse, we may be creating future dysfunction. According to University of Minnesota sex therapist Margretta Dwyer, "Touch-deprived children will become the next generation's sexually dysfunctional adults."

She encourages fathers, teachers, and other caretakers to continue to touch children in normal ways. "Because caretakers fear being accused of sex abuse," observes Dwyer, "many children grow up touch-deprived."

Until we change our attitudes, men's fear of touching will continue to increase. All men are vulnerable. Some men are even afraid to change diapers or bathe their children for fear of being accused. Are men being paranoid? Irrational? Dr. Farrell thinks not.

Farrell notes that by 1986, department stores like J.C. Penney routinely allowed mothers into their sons' dressing rooms, but not the fathers into even a 5-year-old daughter's dressing room. When sued for discrimination, J.C. Penney and Company responded: "The public perception is that men are voyeurs and molesters."

Farrell says, "In the past decade, liberation has meant fathers going from 'Daddy knows best' to 'daddies molest.' "

What are men to do? One of the men in my group said it this way. "It's time that we broke our silence about ways in which we are labeled as 'jerks.' It's time we stopped accepting and laughing at jokes that classify men as less than human. It's time we spoke out in the classroom and with our friends and family. It's time we gathered support from men and women who are opposed to sexism directed at men, not just that directed at women. It's time we loved and touched our children without fear."

It's time we put to rest, forever, the "myth of the dangerous dad." [32]

❊   ❊   ❊

When I first received the following article from David, I respected the author for sharing an aspect of his life that most of us tend to be so very private and often embarrassed about.

Here is a story about an intimate, "everyday" (or thereabouts) aspect of our lives, written with sensitivity and grace.

The Very First Time
David Goff

One afternoon, in early spring two years ago, I touched myself in a new way. Looking back to that afternoon, I am now amused to realize that despite having masturbated since I was six years old, this was like the very first time. Through the power of emotional crisis I had the opportunity to rediscover and repossess myself through the simple act of making love to me. This simple hour I spent in bed exploring my own passionate longing, erogenous zones, and expanding sensitivity to love totally changed my love life.

What I experienced that day, and in the months that followed, was a powerful sense of love for "something" in myself that fulfilled and healed me. After two years of examining this on-going, intrapsychic, erotic love affair, I have come to believe that masturbation contains the potential for something of greater significance to well-being than mere sexual release. I believe auto-erotic love provides an opportunity for the inner feminine and masculine to merge in an act of harmony that diminishes the powerful emotions of a love affair. I want to share with you how this process came about in me, and why I think it meaningful, and replicable, for those who are seeking better relationships.

I started "playing with myself" consciously around age six. By eight years of age it became part of my morning and evening rituals. And somehow, I had already developed the good sense to keep this delicious activity to myself. I found great solace in the warm tickling sensations that both excited and relaxed me, and assured me that wherever I was, I always had a secret friend with whom I could play. By the time my mother (indirectly) and the church (directly) began their urgent warnings about the dangers and corruption of self-abuse, I was already addicted to myself.

They never succeeded in getting me to abandon my first lover. But they did succeed in making me feel guilty, dirty, and very paranoid that anyone (especially my mother) should find out about my "disgusting" habit. The pleasure from my secretiveness made it even more delicious.

I have masturbated more or less regularly ever since those early years. Touching myself provided a necessary release that helped me survive adolescence. Later, it got me through times of loneliness and complemented the times of plenty in my life. The guilt remained, but declined significantly after I darted out from under the heavy-handed wing of the Church. I remember one priest telling me in the confessional, that no woman would ever want to marry me if I continued. I found no shortage of potential marriage partners, though my "self-abuse" continued unabated.

In my early adulthood I kept my auto-erotic activity a closely guarded secret. As I became capable of deeper and more intimate relationships with women, I found that they were often open-minded about masturbation as a phenomenon, but none too pleased to know that I practiced it despite the quality of our relationship. My observation was that it was cool to acknowledge that we "normal" people did it, as long as there was no discussion of the hows, whys and the frequency. It seemed that what one did with one's self was much more private and taboo than what one did with others.

I have since come to wonder why, in a sexually liberated age like ours, masturbation, now considered normal behavior, still carries the stigma of being associated with unsatisfied passion, sexual insatiability and self-absorption.

Having reflected on that question for some time, it occurred to me that masturbating always provided the physical release from sexual frustration I wanted, but it frequently left me feeling empty and lonely. This feeling of emptiness seemed inherent in the experience and resulted in my feeling less than complete. This feeling of being incomplete somehow translated into un-wholesomeness, and contributed directly to my unwillingness to openly and freely discuss masturbation and its rituals. As a man, acknowledging my feelings of being less than whole remains a difficult task. Despite all that I know about myself, admitting that I am missing something still seemingly threatens the self-image that permits me to function as a man in the world.

In the last two years, male friends willing to discuss their experiences with masturbation have duplicated my experience. And I have no doubt the popular euphemisms, "jerking off" and "whacking off," are indicative of attitudes that are widespread. There is an aura of derision surrounding masturbation, such as references to people as "jerk-offs." The hand motions associated with masturbation occasionally crop up as a means of put-down, offering a strong insult.

My experience with women, both as intimates and in therapeutic situations, suggests that their attitudes toward masturbation are similar but perhaps less self-destructive. The women's movement, and the relatively new (last 20 years) demand for sexual satisfaction and orgasmic fulfillment, has tended to bring women into a more endearing relationship with their bodies. Women are encouraged by sex therapists and popular women's magazines to touch themselves, to get to know their bodies, their erogenous zones, etc. For many women, the road to becoming orgasmic includes a great deal of self-love. Still, by and large, the women with whom I have discussed masturbation admit to infrequent practice and solely as a means of release.

So it is with some wonder that I look back on my experience two years ago, and marvel at the circumstances which constellated a whole new approach to, and deeper respect for, self-loving. I was two months into a very painful separation from my wife. I was experiencing agonizing feelings of being rejected and abandoned. Our 12-year relationship had totally capsized. Emotionally, I was deeply wounded and enduring incredible doubt about myself. Additionally, for the first time in my life, I was suffering from prostatitus, an inflammation of the prostate gland, that can result in painfully swollen testicles. The urologist I consulted suggested regular intercourse as the best available treatment for what was essentially a stress-related problem. Sexual intimacy with another was impossible. The pain and discomfort could only be relieved by regular masturbation. The only sexual fantasies I had were obsessively about my wife, and these were emotionally painful. Arousal itself was intensely painful, physically. I was faced with an incredible dilemma. I had to masturbate, but I could not do so as I always had. My initial attempts were so difficult and painful that I simply could not continue. I was very unhappy.

I persevered through those dark hours and days thanks to the support of some loving and nurturing men friends, and a real determination to accept and be transformed by this experience. Without my wife to love, I soon chose to give that love to myself and to explore new ways of loving myself. A man friend told me of a feminist adage he had heard. "A woman should become the man she wants to marry." I decided that made sense for me as a man, and that I could become the woman I wanted to love. The desire to heal myself physically and emotionally, combined with the stimulus of reading, thinking about, and experiencing the feminine I embodied, culminated in my creating a whole new masturbatory ritual, organized more around my need to love and be loved than around sexual release.

One spring afternoon, in my bed, with time to be with myself, I created an environment rich with textures, music, incense, and massage oil that would stimulate and please the one I chose to be with. Very slowly I began to touch and explore my body, as if I were the woman I had longed for, loved, and now had the opportunity to experience and express those feelings with. With the excitement of discovery I ventured into my erogenous zones and found feelings and sensations that were sometimes familiar and sometimes new. I became quickly aroused and anxious. It was still painful, but instead of driving myself over the threshold of orgasm, I slowed my breathing and pace and re-explored my body, connecting all of myself with the excitement I felt. For nearly an hour I repeated this drama of approaching release and retreating. In so doing, my excitement spread throughout my body. My body sang to me in ways that I had known only in my most incredible moments with a lover. As I let myself slip over that threshold, I was released into a full-bodied orgasm that washed away all my fears of lost and unrecoverable love. In the afterglow, I knew my self as well-loved, and as complete as I had ever felt. [**33**]

Quartet
David Steinberg

(1)
Undoing the knots
one by one
like untangling an old pile of string.
I want to be at home in my body again.

(2)
I remember
watching the film
when the tears would not hold back.
It was when the beautiful boy
14-year-old gymnast
graceful as a swan

> talked of being a sissy
> (fear and doubt suddenly in his eyes)
> and I could not find a way
> to care for him enough
> or for me.

(3)

> The young man looks for sensual men to imitate.
> Finding none he must choose
> between hard strength
> and a feeling he doesn't know well enough
> to trust.
> He is sad to separate from his body.
> The loss is deeper than consciousness,
> the pain matched only by the agony
> of finding himself suddenly alone
> in a thick and unexplored forest.

(4)

> Who then will celebrate the beauty
> of the man's body
> that we can love our physical selves
> and not turn to women
> for second-hand sensuality?
> Let me be clear:
> I do not wish to separate from women,
> only to stop looking for them to fill
> that part of myself. [34]

Here's a story all men know well in one form or another. There's only one first time . . .

My First Condoms
Eric Small

I didn't expect high drama at the breakfast table. Even though this was the morning I was leaving for summer camp, it was early and it was just my dad and I in the kitchen. He had come down first and laid out breakfast as he often did. Mom would need more time to dress.

Before we started to eat, without any warning, Dad reached across the table and drug-connection-style uncovered three condoms under his hand. His only words were, "I thought you might need these." My mind flew. All of the anticipation of doing it, never shared with Dad, and now there they were. I felt defensive. Did he think I needed him to get these for me? I was fifteen years old. The truth was, I had put off buying them myself because I was deathly afraid of fucking.

I accepted them in silence. What else was I supposed to do, tell him I felt invaded? It was our first communication about sex. There was so much he didn't know about me. What should I do with them? I knew my mom would be down soon and I knew my duty was to accept the offer man to man. I put them in my pocket and mumbled thanks.

I assumed that was Dad's way of giving me permission to do it. At least it was his way of asking me to be careful. Having them just felt like more pressure. I was already weighed down with fear. I thought what I needed was a new dick, not rubbers. No one knew, except my girlfriend, that the moment she'd put her hands in my pants, I'd come. I wasn't even always hard. It was humiliating. I knew staying hard was all there was to it, the measure of the man. I dreaded the day when I'd be expected to fuck.

I resented having to deal with the condoms. I was also curious about them. When I was alone in my cabin after my parents left, they were my first order of business. I took them out to examine them. They were wrapped in red foil and they were all in one strip. They were Trojans. There was a picture of a helmeted warrior on the wrapper. I had never put together the word Trojan (everyone knew what Trojans were) with fighting men. It seemed strange.

I wondered if I'd really use them. I wondered how to use them. I had a surge of anger. If my dad was going to give me these things, he could have at least given me instructions. Then I remembered how angry I had felt that he had given them to me at all. Thank God he hadn't tried to teach me how to use them. I wondered what they looked like. I knew they were sort of like balloons. I wanted to open one. Then I thought, I mustn't waste them; I only have three. Only three? I didn't even want one.

I stuck them at the bottom of my Kleenex box which I put at the head of my bunk bed. I was paranoid about someone finding them. What if a bunkmate had a sneezing fit and used up an entire box? What if a counselor looking for dope made a thorough search of the cabin? I checked on them occasionally to make sure the foil wrappers still lay at the bottom of the box.

It wasn't until the last week of camp that I dug them up for use. I had come to camp that summer with my girlfriend from home. For the first seven weeks I had managed to keep myself pre-occupied making pottery. I avoided what I imagined would be awful humiliation.

Certain evenings there'd be tension in the air. The question, "Why aren't we off doing it?" hung heavy. I can remember jealousy towards my best friend who would mysteriously disappear with his girlfriend. I would joke nervously with Sarah about where they were, sensing her desire to be there too.

I don't remember if it was their invitation or ours, but a plan was finally made for John and his girlfriend to meet Sarah and me early in the morning on Chicken Hill. This was the notorious spot for going all the way. I suppose I had resigned myself to the inevitable.

I woke up before I needed to that morning. I was thinking about the details. Should I bring a blanket? How close would John and Amy be to us? Did they know we had never done it? How many condoms should I bring? What if I really didn't know how to use them?

The time to dress had come. Armed with two of the Trojans (I decided that three must be delusions of grandeur and one was somehow risky) I walked to Sarah's bunk to pick her up. She was waiting outside. We kissed hello and began walking arm in arm. I was nervous and quiet. I don't know how Sarah felt.

We began to cross the baseball diamond which led to Chicken Hill. The early-morning mist was thick. The grass was dripping. I was trying not to think. Visibility was ten feet ahead at best. We had made it halfway across the field, nearing the ascent, when smack in front of us, sitting calmly in the grass, was a big skunk. Sarah screamed and ran. I freaked out at her panic and tried to nonchalantly exit. The diversion was all it took to postpone our date.

Two years of avoidance followed. The condoms took up residence somewhere clandestine in my bedroom. Sarah and I navigated evenings, steering clear of intercourse, but I felt guilty for the continued avoidance. I planned an evening with Sarah at my parents' house while they were out.

That evening we fumbled our way to my bedroom. Suggesting sex was awkward. We were sitting on the floor, talking. As the words got dull, I got that sinking feeling that it was time for action. I nervously re-positioned to kiss. We were gentle in our groping. The bed was the next target. Clothes would come off tediously after they had been explored thoroughly. I'm not sure if we ever were completely naked.

At what I imagined was the right moment, when we had done everything we had done before, I choked out to Sarah, "Do you want to make love?" I made out a yes. I reached into my bedside table drawer where I had placed one of the same condoms that had journeyed with me to camp. I wasn't sure if it was still good; I had heard that they disintegrate.

I opened the foil. I could feel myself beginning to go limp. I persisted. I tried to roll the rubber on my descending erection. I quickly tried to position myself on top of Sarah. I could feel that there was nothing going in; that there was nothing left. I pumped a few times anyway. I wasn't ready to concede.

My worst fears had been realized. I had failed the test. I felt ashamed. I didn't speak. Both of us lay there in silence. After a while we got dressed and sat in my parents dimly lit kitchen. I was sitting on the counter. Sarah was sitting on the telephone table. We were staring into space, avoiding each other, protective.

I imagined that she thought I was a loser. I certainly felt like one. I was scared that it was over. After six years together, six years of trying to avoid this moment, it had happened. Now I imagined the inevitable consequences must follow.

Sarah didn't break up with me. We stayed boyfriend and girlfriend through high school. The only mention of intercourse was months later when she said she had talked to a gynecologist to get fitted for a diaphragm. I didn't like the implications, but if she got it I never saw it. We never attempted intercourse again.

The remaining two condoms followed me to college. I used one of them for practice just to see how it worked. I retired the other of old age. [35]

CHAPTER VII

BELIEFS, REVELATIONS, FORGIVENESS

Self-Fulfilling Prophecies

Yevrah Ornstein

Both in my job as publisher of the *Journal* and as a participant in men's groups, my ideas and beliefs about male/female delineations have changed over time.

The definitions and assumptions we draw along gender lines are arbitrarily created to the point where I don't think, in larger terms, the kinds of separations we are familar with truly exist. I think we have placed divisions randomly to afford ourselves certain specific types of experience. Some of these boundaries have afforded our species opportunities to grow and to explore definite aspects of reality and experience; and some have proven to be deeply devisive – even life threatening.

More and more, I am convinced that many of our definitions about gender are subjective, willful, and idiosyncratic. We are imprisoning ourselves unwittingly.

There was a brilliant conversation statement along these lines in the movie *My Dinner With Andre*. It illustrates the transparency of assumptions and the imprisoning potential of our unawareness:

"*Where do you come from?*"
"*New York.*"
"*Ah, New York, yes, that's a very interesting place. Do you know a lot of New Yorkers keep talking about the fact that they want to leave but never do?*"

> *"And I said, oh yes."*
> *"And he said, why do you think they don't leave?"*
> *"I gave him different banal theories."*
> *"I don't think it's that way at all. I think New York is the new model for the new concentration camp, where the camp has been built by the inmates themselves, and the inmates are the guards, and they have this pride in this thing they built. They built their own prison, and so they exist in a state of schizophrenia where they are both the guards and the prisoners, and as a result, they no longer have (having been lobotomized) the capacity to leave the prison they made or to even see it as a prison."*

❄   ❄   ❄

Have you ever met someone who has visited New York City? New York is a good example because it is a city of extremes, and extremes help illuminate this process.

I have an Australian friend who goes to New York about once a year if he can afford it. He loves New York. Waric believes New Yorkers are friendly, warm, generous and go out of their way to be helpful; he hasn't a disparaging word to say about the place.

He enjoys theater and art, and of course New York is renowned for its culture.

The buzz of the City isn't a put-off for Waric, just the opposite. It's vital, alive and tremendously exciting.

Anyway, you get the idea. Waric's real hot on "the Big Apple."

Then there are others, who perhaps visit or live in New York, who get accosted, jostled in the subways, hit up for change, step in dog you-know-what, feel inconsequential, fear for their lives when they cross the street, ramble on about the crime infestation, are revolted by the graffiti, etc. This person may walk down the street and be revolted by a drunk a block away and most likely not notice the love and kindness of a grandparent nearby.

Who's right? Who's telling the truth about New York City?

Here's what the Random (ironically) House dictionary says about belief.

Belief: 1. something believed. (Don't you just love these kinds of useless definitions?!) 2. confidence, faith, or trust. 3. a religious tenet or tenets. – Syn. 1. conviction, opinion, view.

❄   ❄   ❄

I learned something very important about the relationship between belief and experience while I was living on the coast in Ecuador. I was still in the Peace Corps, with four months left in-country. Remember, I talked about all of us American Peace Corps volunteers having our bouts of disliking Ecuadorians? Well, I was in the throes of a real humdinger. I had finished working on two schools and had not been away or out of the country for a while. These negative feelings seemed to be a cumulative deal – directly proportional to the amount of time spent in-country without a break.

I was really into hating Ecuadorians at the time. I spent so much time being gawked at, laughed at for my foreignness, that I had become obsessed with the issue.

I accepted totally, absolutely all my mental ramblings and rumblings; I totally accepted my ideas and beliefs about Ecuadorians as inviolate facts. I was totally blind to my inner dialogue as being my beliefs and opinions about them. I was completely ignorant of the self-fulfilling prophecy implications of what I was doing.

Then, I had read something that went like this –

> *No matter what world*
> *consciousness finds itself in,*
> *it's experience*
> *is a function of its belief about itself*
> *and the world around it.*

That was a real eye opener for me. I could have easily come across that quote at another time and have been totally unaffected by it – water off a duck's back. But that day, that quote – the sensibility and wisdom of it – hit home. With what was going on in my life, I was in need and primed for its lesson.

I tried a 5-minute technique that its author suggested that involves conjuring up pleasant memories that are along the lines of the kind of experience you would rather be having and then fantasizing, imagining future experiences that are in harmony with your desires or new belief.

It was exceptionally easy for me to recall warm, fun, touching, delightful memories because I had had so many. After a couple of memories I began smiling and laughing, oo-ing and ah-ing.

I found that the feelings were the propellent to creating new images; images were emerging, inspired by my feelings. It was effortless, and imaginings simply grew and were self-generated from the feelings elicited by my memories. It was not necessary to talk myself into anything. I was not repressing or denying anything. I had shifted my attention, knowing, trusting that I could do so; most of all, I wanted to, because intensely disliking Ecuadorians was no fun.

So I did this little process and then put it out of my mind as was suggested.

Afterwards, I was off to the neighboring fishing village, where there was a harbor and docks, and facilities for unloading the day's catch. It was a great place to buy fresh fish.

When I walked onto the bus and paid my one sucre (4 cents), the very first thing that happened was, an elderly gentleman sitting in the first row got up and insisted that I take his seat. I felt kind of strange about taking the seat of an elder, but with his continued persistence, I gratefully accepted his touching offer.

Being 6' 4", Caucasian, bearded and long haired (at the time), it was no secret I wasn't Ecuadorian.

After I got off the bus, I walked down to the docks and began talking with one of the fisherman who was cleaning and selling his fish. I asked him what he recommended, and when it came time to pay him, he refused to accept my money. In spite of my insisting, he absolutely refused to accept my money – incredible!

After some conversation, I headed back towards the bus stop; a car pulled over and the driver offered me a ride. I hopped in and he went out of his way to take me back to my house.

I walked inside, glowing from all those pleasant experiences, and all of a sudden, I remembered the 5-minute exercise I had done before I left.

My teeth almost fell out! "Do you know what just happened?! Do you have any idea what this means?"

❈   ❈   ❈

In the area of self-fulfilling prophecies, our cultural and religious beliefs about who we are are instrumental in affecting and effecting results.

As we reach out to new territories of selfhood, new models of gender and sexuality, I think it behooves us to critically re-examine and question the old definitions. We are trying to build something new all too often with archaic and degrading notions of who we are.

Beliefs and feelings are the building blocks from which we mold our visions of who we are and what we hope to become. But just what are those beliefs that leaven our sense of selfhood, of personhood? What are the concepts that enhance and/or imprison our inner blueprints of the greater self?

Are we but souls "slumming it" in these carnal, heathen bodies of ours, as many of our religions would have us believe? Have we fallen from grace, have we been evicted or have we perhaps risen from the garden. Was this punishment meted or a gift bestowed?

I am man. Am I therefore competitive by nature? I am strong, but can I use my strength compassionately? I am man, but what is man?

These are the building-block beliefs of how we perceive ourselves. For this reason, it behooves us to look with discerning eye upon our beliefs, for as a man believes, so it is; and as we believe, so it is for our culture.

❋   ❋   ❋

Earlier in the book I included material from a source I described as being of singular inspiration in my life. Once again, Seth discusses provocative ideas on the nature of beliefs and the role they play in forming our ideas and, hence, our experience of gender differentiation:

Beliefs And Gender Identification
Seth

The psyche is not male or female. In your system of beliefs, however, it is often identified as feminine, along with the artistic productions that emerge from its creativity. In that context, the day hours and waking consciousness are thought of as masculine, along with the sun while the nighttime, the moon, and the dreaming consciousness are considered feminine or passive. In the same manner, aggression is usually understood to be violent assertive action, male-oriented, while female elements are identified in terms of the nurturing principle.

Your psychological tests show you only the current picture of males and females, brought up from infancy with particular sexual beliefs. These beliefs program the child from infancy, of course, so that it behaves in certain fashions in adulthood. The male seems to perform better at mathematical tasks, and so-called logical mental activity, while the female performs better in social context, in value development and personal relationships. The male shows up better in the sciences, while the female is considered intuitional.

It should be obvious that this is learned behavior. You cannot teach a boy to be "the strong, silent male type," and then expect him to excel verbally or in social relationships. You cannot expect a girl to show "strong, logical thought development" when she is taught that a woman is intuitional – that the intuitions are opposed to logic, and that she must be feminine, or nonlogical, at all costs.

. . . it is natural to express love through sexual acts – natural and good. It is not natural to express love only through sexual acts, however. Many of Freud's sexual ideas did not reflect man's natural condition. The complexes and neuroses outlined and defined are products of your traditions and beliefs. You will naturally find some evidence for them in observed behavior. Many of the traditions do come from the Greeks, from the great Greek play-writers, who quite beautifully and tragically presented the quality of the psyche as it showed itself in the light of Grecian traditions.

The boy does not seek, naturally, to "dethrone" the father. He seeks to emulate him; he seeks to be himself as fully as it seems to him that his father was himself. He hopes to go beyond himself and his own capabilities for himself and for his father.

As a child, he once thought that his father was immortal, in human terms – that he could do no wrong. The son tries to vindicate the father by doing no wrong himself, and perhaps by succeeding where it seems the father might have failed. It is much more natural for the male to try to vindicate the father than it is to destroy him, or envy him in negative terms.

The child is simply the male child. He is not jealous of the father with the mother, in the way that is often supposed. The male child does not possess an identity so focused upon its maleness. I am not saying that children do not have a sexual nature from birth. They simply do not focus upon their maleness or femaleness in the way that is supposed.

To the male child, the penis is something that belongs to him personally in the same way that an arm or leg does, or that his mouth or anus does. He does not consider it a weapon (humorously). He is not jealous of his father's love for his mother, for he understands quite well that her love for him is just as strong. He does not wish to possess his mother sexually in the way that adults currently suppose. He does not understand those terms. He may at times be jealous of her attention, but this is not a sexual

jealousy in conventionally understood terms. Your beliefs blind
you to the sexual nature of children. They do enjoy their bodies.
They are sexually aroused. The psychological connotations,
however, are not those assigned to them by adults.

The beliefs involving the son's inherent rivalry with the
father, and his need to overthrow him, follow instead patterns of
culture and tradition, economic and social, rather than biological or
psychological. Those ideas serve as handy explanations for
behavior that is not inherent or biologically pertinent.

In a manner of speaking, humanity deals with different
predominant themes at different times. There may be minor
interweaving ones, but the nature of personality, religion, politics,
the family, and the arts – all of these are considered in the light of
the predominating theme.

In usual historic terms, humanity has been experimenting
with its own unique kind of consciousness, and as I have
mentioned many times, this necessitated an arbitrary division
between the subject and the perceiver – nature and man – and
brought about a situation in which the species came to consider
itself apart from the rest of existence.

<u>What you think of</u> as male ego-oriented characteristics are
simply those human attributes that the species encouraged, brought
into the foreground, and stressed. Using those actually as
guidelines, you have so far viewed your world and formed your
cultures. There are some exceptions of note, but here I am
speaking historically of the Western World with its Roman and
Greek heritage. Your gods became masculine then; competitive.
You saw the species pitted against nature, and man pitted against
man. You consider the Greek tragedies great because they echo so
firmly your own beliefs. Man is seen in opposition in the most
immediate fashion with his own father. Family relationships
become a mirror of those beliefs, which are then of course taken as
statements of fact concerning the human condition. You thus have
a very polarized male-female concept.

Those characteristics <u>that you consider female</u> are, then,
those that did not predominate because they represented the source
of nature from which the species sought release. To some extent
this was a true, creative, sexual drama – again, of high pretense, for

in its own way the consciousness of the species was playing for high stakes, and the drama had to be believable.

It was seeking for a multiplication of consciousness, forming new offshoots from its own source. It had to pretend to dislike and disown that source in the same way that an adolescent may momentarily turn aside from its parents in order to encourage independence. Before the so-called flowering of Greek and Roman cultures, consciousness had not as yet made that specialization. There were gods and goddesses galore, and dieties in whose natures the feminine and masculine characteristics merged. There were dieties part human and part animal. The species, then, had not yet taken up the theme that has been predominant in Western culture.

These changes first occurred in man's stories of the dieties. As the species divorced itself from nature, so the animal gods began to vanish. Man first changed his myths, and then altered the reality that reflected them.

Any deep exploration of the self will lead you into areas that will confound conventional beliefs about sexuality. You will discover an identity, a psychological and psychic identity, that is in your terms male _and_ female, one in which those abilities of each sex are magnified, released, and expressed. They may not be so released in normal life, but you will meet the greater dimensions of your own reality, and at least in the dream state catch a glimpse of the self that transcends a one-sex orientation.

Such an encounter with the psyche is often met by great artists or writers, or by mystics. This kind of realization is necessary if you are to ever transcend the framework of seeming opposites in which your world is involved.

The overly specific sexual orientation, then, reflects a basic division in consciousness. It not only separates a man from his own intuition and emotions to some extent, or a woman from her own intellect, but it effectively provides a civilization in which mind and heart, fact and revelation, appear completely divorced. To some degree each person is at war with the psyche, for all of an individual's human characteristics must be denied unless they fit in with those considered normal to the sexual identity. [36]

Dad Didn't Love Me
Yevrah Ornstein

Many years later the cover got blown.

I had endured a childhood believing my father didn't love me. We lived a relationship that was father and son by default; one that at its best moments was cool and superficial.

It was a late wintry afternoon, the kind of day that nudges one to go inside – the introspective kind of inside, sober with thoughts that reflect the absence of leaves, sunny skies and warming rays. I was resting with my eyes closed, letting my thoughts drift. Of their own accord, they nestled upon the mournful topic of my dad, and the distance between us. They were memories and scenes that had become unstuck in time; pictures that would linger for a moment and then dissolve into another image, another memory.

After watching this for a few minutes, I began to realize that there was a connection amongst all these pictures. They weren't linear or sequential; one did not follow the other, and their actual dates were scattered so they seemed to be random events. All of a sudden it dawned on me that there was a common denominator, a thread that undulated in and amongst the emotional ambiance of each memory.

At that point I simply asked myself – what is it? What ties these images together? I knew they shared a bond. And what was the glue that kept them alive within me?

Then I understood that I had lived my life believing, *believing*, that my father didn't love me! It seemed so obvious in that moment, and yet the pain and suffering of that one thought was more than I chose to remember. Bringing it forward felt like a stab in the back, and yet I knew I could now remove that knife with understanding.

This was a major revelation because for so many years I had felt myself to be the victim of his insecurities, his inadequacies, his anger, his withholding, his inability to love; that these were traits and realities I had no control over and in a sense "no part in." I had always felt myself to be on the receiving end of his problems, his dilemmas, his inability to share and express himself emotionally. I bore the crucible of being scared by my father's "problems" for some 25 years.

Once, on a visit home from college my mother said to me that I knew how to "get" to my father. It would be several years before I would come to that awareness myself. Dad and I had entered a two-way partnership, and from my side of it there were things that I was doing – unconsciously – to elicit unloving and hostile responses. Unbeknownst to me, many of my ways were cunningly effective at getting the kinds of responses that confirmed my belief that he didn't love me.

At the time, my mom was referring to my being a hippie. I had long hair and wore jeans with lots of patches, some of which were pretty outrageous. Interestingly enough, I would always pick the more outrageous jeans, the ones with the most patches, to wear home on my occasional visits. I guess it didn't take a Perry Mason to see through my act but I was so sucked into the drama, I couldn't see the forest for the trees.

So the dynamics and the scenario went like this: I simply pushed him beyond where I sensed his boundaries lay. Those jeans, that hair, violated values he dearly held; the symbols by which he defined manhood.

From my perspective he was being superficial; too caught up in appearances, not sensitive to my essence; and on and on.

The point is, I was intentionally/unintentionally pissing him off, and what I got out of the whole deal – my pay-off – came in the form of being *right*. Hence the relationship was one based on who was right and who was wrong. If I couldn't have his love, then at least I got to be right, which brought along with it some perverted sense of winning and justification.

What is also obvious in all of this is, I was really hurt and angry, and my actions had an implicit message of *fuck you, Dad!* It was my way of getting back at him. It was my most potent and effective form of revenge.

The revelation of my role, my responsibility in the partnership was thunderous, and in that moment I saw that being "right" had granted me an empty victory.

When I fully realized that I believed my father didn't love me, that revealed to me the basis for our way of relating to one another. This insight paved the way for me to release it, if I wanted to. Given how painful and miserable our non-relationship was, I very much wanted to let it go.

What was fundamental to the whole experience was my understanding that it was *my* belief and *my* choice and *my* attachment to being right that kept the entire package "alive and well." To blow the cover, to dissolve this diseased relationship, owning up to my actions was essential. This revelation already contained within it the seeds of self-responsibility and freedom; freedom, because I was free to let it go and to enter into a new and different kind of relationship with my father.

This all happened when I was living in Ecuador. Afterwards, I wrote him a letter saying I wanted him to know I now understood that I had grown up believing that he didn't love me; that I now saw all the ways in which I had contributed to that kind of relationship with him.

(As for his contributions and beliefs, well, that was for him to discover if he wanted to, although it wasn't necessary as far as I was concerned).

I closed my letter by telling him that I was ready to turn over a new leaf, to begin once again.

In the year and a half I had been in Ecuador, I had received a couple of short notes from him and that was all. His silence was loud and clear, and when I thought about him occasionally, I usually felt pissed off, sad and resigned to this-is-how-it-is-with-this-guy.

A few weeks after I sent him my letter, I received an incredibly beautiful and touching response. He told me that he, too, wanted to start over; that the past was behind us. The greatest surprise came when he revealed that he knew I had always believed this about him and that he just did not know what to do about it.

What a shock! I was so taken aback by his honesty, his vulnerability, his humanness and his awareness. Dad had always seemed so capable, so on top of things, so all knowing. I remember my deluge of "why" questions as a child; and there always was an answer. How could it be possible my father didn't know what to do, how to cope, find a solution, an answer or a way to break through to reunite our hearts and spirits. In that one sentence he seemed more real, more human and more deserving of love than I had ever felt towards him before. That honest statement dismantled any remaining walls and opened my heart even more to him. For the first time in my life my father became real to me, real in his admission of not knowing what to do, a fellow human being capable of confusion, hurt and feeling lost.

The remainder of the letter was a major learning experience as well, for all the things that I had tried to drag out of him over the years, all the words of encouragement that I had yearned for, now came to me.

There was a powerful lesson here; that when I stopped *trying,* when I stopped pushing, the love and respect and encouragement that I yearned for from my father came freely. I had carried in silence a desire, an emptiness and a numbness that concealed much pain and longing. I had covered it over with layers of blame and rationalizations of not needing or wanting him, attempting to find satisfaction and fulfillment elsewhere. It just ain't so. These people, our parents, hold the original keys to our self-esteem and sense of self-worth as do no others. We only have one mother and one father in this life, and I see so many people attempting to fill that void, the absence of nurturing and loving relationships with their parents, with objects, food, lovers, alcohol, ever-increasing salaries, numbness and denial.

An internationally respected Eastern teacher remarked upon his visit to the United States that in all his travels throughout the world, he had never seen such material wealth and yet such emotional and spiritual poverty.

For the first time in my life, I really heard my father say, I love you.

After I returned from Ecuador, Dad and I did indeed begin anew. Over the years, things just got better between the two of us. We enjoyed each other's company, loved to laugh together and we each took an active interest in the other's life.

❃   ❃   ❃

I gained more insight into my father during an emotional men's retreat. Ninety men were packed into a log cabin room. There was a heaviness upon us, a rawness, an intensity; irritability was in the air. Things were heating up as we were approaching "critical mass."

Much had gone by in the first two days, and for the first time, men were getting angry. So many of us felt ripped off about having wretched, non-existent relationships with our fathers. Our numbness and avoidance of that was beginning to dissolve; blood was beginning to flow once again, and feeling was returning. In that room, it was at an epidemic level: physically and emotionally distant fathers were something almost all of us had in common.

The gathering had convened in an old, rustic camp built in and amongst the majestic redwoods of northern California. Redwoods are enormous, ancient, grandfatherly, wide of girth and majestically tall. Not much light filters down to the ground. Earth and sky spirits unite as one in these giants of the forest. Our meeting room was simple and basic, like everything else in the camp.

Most of the guys had taken their squeaky, sagging, rickety bed frames and had dumped them outside, putting the thin, moldy mattresses on the floor. With three days of stubbly beards, intense inner work and sporadic eruptions, in an intense environment like this, it doesn't take long for you to know who you like and who you can't stomach.

It was about midday, and Robert Bly was spinning tales, using masks to play different characters in his stories; showing slides of Grecian statues and slides of other art forms along the lines of the themes he was developing. It was a masterful performance.

I had never been a fan of poetry. For me it all too often was like reading the Bible or seeing the movie "2001 – A Space Odyssey" – great visuals, but with large blocks of comprehension passing me by. For me, hearing a poet read his poetry is an entirely different experience from reading it myself.

The poem comes alive, and the symbols and associations make themselves known and are felt in ways that don't happen when I read it. Perhaps it's the added presence of the poet that accounts for the profound difference, the added dimension.

Robert recited a poem he had written about his father, while looking at a jagged log – a log that raised many memories.

He played the dulcimer as he recited his poem, and this cradled the poem's feeling into an even deeper poignancy.

Here is that poem.

My Father's Wedding

1924

Robert Bly

Today, lonely for my father, I saw
a log, or branch,
long, bent, ragged, bark gone.
I felt lonely for my father when I saw it.
It was the log
that lay near my uncle's old milk wagon.

Some men live with an invisible limp,
stagger, or drag
a leg. Their sons are often angry.
Only recently I thought:
Doing what you want
Is that like limping? Tracks of it show in sand.

Have you seen those giant bird-
men of Bhutan?
Men in bird masks, with pig noses, dancing,
teeth like a dog's, sometimes
dancing on one bad leg!
They do what they want, the dog's teeth say that!

But I grew up without dogs' teeth,
showed a whole body,
left only clear tracks in sand.

I learned to walk swiftly, easily,
no trace of a limp.
I even leaped a little. Guess where my defect is!

Then what? If a man, cautious
hides his limp,
Somebody has to limp it! Things
do it; the surroundings limp.
House walls get scars,
the car breaks down; matter, in drudgery, takes it up.

On my father's wedding day,
no one was there
to hold him. Noble loneliness
held him. Since he never asked for pity
his friends thought he
was whole. Walking alone, he could carry it.

He came in limping. It was a simple
wedding, three
or four people. The man in black,
lifting the book, called for order.
And the invisible bride
stepped forward, before his own bride.

He married the invisible bride, not his own.
In her left
breast she carried the three drops
that wound and kill. He already had
his barklike skin then,
made rough especially to repel the sympathy

he longed for, didn't need, and wouldn't accept.
They stopped. So
the words are read. The man in black
speaks the sentence. When the service
is over, I hold him
in my arms for the first time and the last.

After that he was alone
and I was alone.
No friends came; he invited none.
His two-story house he turned
into a forest,
where both he and I are the hunters. [37]

❋   ❋   ❋

Tears slid down my cheeks as Robert performed his pulsating recital of a poem that is very dear to him; a poem that comes from the depths of his heart, and reveals and shares the pain of a relationship that never was.

For me, it was the first time in my life that I had ever, ever thought of my father as a son.

That's pretty amazing in hindsight.

As I said, I had always felt myself to be the victim of my father's inability to express his love and concern for me. What I now knew and felt was that my father had been a son, *too*, and that realization, that empathetic feeling was shattering.

It's hard to recreate and describe what this was like, what it meant then and what it means to me today.

My grandfather died when I was five years old. I remember him although I hardly knew him.

I remember the pungent cigar that he smoked. I remember his whopper pinches on my cheeks, and his looks of delight and encouragement that my small body was larger than the last time he had seen me. I also remember that he pinched me too hard and my wishing I was older so that I might have had the where-with-all to break that vise-like grip that was squeezing the blood out of my face. I also remember my neck craned back, the back of my head touching my shoulder blades, looking up at this abnormally tall human being.

What I know about my grandfather comes mostly from my father and from other members of my family. There's a legend about "E.O.," as he's known, and it's never told in modest terms.

The man was intense and extreme, and so was his past. His was a true Horatio Alger story. He was one amongst many brothers and sisters who left his family in Czechoslovakia, when he was 15. He came to New York City with change in his pocket and didn't speak English. No family or friends here – just a kid, on his own.

The times I've thought about his story, I am blown away by what he did, against those odds and under those circumstances. In time, he married, had four sons, was a butcher for a while (one of my uncles became a vegetarian at a young age because of this), and eventually ended up in the real estate business. Through years of hard work and perserverance, he built a substantial business.

His life was his work and his work was his life – seven days a week. I've heard my father say that it amazed him (later on) that his father considered going to a baseball game with his boys a waste of time – time that could be used productively for business.

My father's feeling for his father was an intense love/hate relationship and I understand why, completely.

My father was the first generation Ornstein born in America, and so he was raised here with values that were in flux as Europeans settled down and began to take on the ways of the New World. But he was raised by a man still very much in the throes of the Old World order, and lines of authority were strongly drawn. A child did not speak back to the father and never questioned or disobeyed orders; and the wishes of the father never took the guise of requests – they were: *do this or do that,* period, end of conversation!

Times change, and my father was somewhere about midstream, having internalized a formidable, adamantly strict, completely unemotional father while growing up in a rapidly changing America.

Young America grew into a cultural milieu that challenged and questioned and strove to unfurl its wings according to its own design and desires. Individuality and freedom of choice are the cornerstones of our democratic system.

I remember well the clashes my brothers and I went through with Dad when we came of age and asserted our individuality – which at times ran counter to some of his notions of the ways things were to be done.

Times change, and as my father's best friend said to me (after the one and only time I ever spoke to him about the problems I was having with Dad; I was about 19 or 20), "Your father has a hard time letting go."

After hearing Robert's poem, I knew for the first time that my father had experienced incredible loneliness, that he didn't get what he wanted either. I realized my father was a son *too* and that he had lived with and gotten the authoritative, rigid, uptight, European male model in spades . . . I had been preoccupied years back with being victimized and scarred by him – Robert's poem opened my heart wide.

I began to think of what Dad had inherited, not only in terms of role model and experience, but societal legacies and definitions of how a man, a father, expresses his love and caring for his family.

I could now feel what it was like to come home at the end of the day to a family that did not appreciate the day-to-day sacrifices, the three hours of daily commuting to and from New York City (that turned me into a raving lunatic the few times I got caught in it), the endless crap he no doubt had to deal with.

❄   ❄   ❄

As the man of our culture strives to be father and to understand his father – the generic and emotional source of his manhood – he is filled with contradiction and paradox. Crippled with anger and disappointment, he reaches for understanding and love. He sees within his father the painful reminder of unmet longings and needs; the mere approximation of the man he wanted in his life and the man he knows at some level within, he wants to be. This New Man of our culture finds himself confronted with the paradox of needing to stop holding his father hostage for all that he was not and could not be for him. He realizes that through the

*letting go of the father he never had, he will be able to
forgive and accept the father that he really had.*

*Through these new eyes, the New Man begins to see
that his father was also filled with expectations for being
a man. He comes to know that what he wanted and
wished for in his father was in many ways <u>potentially</u>
present. This understanding will enable him to realize
that residing within himself and within his father are the
same potential for everything he has ever wanted to be;
a potential for power, for the roots and source of his
ancestral manhood. This potential, this source of
manhood, lies within the New Man just as it lay within
his father. It awaits only the acknowledgement that his
father is the true source of his own, manly life.* [38]

Dad Was Also A Son

There seem to be plateaus, levels that many of us go through
in terms of our growth and development.

Coming out of unawareness or reversing a refusal to face
certain kinds of memories, feelings and thoughts often unleashes
anger or rage. If one truly feels the sadness that is often buried
beneath and shielded by anger, there may be a moving into a fuller
understanding, which often leads to compassion by way of
empathy.

These seem to be common and key components of healing,
integration and growth.

I've heard other men talk about what it was like for them to
realize, fully, that their fathers were sons, too; and in each story,
there were new understandings and in the aftermath, deep
compassion and love.

I have also heard other men talk about their surprise and
amazement over their not having seen this sooner.

Here's a letter and a beautiful story/poem written by a friend
along these lines.

Dear Yevrah,

In the process of "finding our fathers" we meet frustration, anger, confusion and desperation. I'm beginning to appreciate these "fateful detours and wrong turnings" (Jung's phrase). They beg to be let in, "hosted" and spoken to. I find them to be most helpful and friendly guides, and messengers on the journey – *if* I don't fret and worry them back into dark corners where they, too, often, take on monstrous proportions. The over-sized shadows they project seem to be their way of knocking more loudly at the door.

I remember when I was a boy, riding my brother's huge horse. After taking me under numerous low-hanging branches, he turned back towards the corral. He was off like a shot, and as he made the last sharp turn he went one way and I went the other, into a mess of brambles that cut my left eyelid open, requiring four stitches. To this day when I get particularly stressed, that eye twitches. But in my imagination I've gotten back on that huge horse, and I've found him to be not so huge. For so many years I feared him – the uncooperative, competitive sonofabitch. But I learned a secret of his when I got back on him: he *wants* a rider as badly as I want to ride him. He wants to move along in tandem, too – he just isn't real sure how to do that. But we can learn. Ain't no doubt about it.

Recently, after a *long* period in therapy, digging around my relationship with my father, I realized the obvious (funny how that works); that my father and I are both *sons!* Let's not be embarrassed about learning the obvious. Besides, coming to those realizations promotes healthy, outright, prolonged giggling.

I did a lot of thinking about my grandfather then. What all did he mean to my father? And what about my greatgrandfather and *his* son? I decided to put *all* those guys into my boat (they were already there; I'd just been too busy, desperately looking for shoreline to stand on and hadn't recognized them). So, we're all sitting in the "boat of sons" where we get a better look at one another. Wonderful company to be keeping. And when it came time for *my* turn to tell a story to them all, the poem, "Pencil Stubs," came bubbling up. So I send along the poem to you and *The Men's Journal*.

Pencil Stubs

(for my father)

Bill Roberson

Here in the city tonight
it is cold and clear.
It is a perfect night for
a winter story. I want to tell you
a story and I hope
the story tells itself.
The room this story is told in
is full of a smell,
the smell of Alder and Fir dust
lightly wet and deep in the nose.
The smell is mixed with another smell,
the smell of the sweat of a man
who has ripped, joined and nailed
all his life: the bittersweet smell of work.

Once, a long time ago,
(I remember this clearly)
I was in your shop alone,
the lights out, late at night,
and I was overwhelmed with the urge
to take sledgehammer and fire
to boards, cabinets, saws and nails,
to raze the business to the ground,
to destroy everything you had made.

I wanted some piece of you,
something I could keep with me,
or ruin you in the bargain.
I never raised the hammer nor
lit the fire I had intended.
Instead I swiped your pencil,
one of those stubs of pencil,
worn and shiny from your hands
that you sharpened with a knife

it was so short. But it was you
and your ethical economy.
I put it in my pocket and made sure
the door was locked behind me.
But the next morning
I was so anxious that you'd miss it,
(you always knew when your things
had been touched) I returned it,
Right there where it had been.

Years later,
cleaning out Grandpa's garage
the day after the funeral
I took his old work jacket
as a momento. When I got home
I found, in the left hand pocket,
an old black worn stub of a pencil.
I left it in the pocket and it is there
right now.

But on a night like this,
somehow I feel wrong about having
his pencil stub. It should be yours.
You should have this piece
of your father to keep with you.
Sons need the stubs of pencils their fathers
have used, to have some sense
of how their lives were drawn and worked,
to keep with them some essence
of what it means to be a man,
a father, a son. So that our stories
will continue to tell themselves. [39]

From *The Prince Of Tides* by Pat Conroy:

For a week we lived alone in the center of the Great Salt
Marsh. We spent the time renewing those fragile, tenuous bonds
that are both the conundrum and the glory of facing the world as

twins. By day, we remained hidden inside the hut, and we passed the time telling and retelling the stories of our life as a family. We told every story we could remember about our early childhood and we tried to assess the damages and the strengths we brought to our adult life after being raised by Henry and Lila Wingo. Our life in the house by the river had been dangerous and harmful, yet both of us had found it somehow magnificient. It had produced extraordinary and somewhat strange children. The house had been the breeding ground of madness, poetry, courage, and an ineffable loyalty. Our childhood had been harsh, but also relentlessly interesting. Though we could draw up passionate indictments against both our parents, their particularity had indemnified our souls against the wages of tedium and ennui. To our surprise, we agreed that we had been born to the worst possible parents but we would have it no other way. On Marsh Hen Island while waiting for Luke, I think we began to forgive our parents for being exactly what they were meant to be. We would begin our talks with memories of brutality or treachery and end them by affirming over and over again our troubled but authentic love of Henry and Lila. At last, we were old enough to forgive them for not having been born perfect. [40]

❈   ❈   ❈

At a certain point in a man's life he must decide when he's going to stop interfacing with the world as a son who is owed things, and when he's going to start acting like a father who wants to protect the almost heartbreakingly fragile world, a world he wants to yelp "good boy!" to, coaxing it forward. Thereafter, from that instantaneous midair moment on, new questions will engage him.

Daniel Asa Rose

As a friend once said, wounds may heal, but scars always remain.

But when we can release the hold we have on our personal point of view, especially one in which we feel ourselves grievously wronged by another; when we *feel* what it's like for another, then something new and sweeter may take root.

The tragedy, of course, is the absence of the father. It's important to feel and understand the loss this represents for the father, too.

Although we often have different values, looking at the intention of another is always very liberating; it is an impetus that brings fluidity to a relationship or a situation in need of movement; it brings transformation.

❋   ❋   ❋

In working on the *Journal* for three years, the bulk of the articles and poems that came my way were laments about fathers and sons. Occasionally, I received articles from fathers who felt remorse over their poor performance as dads, yearning to recapture a relationship that didn't exist or was badly damaged. More often than not it was the other way around. It was the son who openly grieved for a bonding with his father.

When the following article came to me, I was especially touched. There was a beautiful letter accompanying this article, written by a fine gentle-man who ran a counseling center for men in North Carolina. Sherman was at the tail end of that endeavor when I received his article. Sherman truly was a pioneer in the field of working with men, exploring men's issues from a deeply gounded and sensitive position. Here was a man who valued wholesome male values; someone who didn't apologize for being a man, and who helped others discover their own positive male sensibilities and strengths.

What I loved so much about the article he sent was that for the first time, as publisher, I was hearing about a father coming clean. All too often it is the son who exposes, explores and makes vulnerable his negative contributions, hurts, and anger.

I understand the inertia and oppressive power of the conventional male conditioning and yet here was a father, a man who had the courage, the strength and the guts to come out and admit: "I flat out blew it."

I greatly appreciated this addition to *The Men's Journal*. It was my hope that just such an admission would inspire other fathers to get honest, to get off of their self-righteousness, and to acknowledge their version of self-inflicted victimhood.

One Magic Day
Sherman Burns

I am a very fortunate human being, for I have been given great treasures in my life; treasures of the truth. This is a column about the heart of my life, about my relationship with my father. Up to April 1983, my relationship with my father had been the too-busy father and the-son-who-grew-up-pretty-much-alone story you've heard in popular songs. That's usually where the story ends, with the singer going on about how he's too busy for his own kids now; ain't it a shame? But as I said, I've been given a treasure, so read on.

It happened on April 4, 1983. My father called me over to his home to talk. His request was unusual and got my attention.

I arrived at 6:30 p.m., just as the news was starting on TV. He turned off the television and said he needed to say something to me. At that point, I was nervous, because I'd never known him to turn off the TV news.

I knew he'd been going through some real changes in his life, but I was totally unprepared for what must surely be one of the rarest gifts any father has ever given his son. He began to tell me that he had not been available to me in my childhood, that he'd been a workaholic, too busy to teach me the things that men need to learn in the world. He talked of how he had provided the basic food, clothing and shelter, but that he had not been there for me when I needed him; that he had just flat blown it.

In the shock wave of his confession, I have forgotten his exact words, but his closing statement will live in me always: "Sherman, I take little credit; you are who you are by a miracle of your own courage."

At that moment . . . as I am at this moment of sharing the rich, painful gift, my father and I "broke down in a blaze of tears." I look back at that time and see that, even in my shock . . . I began to love him in a new way, much less because I was *supposed* to, much more because I *wanted* to, as a human being whose courage I respected.

Although I'll probably never fully understand what he gave me, I know that it has made a considerable change in my life, has given me more courage to keep going and growing than I ever knew I had.

There is no other relationship like the parent/child one. It has a lifetime of possibilities. It is never too late to know that you are loved, respected and admired by a parent. Thirty-seven years old is not too late to have a father. *It is never too late to have a father.* April 4, 1983, will always be Father's Day for me.

Six months later, I was the volunteer coordinator of a peer support group for men. We were going to have a discussion of fathering, so I summoned all the courage I could. I invited my father into that group to tell the story of our earlier conversation.

Boy, was I nervous! He seemed pretty cool and collected. He said even more than he'd said the first time: "I was a 21-year-old medical student. It was wartime. I was working 14 hours a day. I couldn't find time to be with my wife, then he (pointing at me) came along. I deeply resented him." Then he went on to say what he'd said to me that April.

You could look around the room at that point and see the jaws hanging slack on 20 men. Without their saying a word, I knew those men wanted to know my reaction to what he'd said. I spoke of how loved I felt at his gift of the truth, of what new respect I felt for his courage, of how I was beginning to build a new relationship with him. Several of them afterward told me and my father they'd never heard one man talk to another with such honesty.

As I look back at my father's confession, I see that I wasn't surprised at what he told me. I'd known that all along. I was simply stunned that he told me. I will always respect that he said, "I blew it!" not the tired old, watered-down, "I did the best I could."

Like many of you with absent fathers, I picked up things along the way as best I could from male teachers, coaches and mentors. Today, my father can be one of your inspirations, as he is for me. Do you have something to say to your own children? Things unsaid to loved ones can fester like wounds.

However, you must not expect any response. I happened to be ready for what my father said. We each have our own timetable. You could well incur considerable anger of the why-didn't-you-tell-me-this-when-I-needed-it variety. You may have to be very patient and know that all things have their time.

Now, my father and I are in similar situations. He doesn't know how to have a son, and I don't know much about having a father. We are both learning, one step at a time. There are no words for how I value each new step. **[41]**

❋   ❋   ❋

We all get caught-up in our stereotypic definitions. If there was one thing I wanted to convey, one flavor I've wanted to imbue this book with, it's the belief that we are a benevolent, loving and caring species.

We make mistakes out of ignorance. We exercise poor judgment at times. But for me, one of the most important things about the way we behave is *intention*.

It is the essence-level stuff, and although we may differ with one another about choices made, paths chosen and actions taken, a person's intention is in most cases based upon a desire to love and be loved.

Look at your own actions and look at the "heart" of your intentions. How often have *you* intended, premeditatively intended, to do harm to another? Not often. Of course we all have hurt other people and there are consequences to our actions that may adversely affect others, but were these our original intent? I think not.

CHAPTER VIII

MOTHERS AND SONS

The Mother Turns To One Of The Sons . . .
Yevrah Ornstein

In our modern culture, as fathers leave for their distant workplace, children remain at home to be reared primarily by their mothers or by mother-surrogates. The father's role has diminished, and when that void is coupled with society's notion of "appropriate" maleness, the emotional development within the son is profoundly affected and influenced.

What does it mean for sons to be reared predominantly by their mothers?

❄   ❄   ❄

The men's retreat I have referred to explored the meaning of masculinity by looking at Greek mythology; what it symbolized, revered and revealed of male psychology. Each day of the week we engaged a different male god (the diety that the Greeks equated with that day of the week) and discussed the aspect of male personality he represented.

We explored the meaning of these dieties as portrayed in story, and pondered the aspects of male personality and masculine energies that these characters brought to life. We delved into our own mythological roots and looked to our ancient ancestors for guidance. Theirs was a brilliant and profound psychology; an astute study of human nature. There was much here for us to learn.

We were inspired to personalize this material in ways that taught me a lot about other men as well as shedding light upon

143

some corners of myself that had been dimly lit. In time I came to understand that we were speaking the psyche's own, innate language; for portions of the mind and psyche communicate and create with emotionally-impregnated images.

It was a fascinating and, at times, deeply unsettling experience to compare my real self to these mythological archetypes. Sometimes it felt like my conscious ways were out of synch with my deeper patterns; my real self was out of synch with a deeper sense of my capabilities and potentials, with my inner blueprint of optimal selfhood. When the conscious patterns were held up to the light, these discrepancies from a more profound sense of balance, began to show themselves. The differences between my potential and real selves made themselves known not in rational but visceral ways. This is all very difficult to describe so please bear with me.

One week after this retreat, I spoke with six other men who had been there. My first question was, "How ya doing?" The answers ranged from "shitty" and "depressed" to "really angry." For me, I felt somewhat confused and disoriented – not a particularly bad feeling, but an uneasy one, as though I was on shifting ground. Although my normal day-to-day foundation seemed to be eroding, I basically trusted whatever was happening to me. I believed in the value of what had gone on. The moving about and rearranging inside seemed to have its own sense of internal wisdom and direction.

As I wondered about what was happening, I came to recall what we had done. I began to hypothesize that we were immersed in the psyche's own language, where communication is purer, simpler and more direct than we are usually accustomed to. I think much of our dialogue often serves as a camouflage for what we really are thinking and feeling. I think we spend more time and energy covering up, protecting and shielding ourselves than revealing and sharing who we are. Vulnerability has not been prized as a virtue, especially for men.

There seemed to be a realignment happening, as broader senses, grander visions, truer pictures of selfhood were brought to consciousness, and as we cleansed our notions of who we are, in ancient and wiser versions of manhood.

It was a powerful week and there was a revelation that came to me two weeks after the retreat, a revelation whose seeds had been planted in the time we spent together. It just took a bit of letting the dust settle for me to put together the seemingly random and unorganized pieces.

Occasionally, Robert, who guided us, would say something that had a major impact upon me; food for thought and grist for stirring the soul and psyche.

One of the bombshells was: "When things are shitty between the husband and wife, the mother turns to one of the sons."

Sometimes the truth is so piercing, the Walls of Jericho come tumbling down – *pronto*.

I asked Robert: "What if there is more than one son in the family?"

His answer was equally piercing; one that brought out a burst of laughter which then quickly subsided into groans of collective recognition (oh shit, he's right!).

His answer was; "*That* son is sitting in this room today."

Robert had just finished telling a fairy tale and we took a break. I was outside with three or four guys, and I said to the men there that I felt as though I was holding the pieces to a puzzle but something was missing.

I knew that the big *ah ha* that crystallizes the mosaic into comprehension hadn't come yet. I didn't know what the key was, but I knew I didn't have it.

I asked if anyone else was in a similar place, if they knew what I was talking about.

Yep, I was definitely not alone.

I was in New York a couple of weeks later visiting my folks, and I wanted very much to talk with my parents about many of the insights and feelings that had surfaced from my time at the retreat.

When it came to my mom, it wasn't time yet. I knew something hadn't solidified; that what I'd have to say would be jagged and incomplete.

Having grown up in a hostile home environment, Mom was my quiet ally, the one who gave the emotional support that was not forthcoming elsewhere. So partly out of a sense of gratitude and loyalty, I just felt too inhibited to say anything, and I didn't know what to say even if I wanted to. The dilemma was such that I could not point to anything, something concrete, – there was nothing visible.

So I was sitting, overlooking a gorgeous vista, totally oblivious to the beauty all around me, feeling kind of crappy and strange. I suddenly flashed on the the retreat – the fairy tale we had heard, and the missing key.

What sparked my attention was the *invisible force field* that captures so many of the young boys in so many fairy tales. The riddle in the fairy tale is how does the youngster find his way out of the labyrinth and all of a sudden, I realized that the invisible force field with mom was related to Robert's line about the mother turning to one of the sons; "When things are shitty between the husband and the wife, the mother turns to one of the sons . . ." *BINGO!*

The umbilical cord with my mother had been cut physically, but the psychic/emotional cord was still very much intact, which accounted for the invisibleness and the seemingly "irrational" feelings that were going on in me.

As the pieces began to fall into place, I began to understand some of the things we talked about at the retreat.

Withholding feelings; resentment towards women; sometimes feeling suffocated by woman; lifetime strains of never being able to fulfill an olympian expectation – replacing the father in all his multi-faceted roles; unwilling and unable to fully put myself into a relationship with another woman, etc. This was the tip of an iceberg as I began to see these kinds of frustrations from a very new and helpful perspective.

I met with my friend Steve that afternoon and told him about my unfolding realizations as best as I could, which was pretty rough as it was all so new and recent.

He cut me off mid-stream and told me he knew exactly what I was talking about; that he had gone through it with his mother. In the most stunning, succinct terms, he laid out his version and understanding of the mother/son bond, its potential entrapment, and what he did about it.

Steve's story is one of the most unusual and dramatic I've ever heard.

He had been a practitioner of Primal Scream Therapy. I'm not going to go into the specifics of Primal Scream, but he believes that the technique works extremely well for him.

He was visiting his parents many years back, and one evening they threw a party for their friends. Steve was upstairs in his old bedroom, rolling around the floor, buck naked, Primal Screaming.

I have heard Steve Primal Scream once. I was with Steve and Tracy in their living room late one night when Steve excused himself to go into the bedroom. After a couple of minutes I heard what I was sure was a wolf howling off in the distance. Now I've never heard a wolf howling in or around Ithaca, and I turned to Tracy, kind of amazed and thrilled, and asked her if she heard it too.

She smiled and casually said, "Oh yeah, that's Steve Primal Screaming."

Wild, I thought, and then Steve came bursting out of the bedroom, exhilarated and wired from some insight that had just come as he pushed through some inner barrier.

Back to the original story: Steve was rolling around the floor upstairs, Primal Screaming, and his parents were downstairs entertaining their friends and probably trying to downplay their son's howls with: "That's just Steve involved with some new fad of his." (You can imagine what a scene this must have been.)

After a while, Steve's mother went upstairs to see what the hell was going on, and as she opened the door, Steve lunged for her, tackled and wrestled her down to the floor, and tied her up into a full nelson, immobilizing her. Steve is one hell of a powerful guy and Mrs. B. wasn't going anywhere if that's what Steve had in mind and that's exactly what Steve had in mind. After a few attempts to get free she stopped. Steve grabbed her hand and jammed it onto his balls and screamed; *"They're blue, they're blue, they're blue, because of you!"*

Then, he released her so she could return to her party (???).

That was one astounding story, and I sat there, stunned, with my jaw in my lap.

That's called severing the mother/son conspiracy by taking matters into your own hands. I said to Steve, "Things must have been mighty weird at breakfast the next morning." He didn't elaborate on that.

Then Steve proceeded to lay out a brilliant, concise, precise, articulate map on this arrangement between the mother and the entrapped son. I was absolutely mesmerized with his synopsis and story, and I told him: "Steve, you have no idea what a gift you have just given me."

Up until that time, I had never heard another man talk about these interrelationships in such depth . . . and to have the "balls" to act on it as he did . . . whoa!

The key was in place, the mosaic was in focus, and I was now equipped to go back to New York City and bring it up and out with my mom.

She and I sat and talked for two and a half hours in the kitchen on my return. I explained as best I could my emerging understanding as to what had happened between us, how my mom turned to me from dissatisfaction with my dad, and how it had affected my life; how these interweavings related to my sexuality; ways in which I held back with the women in my life; feelings of inadequacy as I felt subconsciously that I could never fulfill a role that was not mine to fulfill, but my father's; how this had affected my relationship with my dad and other men; the list went on and on.

She was incredibly open to hearing me. There were tears and an apology, and an acknowledgement of the truth. These things had not been conscious or intentional, but she recognized that what I was saying was accurate; it was, in fact, what had gone on.

Mom went on to tell me something that speaks for the extraordinary person that she is.

She said that she knew there was something deep down inside of me that she had not been able to unearth, that there was something holding me back. She said she had spent many hours trying to get to it but she wasn't able to solve the mystery. She said I had done it and that I had gotten to the essence of "this thing." She also said she was very sorry, that it was not something she had done knowingly.

I do not take the position that entanglement of this kind is present between all sons and mothers, but I do know it is there for many men, and those men would benefit from examining this further.

The time was ripe to get something else off my chest with my mother. In the course of our conversation my mother had mentioned the not so magic word, hypersensitive.

As a child I had been told many-a-time that I was "hypersensitive."

If you've ever seen a movie written by Jules Pfeiffer entitled, *Little Murders,* you'd get a sense of what this is like. The movie takes place in New York City, and Alan Arkin is investigating a murder (which are as common as house flies in this particular neighborhood). He's questioning a family in an apartment complex where the murder took place.

The living room walls are lined with steel plates and there are tiny peep holes for windows, which can also be used as rifle sights. In the course of the interview, someone opens one of these tiny windows and a bullet shatters the glass Arkin is holding. The peep window is casually closed and the conversation continues unabated. No one blinks an eye or pauses in conversation; such is life. The only visible sign of stress is that Arkin's eye begins to twitch; he continues his inquiry as if nothing out of the ordinary has happened, while the entire family conducts itself in a civilized, contained, calm manner.

The son in the family, depicted as the "crazy" one, drops to the floor and begins rolling around in a fit of uncontrollable laughter. He's the only one who is reacting, responding in some way to what happened, to the world around him.

In time, I felt like the crazy one in my family, as I reacted to events around me by being "hypersensitive."

This is the kind of message that pushes one into emotional paralysis. It's the stuff that sends some people to the top of the Texas University Tower with a rifle, taking out targets like one does at a boardwalk arcade.

We all enact different roles in the family drama, and I drew straws on acting out (and subsequentally internalizing) the emotional upset. Because there was so much discomfort and denial going on, my hypersensitivity was a painful reminder of the pain that coursed through our family life, not so neatly swept under the rug.

I began to loosen the cork on this one with my mom. Releasing this one slowly, rationally was out of the question. I blew, as years of hurt and outrage vomited to the surface.

A gale was unleashed as I told her of the enormous damage that had been done to me with this unknowing weapon and that it was *their* inability to deal with the situation and *their* feelings and *their* fury . . . all of which was their problem.

"DON'T YOU EVER, EVER, TELL ME I'M HYPERSENSITIVE – thank God I can feel; I'm trying my damnedest to come back to life once again, and that means allowing myself to feel . . ."

Mom hung in there with me and she understood.

I told her I was no longer her baby on the end of an umbilical cord, and that that relationship was over. It was time to enter into a new arrangement, a new relationship.

The genesis of that new relationship was to come a few months down the road. I told her I had no teachers in this area, no guides to point the way, and that I was doing the best I could at the moment; and that meant getting this pus out.

The men's retreat was the first of three segments of this drama. The episode with my mom in the kitchen was the second part. Part three was to be the acid test, the putting of theory into practice.

On the other side of these kinds of feelings, there needs to be understanding, compassion and forgiveness. It was important that my mother understand that I knew all of this "stuff" was subconscious behavior. I told her I knew that she had not been fulfilled with my father in many of the ways that she deserved and wanted, but that this was an impossible burden to place upon me, especially when I was young.

I told her the buck stops here, and that what has passed from one generation to the next, which accounts for much of this unconscious pain and garbage, is over.

[*All my childhood I had been called hypersensitive and had reacted defensively to that. Recently I realized something – perhaps obvious to others but a revelation to me. Guess what? I really am hypersensitive.*]

Several months after our talk in the kitchen a family crisis came to pass – one of my brothers had a nervous breakdown. Everyone in the family reacted and responded differently, which included not responding.

It was my mother who came to my brother's rescue and with my living near him, I was asked to help.

This *is* touchy material . . .

I limited my input because I strongly felt my brother was long past the time to stand on his own two feet.

There was a strong and emotionally charged difference of opinion here, especially with my mother. She felt he badly needed nurturing and guidance, by me as well.

I felt my brother had a golden opportunity to begin anew and that meant he needed to pull himself up, on his own. My mother viewed me as a traitor and someone who couldn't be turned to, relied upon in an "emergency" such as this.

I was involved in the beginning but then after much introspection and reflection, I decided to exit from the drama.

I was absolutely convinced that my participation was feeding and sustaining destructive patterns. I did not want to be a part of perpetuating my brother's dependencies.

The turning point came after I announced my withdrawal from the trio.

Mom and I went for a walk and after explaining as best I could my reasons, she asked me to "do it for her, if not for my brother."

It was the first time my mother had ever come right out and said "Do this for me."

I felt myself on the verge of a tailspin. The focus had shifted from my brother to my mother and the situation was being reframed. Now I understood that I couldn't remain loyal to my mother and at the same time do what I knew was right for my brother.

I told her with a heavy heart – no, that I was committed to my decision.

I strongly felt that a continuation on my part, ultimately, was a grave disservice to my brother, short circuiting him of the opportunity he desperately needed in his life; and that the crisis was orchestrated by his own actions and he had unconsciously brought about these auspicious openings to move on in his life.

I knew beyond the shadow of a doubt that a deep, deep wound would be inflicted by me upon my mother, or at least she would interpret it in that way. I knew that I was risking permanent scars in what had been a very loving and caring relationship. I knew I would be seen as a traitor and someone who couldn't be depended upon in a crisis, ergo, selfish and self-centered.

The silence was nearly devastating and we headed back to my house with no further words between us.

One of the most difficult things about all of this was that I felt very much alone. I spoke with a friend and three weeks later she sent me the book *He* by Robert Johnson.

When I came across the following passage, I felt I had found what I was looking for.

He
Understanding Masculine Psychology

Robert A. Johnson

Then Parsifal goes to Gournamond's castle. Gournamond is Parsifal's godfather, so to speak; he trains him, takes some of the rough edges off and teaches him the things a boy needs to know for the pursuit of chivalry. He urges Parsifal to stay with him for another year to study, but Parsifal refuses and goes off quite suddenly because he thinks his mother might be in trouble.

Gournamond has taught Parsifal two specific things, and much of the myth (the Story of the Holy Grail) revolves around these two instructions. The first is that if Parsifal is to search for the Holy Grail, the only proper pursuit for a knight, one primary requirement lies upon him: He must never seduce or be seduced by a woman, or there is no hope for the Grail.

The second instruction is that when Parsifal gets into the Grail castle he must ask the specific question "Whom does the Grail serve?" This is a curious question, which we do not understand for a while, but these two instructions are drummed into Parsifal's head by Gournamond.

So he goes off to hunt for his mother. He finds that soon after he left his mother, she died of a broken heart. You remember that her name was Heart Sorrow. Naturally, Parsifal feels dreadfully guilty about this, but this also is part of his masculine development. No son ever develops into manhood without being disloyal to his mother in some way. If he remains with his mother to comfort her and console her, then he never gets out of his mother complex. Often, a mother will do all she can to keep her son with her. One of the most subtle ways is to encourage in him the idea of being loyal to mother, but if he gives in to her completely on this score then she often winds up with a son who has a severely injured masculinity. The son must ride off and leave his mother, even if it seems to mean disloyalty, and the mother must bear this pain. Later, like Parsifal, the son may then come back to the mother and they may find a new relationship on a new level; but this can only be done after the son has first achieved his independence and transferred his affections to a woman of his own age. In our myth, Parsifal's mother had died when he returned. Perhaps she represents the kind of woman who can only exist as mother, who, psychologically, "dies" when this role is taken from her because she does not understand how to be an individual woman, only a mother. [42]

❊   ❊   ❊

I sent this passage along to my mother with a note, saying, "The enclosed says what I want to express but says it far better than I can."

The next year was a tense one between us. It was the first time in our lives that a hardness had entered our relationship. Phone conversations were stilted, uncomfortable and the old familiar warmth wasn't there.

I decided I had done the proper thing, and I consciously accepted the consequences of my actions – which at the time I knew were inevitable. I knew I was inflicting a wound; there was the possibility the scars would be everlasting, her distrust of me always there, but I was absolutely convinced that for who we were and for our situation, this was necessary for both of our sakes.

Almost a year had gone by since the episode with my brother, the schism with my mom. My dad and I had never talked about what had happened. He was back east and we hadn't seen one another since the problem broke.

One evening, I decided I wanted him to hear my side of the story. I had kept it all to myself and had endured the reputation of having betrayed the family, in solitude. Word had come to me that this was the consensus, the judgement passed.

He listened quietly, acutely to what I had to say. I gave him the Parsifal passage to read. After reading it, he said he found it very interesting and enlightening, and now he understood my side of it. He confirmed all the damage and disappointment I knew my mother had felt.

I found out months later from my mother that my dad had returned home and had played the part of peacemaker. I don't remember the specifics, but I got the impression that he was gentle and impartial in mediating the rift that had taken place. Somehow he was able to speak to my mother and say things that I don't think she could hear or receive from me.

❊ ❊ ❊

I think motherhood is one of the greatest and most difficult tasks any of us are called to. To take a human being from your body, nourish it physically and emotionally for some 18 years and then to have to let it go requires a supreme act of courage and trust. If some of our mothers had difficulty with that, we should not be surprised. That some mothers carried off that separation successfully is a tribute to the spirit of woman. Older and wiser cultures had rites of passage that supported this separation with years of tradition and the energy of the entire tribe. What they did with all that support, our mothers attempted to do alone. I salute all mothers who must make that attempt and assure you that that separation is the most healing and loving thing you can do for your children.

Bob Trowbridge

*Let the beauty
of what you love
be what you do.*

Rumi

CHAPTER IX

STEPS ALONG THE PATH

In May of 1982, *New Age Journal* published an in-depth interview; a conversation between Robert Bly and Keith Thompson. I've already mentioned my admiration and respect for Robert. Keith is a man with extraordinary depth and clarity, a man with the ability to draw from Robert profound views and insights on men; our history, our contemporary dilemma, along with new possibilities for our future development.

There's magic in this interview and a rare matching of minds and souls. Here is that interview in its entirety.

A special thank you to Keith for giving me permission to include it.

What Men Really Want

Keith Thompson and Robert Bly

Thompson: After exploring the way of the goddess and the matriarchs for many years, lately you've turned your attention to the pathways of *male* energy – the bond between fathers and sons, for example, and the initiation of young males. You're also writing a book relating some of the old classic fairy tales to men's growth. What has your investigation turned up? What's going on with men these days?

Bly: No one knows! Historically, the male has changed considerably in the past thirty years. Back then there was a person we could call the 50's male, who was hard-working, responsible, fairly well disciplined: he didn't see women's souls very well, though he looked at their bodies a lot. Reagan still has this personality. The 50's male was vulnerable to collective opinion: be aggressive, stick up for the United States, never cry, and always provide. But this image of the male lacked feminine space. It lacked some sense of flow; it lacked compassion, in a way that led directly to the unbalanced pursuit of the Vietnam war, just as the lack of feminine space inside Reagan's head now has led to his callousness and brutality toward the poor in El Salvador, toward old people here, the unemployed, schoolchildren, and the poor people in general. The 50's male had a clear vision of what a man is, but the vision involved massive inadequacies and flaws.

Then, during the 60's, another sort of male appeared. The waste and anguish of the Vietnam war made men question what an adult male really is. And the women's movement encouraged men to actually *look* at women, forcing them to become conscious of certain things that the 50's male tended to avoid. As men began to look at women and at their concerns, some men began to see their own feminine side and pay attention to it. That process continues to this day, and I would say that most young males are now involved in it to some extent.

Now, there's something wonderful about all this – the step of the male bringing forth his own feminine consciousness is an important one – and yet I have the sense there is something wrong. The male in the past twenty years has become more thoughtful, more gentle. But by this process he has *not* become more free. He's a nice boy who now not only pleases his mother but also the young woman he is living with.

I see the phenomenon of what I would call the "soft male" all over the country today. Sometimes when I look out at my audiences, perhaps half the young males are what I'd call soft. They're lovely, valuable people – I like them – and they're not interested in harming the earth, or starting wars, or working for corporations. There's something favorable toward life in their whole general mood and style of living.

But something's wrong. Many of these men are unhappy. There's not much energy in them. They are life-preserving but not exactly *life-giving*. And why is it you often see these men with strong women who positively radiate energy? Here we have a finely tuned young man, ecologically superior to his father, sympathetic to the whole harmony of the universe, yet he himself has no energy to offer.

Thompson: It seems as if many of these soft young men have come to equate their own natural male energy with being macho. Even when masculine energy would clearly be life-giving, productive, of service to the community, many young males step back from it. Perhaps it's because back in the 60's, when we looked to the women's movement for leads as to how we should be, the message we got was the new strong women *wanted* soft men.

Bly: I agree. That's how it felt. The women did play a part in this. I remember a bumper sticker at the time that read: "WOMEN SAY YES TO MEN WHO SAY NO." We know it took courage to resist, or to go to Canada, just as it took courage also to go to Vietnam. But the women were definitely saying that they preferred the softer receptive male, and they would reward him for being so: "We will sleep with you if you are not too aggressive and macho." So the development of men was disturbed a little there: nonreceptive maleness was equated with violence, and receptivity was rewarded.

Also, as you mention, some energetic women chose soft men to be their lovers – and in a way, perhaps, sons. These changes didn't happen by accident. Young men for various reasons wanted harder women, and women began to desire softer men. It seems like a nice arrangement, but it isn't working out.

Thompson: How so?

Bly: Recently, I taught a conference for men only at the Lama Community in New Mexico. About forty men came, and we were together ten days. Each morning I talked about certain fairy tales relating to men's growth, and about the Greek gods that embody what the Greeks considered different kinds of male energy. We spent the afternoons being quiet or walking and doing body movement or dance, and then we'd all come together again in the late afternoon. Often the younger males would begin to talk and within five minutes they would be weeping. The amount of grief and anguish in the younger males was astounding! The river was deep.

Part of the grief was a remoteness from their fathers, which they felt keenly, but part, too, came from trouble in their marriages or relationships. They had learned to be receptive, and it wasn't enough to carry their marriages. In every relationship, something fierce is needed once in a while; both the man and the woman need to have it. At the point when it was needed, often the young man didn't have it. He was nurturing, but something *else* was required – for the relationship, for his life. The male was able to say, "I can feel your pain, and I consider your life as important as mine, and I will take care of you and comfort you." But he could not say what *he* wanted, and stick by it; that was a different matter.

In *The Odyssey*, Hermes instructs Odysseus, when he is approaching a kind of matriarchal figure, that he is to lift or show Circe his sword. It was difficult for many of the younger males to distinguish between showing the sword and hurting someone. Do you understand me? They had learned so well not to hurt anyone that they couldn't lift the sword, even to catch the light of the sun on it! Showing a sword doesn't mean fighting; there's something joyful in it.

Thompson: You seem to be suggesting that uniting with their feminine side has been an important stage for men on their path toward wholeness, but it's not the final one. What *is* required? What's the next step?

Bly: One of the fairy tales I'm working on for my *Fairy Tales for Men* collection is a story called "Iron John." Though it was first set down by the Grimm Brothers around 1820, this story could be ten or twenty thousand years old. It talks about a different development for men, a further stage than we've seen so far in the United States.

As the story starts, something strange has been happening in a remote area of the forest near the king's castle; when hunters go into this area, they disappear and never come back. Three hunters have gone out and disappeared. People are getting the feeling that there's something kind of weird about that part of the forest and they don't go there anymore.

Then one day an unknown hunter shows up at the castle and says, "What can I do around here? I need something to do." And he is told, "Well, there's a problem in the forest. People go out there and they don't come back. We've sent in groups of men to see about it and they disappear. Can you do something about it?"

Interestingly, this young man does not ask for a group to go with him – he goes into the forest alone, taking only his dog. As they wander about in the forest, they come across a pond. Suddenly a hand reaches up from the pond, grabs the dog, and drags it down. The hunter is fond of the dog, and he's not willing to abandon it in this way. His response is neither to become hysterical, nor to abandon his dog. Instead, he does something sensible: he goes back to the castle, rounds up some men with buckets, and then they bucket out the pond.

Lying at the bottom of the pond is a large man covered with hair all the way down to his feet. He's kind of reddish – he looks a little like rusty iron. So they capture him and bring him back to the castle, where the king puts him in an iron cage in the courtyard.

Now, let's stop the story here for a second. The implication is that when the male looks into his psyche, not being instructed what to look for, he may see beyond his feminine side, to the other side of the "deep pool." What he finds at the bottom of his psyche – in this area that no one has visited in a long time – is an ancient male covered with hair. Now, in all of the mythologies, hair is heavily connected with the instinctive, the sexual, the primitive. What I'm proposing is that every modern male has lying at the bottom of his psyche, a large, primitive man covered with hair down to his feet. Making contact with this Wild Man is the step the 70's male has not yet taken; this is the process that still hasn't taken place in contemporary culture.

As the story suggests very delicately, there's a little fear around this ancient man. After a man gets over his initial skittishness about expressing his feminine side, he finds it to be pretty wonderful. He gets to write poetry and go out and sit by the ocean, he doesn't have to be on top all the time in sex anymore, he becomes empathetic – it's a beautiful new world. But Iron John, the man at the bottom of the lake, is quite a different matter. This figure is even more frightening than the interior female, who is scary enough. When a man succeeds in becoming conscious of his interior woman, he often feels warmer, more alive. But when he approaches what I'll call the "deep male," that's a totally different situation!

Contact with Iron John requires the willingness to go down into the psyche and accept what's dark down there, including the sexual. For generations now, the business community has warned men to keep away from Iron John, and the Christian Church is not too fond of him either. But it's possible that men are once more approaching that deep male.

Freud, Jung, and Wilhelm Reich are three men who had the courage to go down into the pond and accept what's there, which includes the hair, the ancientness, the rustiness. The job of modern males is to follow them down, and in some psyches (or on some days in the whole culture) the Hairy Man, or Iron John, has been brought up and stands in a cage "in the courtyard." That means he has been brought back into the civilized world, and to a place where the young males can see him.

Now, let's go back to the story: One day the king's eight-year-old son is playing in the courtyard and he loses his beloved golden ball. It rolls into the cage, and the Wild Man grabs it. If the prince wants his ball back, he's going to have to go to this rusty, hairy man who's been lying at the bottom of the pond for a very long time, and ask for it. The plot begins to thicken.

Thompson: The golden ball, of course, is a recurrent image in many fairy stories. What does it symbolize in general, and what is its significance here?

Bly: The golden ball suggests the unity of personality that we have as children — a kind of radiance, a sense of unity with the universe. The ball is golden, representing light, and round, representing wholeness; like the sun, it gives off a radiant energy from inside.

Notice that in this story, the boy is eight. We all lose something around the age of eight, whether we are girl or boy, male or female. We lose the golden ball in grade school if not before; high school finishes it. We may spend the rest of our lives trying to get the golden ball back. The first stage of that process, I guess, would be accepting — firmly, definitely — that the ball has been lost. Remember Freud's words? "What a distressing contrast there is between the radiant intelligence of the child and the feeble mentality of the average adult."

So who's got the golden ball? In the 60's, males were told that the golden ball was the feminine, in their own feminine side. They found the feminine, and still did not find the golden ball. The step that both Freud and Jung urged on males, and the step that men are beginning to undertake now, is the realization that you *can't* look to your own feminine side, because that's not where the ball was lost. You can't go to your wife and ask for the golden ball back; she'd give it to you if she could, because women are not hostile in this way to men's growth, but she doesn't have it anyway, and besides, she has lost her own. And heaven knows you can't ask your mother!

After looking for the golden ball in women and not finding it, then looking in his own feminine side and not finding it, the young male is called upon to consider the possibility that the golden ball lies within the magnetic field of the Wild Man. Now, that's a very hard thing for us to conceive: the possibility that the deep nourishing and spiritually radiant energy in the male lies not in the feminine side, but in the deep masculine. Not the shallow masculine, the macho masculine, the snowmobile masculine, but the *deep* masculine, the instinctive one who's underwater and who has been there we don't know how long.

Now, the amazing thing about the "Iron John" story is that it doesn't say that the golden ball is being held by some benign Asian guru or by a kind young man named Jesus. There's something connected with getting the golden ball back that is incompatible with niceness. In the story of "The Frog Prince" it's the frog, the un-nice one, the one that everyone says, "Ick!" to, who brings the golden ball back. And the frog only turns into a prince when it is thrown against the wall in a fit of what New Age people might call "negative energy." New Age thought has taught young men to kiss frogs. That doesn't always work. You only get your mouth wet. The women's movement has helped women learn to throw the frog against the wall, but men haven't had this kind of movement yet. The kind of energy I'm talking about is not the same as macho, brute strength, which men already know enough about; it's forceful action undertaken, not without compassion, but with resolve.

Thompson: It sounds as if contacting the Wild Man would involve in some sense a movement against the forces of "civilization."

Bly: It's true. When it comes time for a young male to have a conversation with the Wild Man, it's not the same as a conversation with his minister or his guru. When a boy talks with the hairy man, he is not getting into a conversation about bliss or mind or spirit, or "higher consciousness," but about something wet, dark, and low – what James Hillman would call "soul."

And I think that today's males are just about ready to take that step; to go to the cage and ask for the golden ball back. *Some* are ready to do that. Others haven't gotten the water out of the pond yet – they haven't yet left the collective male identity and gone out into the wilderness alone, into the unconscious. You've got to take a bucket, several buckets. You can't wait for a giant to come along and suck out all the water for you; all that magic stuff isn't going to help you. A weekend at Esalen won't do it either! You have to do it bucket by bucket. This resembles the slow discipline of art: it's the work that Rembrandt did, that Picasso and Yeats and Rilke and Bach all did. Bucket work implies much more discipline than many males have right now.

Thompson: And of course it's going to take some persistence and discipline, not only to uncover the deep male, but to get the golden ball back. It seems unlikely that this "un-nice" Wild Man would just hand it over.

Bly: You're right. What kind of story would it be if the Wild Man answered, "Well, okay, here's your ball – go have fun?" Jung said that in any case, if you're asking your psyche for something, don't use yes-or-no questions – the psyche likes to make deals. If part of you, for example, is very lazy and doesn't want to do any work, a flat-out New Year's resolution won't do any good: it will work better if you say to the lazy part of yourself, "You let me work for an hour, then I'll let you be a slob for an hour – deal?" So in "Iron John," a deal is made: the Wild Man agrees to give the golden ball back if the boy opens the cage.

At first, the boy is frightened and runs off. Finally, the third time the Wild Man offers the same deal, the boy says, "I couldn't open it even if I wanted to because I don't know where the key is." The Wild Man now says something magnificent; he says, "The key is under your mother's pillow."

Did you get that shot? The key to let the Wild Man out is lying not in the toolshed, not in the attic, not in the cellar – it's under his mother's pillow! What do you make of that?

Thompson: It seems to suggest that the young male has to take back the power he has given to his mother and get away from the force field of her bed. He must direct his energies away from pleasing Mommy and toward the search for his own instinctive roots.

Bly: That's right, and we see a lot of trouble right there these days, particularly among spiritual devotees. A guru may help you skip over your troubled relations with your mother, but one doesn't enter the soul by skipping. In the West, our way has been to enter the soul by consciously exploring the relationship with the mother – even though it implies the incest issue, even though we can't seem to make any headway in talking with her.

Thompson: Which would explain why the boy turns away twice in fright before agreeing to get the key from his mother's bed. Some longtime work is involved in making this kind of break.

Bly: Yes. And it also surely accounts for the fact that, in the story, the mother and father are away on the day that the boy finally obeys the Wild Man. Obviously, you've got to wait until your mother and father have gone away. This represents not being so dependent on the collective, on the approval of the community, on being a nice person, or essentially being dependent on your own mother. Because if you went up to your mother and said, "I want the key so I can let the Wild Man out," she'd say, "Oh no, you just get a job," or "Come over here and give Mommy a kiss." There are very few mothers in the world who would release that key from under the pillow, because they are intuitively aware of what would happen next – namely, they would lose their nice boys. The possessiveness that some mothers exercise on sons – not to mention the possessiveness that fathers exercise toward their daughters – cannot be overestimated.

And then we have a lovely scene in which the boy succeeds in opening the cage and setting the Wild Man free. At this point, one could imagine a number of things happening. The Wild Man could go back to his pond, so that the split happens over again; by the time the parents come back, the Wild Man is gone and the boy has replaced the key. He could become a corporate executive, an ordained minister, a professor; he might be a typical twentieth-century male.

But in this case, what happens is that the Wild Man comes out of the cage and starts toward the forest, and the boy shouts after him. "Don't run away! My parents are going to be very angry when they come back." And Iron John says, "I guess you're right; you'd better come with me." He hoists the boy up on his shoulders and off they go.

Thompson: What does this mean, that they take off together?

Bly: There are several possible arrangements in life that a male can make with the Wild Man. The male can be separated from the Wild Man in his unconscious by thousands of miles and never see him. Or the male and the Wild Man can exist together in a civilized place, like a courtyard, with the Wild Man in a cage, and then they can carry on a conversation with one another, which can go on for a long time. But apparently the two can never be united in the courtyard; the boy cannot bring the Wild Man with him into his home. When the Wild Man is freed a little, when the young man feels a little more trust in his instinctive part after going through some discipline, then he can let the Wild Man out of the cage. And since the Wild Man can't stay with him in civilization, he must go off with the Wild Man.

This is where the break with the parents finally comes. As they go off together, the Wild Man says, "You'll never see your mother and father again," and the boy has to accept that the collective thing is over. He must leave his parents' force field.

Thompson: In the ancient Greek tradition, a young man would leave his family to study, with an older man, the energies of Zeus, Apollo, or Dionysius. We seem to have lost the rite of initiation, and yet young males have a great need to be introduced to the male mysteries.

Bly: I agree. This is what has been missing in our culture. Among the Hopis and other Native Americans of the Southwest, a boy is taken away at age twelve and led down into the kiva (down!); he stays down there for six weeks, and a year and a half passes before he sees his mother. He enters completely into the instinctive male world, which means a sharp break with both parents. You see, the fault of the nuclear family isn't so much that it's crazy and full of double-binds (that's true in communes, too – it's the human condition); the issue is that the son has a difficult time breaking away from the mother's field, and our culture simply has made no provision for this.

The ancient societies believed that a boy becomes a man only through ritual and effort – that he must be initiated into the world of men. It doesn't happen by itself; it doesn't happen just because he eats Wheaties. And only men can do this work.

Thompson: We tend to picture initiation as a series of tests that the young male goes through, but surely there's more to it.

Bly: We can also imagine initiation as that moment when the older males together welcome the younger male into the male world. One of the best stories I've heard about this kind of welcoming is one which takes place each year among the Kikuyus in Africa. When a young man is about ready to be welcomed in, he is taken away from his mother and brought to a special place the men have set up some distance from the village. He fasts for three days. The third night he finds himself sitting in a circle around the fire with the older males. He is hungry, thirsty, alert, and frightened. One of the older males takes up a knife, opens a vein in his arm, and lets a little of his blood flow into a gourd or bowl. Each man in the circle opens his arm with the same knife, as the bowl goes around, and lets some blood flow in. When the bowl arrives at the young male, he is invited in tenderness to take nourishment from it.

The boy learns a number of things. He learns that there is a kind of nourishment that comes not from his mother only, but from males. And he learns that the knife can be used for many purposes besides wounding others. Can he have any doubts now that he is welcome in the male world?

Once that is done, the older males can teach him the myths, the stories, the songs that carry male values; not fighting only, but spirit values. Once these "moistening myths" are learned, they lead the young male far beyond his personal father and into the moistness of the swampy fathers who stretch back century after century.

Thompson: If young men today have no access to initiation rites of the past, how are they to make the passage into their instinctive male energy?

Bly: Let me turn the question back to you: as a young male, how are *you* doing it?

Thompson: Well, I've heard much of my own path described in your remarks about soft young men. I was fourteen when my parents were divorced, and my brothers and I stayed with our mom. My relationship with my dad had been remote and distant anyway, and now he wasn't even in the house. My mom had the help of a succession of maids over the years to help raise us, particularly a wonderful old country woman who did everything from changing our diapers to teaching us to pray. It came to pass that my best friends were women, including several older, energetic women who introduced me to politics and literature and feminism. These were platonic friendships on the order of mentor-student bond. I was particularly influenced by the energy of the women's movement, particularly because I had been raised by strong yet nurturing women and partially because my father's absence suggested to me that men couldn't be trusted. So for almost ten years, through about age twenty-four, my life was full of self-confident, experienced women friends and men friends who, like me, placed a premium on vulnerability, gentleness, and sensitivity. From the standpoint of the sixties-seventies male, I had it made! Yet a couple of years ago, I began to feel that something was missing.

Bly: What was missing for you?

Thompson: My father. I began to think about my father. He began to appear in my dreams, and when I looked at old family photos, seeing his picture brought up a lot of grief – grief that I didn't know him, that the distance between us seemed so great. As I began to let myself feel my loneliness for him, one night I had a powerful dream, a dream I had actually had before and forgotten. In the dream I was carried off into the woods by a pack of she-wolves who fed and nursed and raised me with love and wisdom, and I became one of them. And yet, in some unspoken way, I was always slightly separate, different from the rest of the pack. One day after we had been running through the woods together in beautiful formation and with lightening speed, we came to a river and began to drink. When we put our faces to the water, I could see the reflection of all of them but I couldn't see my own! There was an empty space in the rippling water where I was supposed to be. My immediate response in the dream was panic – was I really *there*, did I even *exist?* I knew the dream had to do in some way with the absent male, both within me and with respect to my father. I had resolved to spend time with him, to see who we are in each other's lives now that we've both grown up a little.

Bly: So the dream deepened the longing. Have you seen him?

Thompson: Oh yes. I went back to Ohio a few months later to see him. He and my mom are both remarried and still live in our hometown. For the first time, I spent more time with my dad than with my mom. One long afternoon he and I spent driving to old familiar places – the pond where we fished, the country reservoir where we skated each winter, my grandfather's old farm, which is now owned by someone outside our family. The old windmill stood in the field, rusting, same as it ever was. When we got back to my dad's house, I called my mom and said, "I'm having dinner and spending the night over here at Dad's. See you later." That would *never* have happened a few years earlier.

Bly: That dream is the whole story. What has happened since?

Thompson: Since reconnecting with my father, I've been discovering that I have less need to make my women friends serve as my sole confidantes and confessors. I'm turning more to my men friends in these ways, especially those who are working with similar themes in their lives. What's common to our experience is that not having known or connected with our fathers and not having older male mentors, we've tried to get strength secondhand through women who got *their* strength from the women's movement. It's as if many of today's soft young males want these women, who are often older and wiser, to initiate them in some way.

Bly: I think that's true. And the problem is that, from the ancient point of view, women *cannot* initiate males; it's impossible.

When I was lecturing about the initiation of males, several women in the audience who were raising sons alone told me they had come up against exactly that problem. They sensed that their sons needed some sort of toughness, or discipline, or hardness – however it is to be said – but they found that if they tried to provide it, they would start to lose touch with their own femininity. They didn't know what to do.

I said that the best thing to do when the boy is twelve is send him to his father. And several of the women said flatly, "No, men aren't nourishing, they wouldn't take care of them." I told them that I had experienced tremendous reserves of nourishment that hadn't been called upon until it was time for me to deal with my children. Also, I think a son has a kind of body-longing for the father, which must be honored.

One woman told an interesting story. She was raising a son and two daughters. When the son was fourteen or so, he went off to live with his father, but stayed only a month or two and then came back. She said she knew that, with three women, there was too much feminine energy in the house for him – it was unbalanced, so to speak, but what could she do? One day something strange happened. She said gently, "John, it's time to come to dinner," and he knocked her across the room. She said, "I think it's time to go back to your father." He said, "You're right." The boy couldn't bring what he needed into consciousness, but his body knew it. And his body acted. The mother didn't take it personally either. She understood it was a message. In the U.S. there are so many big-muscled high school boys hulking around the kitchen rudely; and I think in a way they're trying to make themselves less attractive to their mothers.

Separation from the mother is crucial. I'm not saying that women have been doing the wrong thing, necessarily. I think the problem is more that the men are not really doing their job.

Thompson: Underneath most of the issues we've talked about is the father, or the absence of the father. I was moved by a statement you made in *News of the Universe*, that the love-unit most damaged by the Industrial Revolution has been the father-son bond.

Bly: I think it's important that we not idealize past times, and yet the Industrial Revolution does present a new situation, because as far as we know, in ancient times the boy and his father lived closely with each other, at least in the work world after age twelve.

The first thing that happened in the Industrial Revolution was that boys were pulled away from their fathers and other men, and placed in schools. D.H. Lawrence described what this was like in his essay "Men Must Work and Women As Well." What happened to his generation, as he describes it, was the appearance of one idea; that physical labor is bad. Lawrence recalls how his father enjoyed working in the mines, enjoyed the camradery with the other men, enjoyed coming home and taking his bath in the kitchen. But in Lawrence's lifetime, the schoolteachers arrived from London to teach him and his classmates that physical labor is a bad thing, that boys and girls both should strive to move upward into more "spiritual" work – higher work, mental work. With this comes the concept that fathers have been doing something wrong, that men's physical work is low, that the women are right in preferring white curtains and a sensitive, elegant life.

When he wrote *Sons and Lovers*, Lawrence clearly believed the teachers: he took the side of "higher" life, his mother's side. It was not until two years before he died, when he had tuberculosis in Italy, that he began to notice the vitality of the Italian working men, and to feel a deep longing for his own father. He began to realize it was possible that his mother hadn't been right on this issue.

A mental attitude catches like a plague: "Physical work is wrong." And it follows from that, that if Father is wrong, if Father is crude and unfeeling, then Mother is right and I must advance upward, and leave my father behind. Then the separation between fathers and sons is further deepened when *those* sons go to work in an office, become fathers, and no longer share their work with their sons. The strange thing about this is not only the physical separation, but the fact that the father is not able to explain to the son what he's doing. Lawrence's father could show his son what he did, take him down in the mines, just as my own father, who was a farmer, could take me out on the tractor, and show me around. I knew what he was doing all day and all the seasons of the year.

In the world of offices, this breaks down. With the father only home in the evenings, and women's values so strong in the house, the father loses the son five minutes after birth. It's as if he had amnesia and can't remember who his children are. The father is remote; he's somewhere else. He might as well be in Australia.

And the father is a little ashamed of his work, despite the "prestige" of working in an office. Even if he brings his son there, what can he show him? How he moves papers? Children take things physically, not mentally. If you work in an office, how can you explain how what you're doing is important, or how it differs from what the other males are doing?

The German psychologist Alexander Mitscherlich writes about this situation in a fine book called *Society Without The Father*. His main idea is that if the son does not understand clearly, physically, what his father is doing during the year and during the day, a hole will appear in the son's perception of his father, and into the hole will rush demons. That's a law of nature: demons rush in, because nature hates a vacuum. The son's mind then fills with suspicion, doubt, and a nagging fear that the father is doing evil things.

This issue was dramatized touchingly in the 60's when rebellious students took over the president's office at Columbia, looking for evidence of CIA involvement with the university. It was a perfect example of taking the fear that your father is demonic and transferring the fear to some figure in authority. I give the students all the credit they deserve for their bravery, but on a deeper level they weren't just making a protest against the Vietnam War; they were looking for evidence of their fathers' demonism. A university, like a father, looks upright and decent on the outside, but underneath, somewhere, you have the feeling that it's doing something evil. And it's an intolerable feeling, that the inner fears should be so incongruous with the appearances. So you go to all the trouble to invade the president's office to make the inner look like the outer, to find evidence of demonic activity. And then, naturally, given the interlocking relationships between establishments, you *do* discover letters from the CIA, and demonic links *are* found!

But the discovery is never really satisfying, because the image of the demons inside wasn't real in the first place. These are mostly imagined fears; they come in because the father is *remote*, not because the father is wicked. Finding evidence doesn't answer the deep need we spoke to in the first place – the longing for the father, the confusion about why I'm so separate from my father; where is my father, doesn't he love me, what is going on?

Thompson: Once the father becomes a demonic figure in the son's eyes, it would seem that the son is prevented from forming a fruitful association with *any* male energy, even positive male energy. Since the father serves as the son's earliest role model for male ways, the son's doubts will likely translate into doubts toward the masculine in general.

Bly: It's true. The idea that male energy, when in authority, could be good has come to be considered impossible. Yet the Greeks understood and praised that energy. They called it Zeus energy, which encompasses intelligence, robust health, compassionate authority, intelligent, physically healthy authority, good will, leadership – in sum, positive power accepted by the male in the service of the community. The Native Americans understood this, too – that this power only becomes positive when exercised for the sake of the community, not for personal aggrandizement.

All the great cultures since have lived with images of this energy, except ours.

Zeus energy has been disintegrating steadily in America. Popular culture has destroyed it mostly, beginning with the "Maggie and Jiggs" and "Dagwood" comics of the 1920's, in which the male is always foolish. From there the stereotypes went into animated cartoons, and now it shows up in TV situation comedies. The young men in Hollywood writing these comedies have a strong and profound hatred for the Zeus image of male energy. They may believe that they are giving the audience what it wants, or simply that they're working to make a buck, whereas in fact what they are actually doing is taking revenge on their fathers, in the most classic way possible. Instead of confronting their father in Kansas, these television writers attack him long distance from Hollywood.

This kind of attack is particularly insidious because it's a way of destroying not only all the energy that the father lives on, but the energy that he has tried to pass on. In the ancient tradition, the male who grows is one who is able to contact the energy coming from older males – and from women as well, but especially male spiritual teachers who transmit positive male energy.

Thompson: I find in your translations of the poems of Rainer Maria Rilke, as well as in your own most recent book of poems, *The Man in the Black Coat Turns*, a willingness to pay honor to the older males who have influenced you – your own father and your spiritual fathers. In fact, in the past few years, you seem to have deliberately focused on men and the masculine experience. What inspired this shift in emphasis away from the feminine?

Bly: After a man has done some work in recovering his wet and muddy feminine side, often he still doesn't feel complete. A few years ago I began to feel diminished by my lack of embodiment of the fruitful male, or the "moist male." I found myself missing contact with the male – or should I say my father?

For the first time, I began to think of my father in a different way. I began to think of him not as someone who had deprived me of love or attention or companionship, but as someone who himself had been deprived, by his mother or by the culture. This process is still going on. Every time I see my father I have different and complicated feelings about how much of the deprivation I felt with him came willfully and how much came against his will – how much he was aware of and unaware of. I've begun to see him more as a man in a complicated situation.

Jung made a very interesting observation: he said that if a male is brought up mainly with the mother, he will take a feminine attitude toward his father. He will see his father through his mother's eyes. Since the father and the mother are in competition for the affection of the son, you're not going to get a straight picture of your father out of your mother. Instead, all the inadequacies of the father are well pointed out. The mother tends to give the tone that civilization and culture and feeling and relationship are things which the mother and the son and the daughter have together, whereas what the father has is something inadequate, stiff, maybe brutal, unfeeling, obsessed, rationalistic, money-mad, uncompassionate. So the young male often grows up with a wounded image of his father – not necessarily caused by the father's actions, but based on the mother's observation of these actions.

I know that in my own case I made my first connection with feeling through my mother; she gave me my first sense of human community. But the process also involved picking up a negative view of my father and his whole world.

It takes a while for a man to overcome this. The absorption with the mother may last ten, fifteen, twenty years, and then, rather naturally, a man turns toward his father. Eventually, when the male begins to think it over, the mother's view of the father just doesn't hold up.

Another way to put all this is to say that if the son accepts his mother's view of his father, he will look at his own masculinity from a feminine point of view. But eventually the male must throw off this view and begin to discover for himself what the father is, what masculinity is.

Thompson: What can men do to get in touch with their male energy – their instinctive male side? What kind of work is involved?

Bly: I think the next step for us is learning to visualize the Wild Man. And to help that visualization, I feel we need to return to the mythologies that today we only teach children. If you go back to ancient mythology you find that people in ancient times have already done some work in helping us to visualize the Wild Man. I think we're just coming to the place where we can understand what the ancients were talking about.

In the Greek myths, for example, Apollo is visualized as a golden man, standing on an enormous accumulation of dark, dangerous energy called Dionysius. The Bhutanese bird men with dog's teeth are another possible visualization. Another is the Chinese tomb-guardian: a figure with enormous power in the muscle and the will, and a couple of fangs sticking out of his mouth. In the Hindu tradition this fanged aspect of the Shiva is called the Bhairava: in his Bhairava aspect, Shiva is not a nice boy. There's a hint of this energy with Christ going wild in the temple and whipping everybody. The Celtic tradition gives us Cuchulain – smoke comes out of the top of his head when he gets hot.

These are all powerful energies lying in ponds we haven't found yet. All these traditions give us models to help us sense what it would be like for a young male to grow up in a culture in which the divine is associated not only with the Virgin Mary and the blissful Jesus, but with the Wild Man, covered with hair. We need to tap into these images.

Thompson: These mythological images are strong, almost frightening. How would you distinguish them from the strong but destructive male chauvinist personality that we've been trying to get *away* from?

Bly: The male in touch with the Wild Man has true strength; he's able to shout and say what he wants in a way that the 60's-70's male is not able to. The approach to his own feminine space that the 60's-70's male has made is infinitely valuable, and not to be given up. But as I say in my poem *A Meditation on Philosophy*: "When you shout at them, they don't reply. They turn their face toward the crib wall, and die."

However, the ability of a male to shout and to be fierce is *not* the same as treating people like objects, demanding land or empire, expressing aggression – the whole model of the 50's male. Getting in touch with the Wild Man means religious life for a man in the broadest sense of the phrase. The 50's male was almost wholly secular, so we are not talking in any way of movement back.

Thompson: How would you envision a movement forward?

Bly: Just as women in the 70's needed to develop what is known in the Indian tradition as Kali energy – the ability to really say what they want, to dance with skulls around their necks, to cut relationships when they need to – what males need now is an energy that can face this energy in women, and meet it. They need to make a similar connection in their psyches to their *Kala* energy – which is just another way to describe the Wild Man at the bottom of the pond. If they don't, they won't survive.

Thompson: Do you think they can?

Bly: I feel very hopeful! Men are suffering right now – young males especially. But now that so many men are getting in touch with their feminine side, we're ready to start *seeing* the Wild Man and to put his powerful, dark energy to use. At this point, many things can happen. [43]

CHAPTER X

MEN AND WOMEN

Modern Day Odysseus

Yevrah Ornstein

Many of the memories within these pages have been buried for a long time, events that have been gathering dust from the time of their birth. It makes an interesting pallette to assemble the pieces with the eyes and mind of who I am today.

Patterns emerge not noticed before; cobwebs reveal secrets into self that may have eluded my awareness at the time of their unfolding.

I like the process of telling stories and listening to those of others. It allows me to draw my own conclusions, allows me to search my own soul in a way that brings the responsibility home, crashing or nestling upon the shore from whence it came.

❀   ❀   ❀

The Grecian isle of Crete floats in a sea of blue azure . . . mostly barren, sun bleached, white stucco homes, creating a smart and striking contrast with the intensely vivid blue waters that cradle this rocky island. Her people are warm, kind and generous. When I think of Greece and her people, being giving and alive are what I recall most of all. The Greeks are extremely animated and expressive, much like Italians but without the melodrama.

A conference on mythology drew me to Crete several years ago. I met a man from Holland whom I liked very much. Raul's English was excellent so we weren't hampered by a language barrier.

Although this conversation took place quite a while ago, I remember the gist of it because of the depth and intensity of the feelings, and because of the confusion we shared at the time.

Perched on a cliff one afternoon, eased by the gentle sounds of waves lapping against the rocks below, we drew parallels from our lives to the plight of Odysseus – a timely conversation for a mythology conference.

Raul had been married for many years and spoke freely of his relationship with his wife; close, warm, loving and supportive. He also spoke of the ways he distanced himself; the parts of him that were on an odyssey – traveling from island to island and challenge to challenge.

The central question that kept coming up for both of us was, why do we run away from the love being offered to us from that special woman in our lives? Why do we feel compelled to travel from island to island, slaying this beast and doing battle against repetitious obstacles, all the time denying the love that awaits us at home?

(Why a woman chooses a man who lives this kind of life is the subject of a book befitting a female author.)

Sitting on this cliff, two men confessed to one another that they felt basically overpowered and overwhelmed by forces that seemed to draw their strength and sustenance from some place "out there," dwarfed by swarming phantoms whose methods taunted us while we foolishly lashed out at shadows.

Perhaps the feeling of not being at the helm is the source of the anger I feel sometimes, feeling frustrated and victimized by something beyond my control. And at times, I sense a large gap between what is potential and what is real. For me, the disparity between what is possible and what *is*, often seeds my anger and frustration.

These were dilemmas for Raul and me to fathom, but we knew it was our private puzzle to unravel and, hopefully, some day, piece together. And yet there was momentary solace in meeting a fellow traveler, cast out upon foreign waters. We were travelers from island to island, searching for and yearning to reunite with a physical woman, with the inner woman, and to know some kind of inner tranquility that we sensed but had never known.

There is a book by Richard Bach that had a great impact on me, entitled *The Bridge Across Forever*. I've read it twice and have re-read portions many-a-time. I need to remind myself often of certain things that strike particularly deep interior chords.

A couple of years ago I went to Tahiti with a friend who was reading Richard's book. We rented a car one day and went out in search of an isolated, idyllic fantasy beach, swaying palm trees, a cool South Pacific breeze, warm, clear ocean, and great waves for body surfing – you've seen the picture.

We found a spot that came mighty close, minus the wave action, and after swimming and sun bathing, Emer took out his book and began reading. Ten, fifteen minutes later, the stillness and tranquility was ruptured with hysterical laughter. Emer does something very funny when he's racked with laughter; he covers his mouth as a child might do if he or she feels self-conscious. It's a very cute and endearing gesture. The story was still quite vivid in my memory and I was waiting for Emer to come to those passages of special impact.

I love Bach's style immensely; his ability to be profound and light simultaneously, and to capture the essence so well, sometimes in a word, a phrase or a few sentences. His book *Illusions* is an excellent example of his skill.

The book provided hours of conversation for Emer and me. Emer would be reading, and all of a sudden there'd be an outburst of laughter or a hum of musing as something hit home in a provocative way.

I'd ask, "What'd you just read, Emer?" and we'd dive into a personal heart-to-heart of our own particulars.

I didn't know where Emer was in the book so I didn't know what he was laughing about, but I was curious to know what had gotten to him. He said two words that had unglued me in exactly the same way when I had read them: "beautiful aliens."

To understand what Richard is talking about, you have to know that after becoming wealthy from his books, he took to the "circuit" – TV, radio interviews, a movie, etc. He was a big, big hit – a true rags to riches story, complete with lovers in every port.

There's so and so with the perfect nose; then there's another with the perfect body but shy on brains; then there's the intellectual one who is woefully handicapped by bad teeth or the wrong colored hair; etc.

Why can't he simply find the ideal composite? So there's "poor" Richard, jetting all over the country, the owner of some ten airplanes (his beloved hobby) fucking his brains out from coast to coast.

He wakes up in the morning lying next to a virtual stranger, wishing he were alone, mired in that crappy feeling in the pit of the stomach: "What the hell am I doing here with this stranger?" . . . "beautiful aliens" . . . brilliant, Richard.

So Emer and I talked about what it had been like for us to sleep with "beautiful aliens," and the changes we've been through over the years.

I told Emer that reading Richard's book felt like someone had been reading my mail. It was so close to home; embarrassingly so at times. And yet, Richard's humor and his willingness to poke fun at himself took some of the sting out of having someone "read my mail."

The essence of Richard's book *The Bridge Across Forever* is his relationship with the woman he ends up marrying; the subtitle is "A love story."

I had recommended this book to many friends and I noticed that the women I know who read it, found it hard to get into. I think it's because in many ways it's the story of a man's odyssey – a man's journey. When I say I felt as if someone were reading my mail, it's because I saw so much of myself in Richard's story. Many of the men I know who have read it have felt the same way.

I don't want to blow the story for you if you haven't read it and intend to but there's a letter from a woman to Richard that is one of the finest, most poetic and touching pieces I've ever read.

Perhaps what follows is a woman's grief and commentary on the male Odyssean sojourn.

Dearest Richard,

It's so difficult to know where to begin. I've been thinking long and hard through many ideas, trying to find a way . . .

I finally struck one little thought, a musical metaphor, through which I have been able to think clearly and find understanding, if not satisfaction, and I want to share it with you. So please bear with me while we have yet another music lesson.

The most commonly used form for large classical works is sonata form. It is the basis of almost all symphonies and concertos. It consists of three main sections: the exposition or opening, in which little ideas, themes, bits and pieces are set forth and introduced to each other; the development, in which these tiny ideas and motifs are explored to their fullest, expanded, often go from major (happy) to minor (unhappy) and back again, and are developed and woven together in greater complexity until at last there is: the recapitulation, in which there is a restatement, a glorious expression of the full, rich maturity to which the tiny ideas have grown through the development process.

How does this apply to us, you may ask, if you haven't already guessed.

I see us stuck in a never-ending opening. At first, it was the real thing, and sheer delight. It is the part of the relationship in which you are at your best: fun, charming, excited, exciting, interesting, interested. It is a time when you're most comfortable and most lovable because you do not feel the need to mobilize your defenses, so your partner gets to cuddle a warm human being instead of a giant cactus. It is a time of delight for both, and it's no wonder you like openings so much you strive to make your life a series of them.

But beginnings cannot be prolonged endlessly; they cannot simply state and restate and restate themselves. They must move on and develop – or die of boredom. Not so, you say. You must get away, have changes, other people, other places so you can come back to a relationship *as if* it were new, and have constant new beginnings.

We moved on to a protracted series of reopenings. Some were caused by business separations that were necessary, but unnecessarily harsh and severe for two so close as we. Some were manufactured by you in order to provide still more opportunities to return to the newness you so desire.

Obviously, the development section is anathema to you. For it is where you may discover that all you have is a collection of severely limited ideas that won't work no matter how much creativity you bring to them or – even *worse* for you – that you have the makings of something glorious, a symphony, in which case there is work to be done; depths must be plumbed, and separate entities carefully woven together, the better to glorify themselves and each other.

We have undoubtedly gone further than you ever intended to go. And we have stopped far short of what I saw as our next logical and lovely steps. I have seen development with you continually arrested, and have come to believe that we will never make more than sporadic attempts at all our learning potential, our amazing similarities of interest, no matter how many years we may have – because we will never have unbroken time together. So the growth we prize so highly and know is possible, becomes impossible.

We have both had a vision of something wonderful that awaits us. Yet we cannot get there from here. I am faced with a solid wall of defenses and you have the need to build more and still more. I long for the richness and fullness of further development, and you will search for ways to avoid it as long as we're together. Both of us are frustrated; you unable to go back, I unable to go forward, in a constant state of struggle, with clouds and dark shadows over the limited time you allow us.

Facing facts as honestly as I can, I know I cannot continue, no matter how much I might wish to do so; I cannot bend further. I hope you will not see this as a breaking of an agreement, but rather the continuation of the many, many endings you have begun.

I am still your friend, as I know you are mine. I send this with a heart full of the deep and tender love and high regard you know I have for you, as well as profound sorrow that an opportunity so filled with promise, so rare and so beautiful, had to go unfulfilled.

Leslie **[44]**

❉ ❉ ❉

A Man's Romance

Colin Ingram

Novels, stories and articles about women's romantic adventures are everywhere. But how often do you see men's romance novels on the bookshelves? Books and magazines for men are about war stories, spy adventures or sports competition – any literature for men on the subject of women is likely to look like *Playboy* Magazine. But many men are as romantic as women, with similar needs, dreams and fears. For what it's worth, this is a romance story told by a man . . . to men.

I was working in Oakland, California as an engineer in a big, modern building when the most extraordinary woman appeared – but I'm getting ahead of my story; I should begin with my marriage. I had been married for nine years – nine long years – to Kathy, who I thought would be my wife forever. When we'd first met in college, we'd had many nights of trembling, passionate petting. But as it turned out, her trembling was not from passion but from fear. And it was only on our wedding night that I found out she was terrified of sex (back in those days, you didn't learn about your fiance's prowess in bed until after the marriage). That night, our marriage was not consummated – my bride was so frightened that she was simply incapable of making love – and our sex life never got much better.

Kathy was marvelous in other ways. She had majored in European history in college, and we spent wonderful months together, exploring remote villages and ruins and cathedrals from one end of Europe to the other – she could speak pretty good French and German, and passable Spanish. We both loved art and music and good books. We spent long hours together talking about culture, politics and peace movements. We even marched together in Berkeley in what was called the "Free Speech Movement," the year that then-governor Ronald Reagan sent helicoptors shooting tear gas to dampen our ardor. In short, Kathy was a great companion and friend – I couldn't ask for better.

But there was no romance between us, and little sex. It may have been my fault, for in my early years I didn't know how to look into a woman's eyes and say, "I love you." But whatever the reason, we stayed married. I rationalized that we were such good friends that I could do without romance and sex – after all, the traveling together and the other sharing was so good. This continued for nine years; years when frustration and yearnings were so deeply buried I thought they had long since gone. And, after all, I was successful and had an intelligent, cultured, friendly wife.

Now I can get back to the story. As I said, I was working in Oakland, and management had hired a bunch of college-age girls to work as general purpose clerks for the summer. We all have our dream images of perfection in the opposite sex, and this girl was mine. She had long, wavy golden hair (naturally gold – not tinted), a fair, rosy complexion bursting with health, and gray-green eyes that looked at you innocently, without even a hint of fear or awkwardness or guile. Her name was Beth, and she had that kind of exquisite figure that you only see a few times in your whole life. In short, this girl was an absolute knockout. She was so electrifying that not only men, but women, too, would turn to look at her when she passed by.

I found out that Beth was twenty-one. I was thirty-one and, while not unattractive, I have never been singled out by women for my looks. So what were my chances with this goddess called Beth?

In engineering, mountain climbing and other endeavors, I've been able to call upon a degree of initiative. But I had never been much good at meeting women. With the arrival of Beth, the compulsion to do something was overwhelming. Through office gossip (and there was a lot of that on the day she arrived) I found out that Beth's birthday was the next day. I made some excuses to leave the office and ran down to the flower shop that was in the lobby of the building. I spent several hundred dollars on flowers and had them made into dozens of large, beautiful bouquets, each with a note that said, "Birthday greetings from a secret admirer." I instructed the flower shop manager to deliver the bouquets that afternoon, one every ten minutes, to Beth.

After lunch they began arriving. There weren't enough vases in the office complex, so Beth and her girlfriends emptied the wastebaskets and filled them with water. By about 4:00 p.m., the office was filled with flowers; flowers on desks, on file cabinets and in the wastebaskets. I hadn't told the people at the flower shop to be secretive – I knew some of the girls would ask around and find out I was the one who had sent them.

You see, since there were already half a dozen handsome young studs around Beth, I didn't want to be seen as just another drooling admirer. I wanted Beth to find out who had sent the flowers, and I knew she would have to come to me! After all, if you had just been overwhelmed with flowers from a "secret admirer," and then you found out who it was, wouldn't you feel curious, if not obliged, to meet and thank him?

It worked. The next morning Beth came over and told me it was one of the most fun things that had ever happened in her life. We talked for a few minutes. I was wonderfully casual. Though my peripheral vision noticed her delicate sweater and her obvious lack of a bra, I did not once look at her breasts or even make the slightest allusion that I was aware she was female. I asked her if she'd like to go canoeing at lunchtime (our building was next to a small, downtown lake with rental boats) – I could get bag lunches and get her back to work on time. She said yes – how could she refuse after all the flowers?

On the lake, paddling around in the canoe, we talked a lot. It was good talk – sincere talk – and most of all, it was happy talk. Beth had a soft, musical voice that made you think you were with a nymph, if not an angel. We raced across the lake, both of us paddling furiously. Then we rested, in silence. I had never before or since seen such a beautiful human being. And I had not touched this thing of beauty that now sat so close to me. I had not even touched her hand. And on a sunny Tuesday afternoon, in a softly bobbing canoe, in Oakland, California, I said to Beth: "How would you like to run away with me to the Caribbean – tomorrow – and go island-hopping in a sailboat?" No teasing, no flippancy. I was serious and she knew it. Beth said, "I can't. There are some things I have to do." There was a pause. Then she said, with a stunningly beautiful smile, "How about Friday?"

Somehow, I was not surprised. Somehow, I knew that she would say yes, and come with me on an odyssey of love. I was filled with a warm glow, the first stirring of an impulse to romance that I had buried for so long.

At this point, I still had a wife to contend with. We hadn't been spending much time together lately, but she was still my wife. The next day we drove out on the coast highway, south from San Francisco. At a beach, near Half Moon Bay, I did the hardest thing I have ever done in my life. I told my wife I was leaving her. She had sensed, of course, that we were growing more distant. But it is one thing to sense that and another to hear your husband or wife tell you that they're leaving.

I'll spare you the agonizing details, except to say that in my ignorance, I tried to justify my decision to her, and in hers, she tried equally hard to change my mind. It was too late for that – much too late.

I had decided to leave everything to Kathy, partly to assuage my guilt and partly because I knew that her having the house, car and possessions would help her to cope with the separation. I took our backup car, an old Chevy, and I made ready to depart for the Caribbean.

Beth was renting a room at a coed boarding house near the UC Berkeley campus. I wanted to get an early start at driving across the desert in the summer, and we had arranged for me to pick her up at dawn, Friday morning. It was dark when I got there and Beth, while awake, was still in bed in her nightgown. She said she was cold and asked me if it would be all right if I stayed with her just a little while before we left.

I had still not touched Beth since meeting her. Now, she arose from the bed and kissed me lightly and started to undress me, with loving caresses. When she was done, Beth pulled me toward her onto the bed. She spread her beautiful legs open, wrapped them around me and whispered in that angel's voice, "Please make love to me before we go. I want you so much."

Nine years. Nine years of frustration erupted from me in a great moan as I slid into her body and held her tight. In all those years of my marriage, my wife had never once undressed me, never once held my genitals, never once willingly opened herself to me, and never, ever said or even suggested that *she* wanted *me*.

And here . . . here was a woman who wanted me. A woman who really wanted me inside of her, to fill her space with strength and passion and love. My God, I thought, my God! I had forgotten what it was to be a man! To be totally accepted and desired as a man!

When I "came," I cried, and I could not stop, it was so sweet. Beth may have had a thousand lovers, but then, at that moment, she was all mine, the most perfect symbol of feminine beauty and softness and love I had ever imagined. My wife, Kathy, ceased to exist after that moment. I didn't hate her – on the contrary, I knew that, like everyone else, she was doing the best she could. And I realized what a fool I had been to pretend, for so long, that we were really man and wife.

Beth and I drove across the United States, took a plane to Puerto Rico and chartered a boat for six months – I had enough money to last us for a while. We sailed from island to island and swam together in spectacular blue lagoons. We slept in thatch huts and hid beneath thundering waterfalls and climbed to the mountain tops in exotic rain forests. The islands and our time there were like a fantasy dream: St. Lucia, Dominica, Haiti, Montserrat, Trinidad, Tobago, Bonaire and dozens more. Beth and I made love two and three times a day, spontaneously, in the water, in cars, on the beach, in restrooms and, once, with circumspection, in the back seat of a public bus.

One of the things I liked best about Beth is that the sexual interplay between us was fun. She would walk by me in a passageway and barely brush her nipples against me as she went by, completely devoid of expression, to see if I would notice. In public places, she would subtly rub my pants to see if she could produce an erection against my will. In the back of crowded elevators, I would place my hand inside her jeans and stroke her clitoris until I could feel her start to squirm, all the while both of us smiling innocently and disarmingly at the passengers around us. A trip to the restaurant was, for us, a great excuse for under-the-table maneuvers.

Until Beth, I had never met a woman with (what I felt to be) a really healthy attitude toward sex. Beth was so open, so loving, so giving and so considerate that it would have been impossible not to be the same in return. One of my most satisfying and loving moments was when I helped Beth to "come" during intercourse – the first time she had been able to do that.

I won't dwell on our physical relationship except to recall something that happened when we were about to cross the toll bridge between two small islands. When we were driving somewhere together, Beth loved to loosen my pants and caress my penis with her mouth – she was an expert at teasing and arousing me, all the while telling me to keep my hands on the steering wheel. This time, with Beth working to arouse me, I put one hand on top of her head to hold it down on my lap. She was used to that and didn't stop. I slowed the car down and pretended to get some coins out of my pocket. Then, still holding Beth's head down between my legs, I brought the car to a stop and said in a loud voice (to no one), "How much is the toll?"

You have never seen anyone squirm like Beth squirmed at that moment. When I finally let her head up, and she saw that no one was there, she was furious. She screamed and scratched and kicked at me as hard as she could and yelled the first bad words I had ever heard her utter: "You dirty bastard! You Goddam shit!" If you had heard her soft, musical, angelic voice shouting these coarse words with such passion, it would have cracked you up. It did me. And then we both started laughing until we were hysterical.

When we had both calmed down, there was a sweet and tender kiss. I told Beth, "You are the best thing that has ever happened to me. I am a whole man again. I didn't know a person as wonderful as you could exist, and I love you with all of my heart." It was the first time I had ever said anything remotely like that to a woman, and I meant every word.

Our honeymoon wasn't yet over. After six months in the tropics, we headed back to the U.S. and spent the Autumn climbing mountains in New England and watching the pageant of the leaves. Beth was an unusual combination. She was the softest, most feminine creature imaginable, but she could put on a pair of cleated boots and scale a vertical slope, leaving me groping for handholds. Then, down on the level ground once again, she would recite love poetry from memory and read me romantic stories from the time of the Druids.

Finally, our money was running out and it was time to head home to Berkeley.

Neither of us could stand the thought of going back to a dreary job again, so we opened a flower shop, in the fashion of the open-air flower markets I had seen in Nice, France.

Within a few weeks of our return, Beth seemed to change. She started smoking joints, occasionally, at first, and then regularly. When she wanted to buy stronger drugs, we had our first real fight – then our second and third. Gradually, I began to realize what was happening. As long as Beth and I were in a fantasy world, she was happy. When we returned to work-a-day reality, she couldn't cope with it, and drugs were a way out.

Beth and I remained together for three more years. Three years of the most glorious and romantic times imaginable, and three years of living hell. We would have a picnic lunch together, and talk of marriage and the future. Later in the afternoon, I would get a call from her, her voice sounding stoned and thick: "Come get me. Hurry. I'm at this dealer's house and I don't have enough money to pay for the stuff. He wants me to make love as payment." And I would rush over to find Beth, stoned out of her head, making out with this guy, and not seeming to mind it.

The drug issue got between us more and more, and Beth was in and out of therapy. I became the "heavy," not allowing Beth to have any "fun." She would leave the house in the middle of the night and wander who-knows-where, looking for a party. And in Berkeley, in those years, parties were not hard to find.

At times Beth would come out of it. During one of these times, she swore off drugs forever. We planned to get married and have kids. Beth stopped taking birth control pills and she got pregnant almost immediately. I was deliriously happy. I had never had nor wanted children before, but to create children with someone you love very deeply is a feeling so profound it can only be experienced – not described. We found a beautiful piece of property in Oregon and set about the first steps of building our own log home, just the two of us. We had devised a plan of doing specialty farming – raising unusual crops that command high prices from posh restaurants – on just a few acres. Beth was glowing from her pregnancy and had never seemed happier.

The house was going up and Beth was in her fourth month. If anything, she looked even more beautiful. Her green eyes held magic, as though she alone knew a great and wonderful secret. When we would drive into the nearby town, every head would turn. I had such a feeling of pride, walking beside Beth, that this was "my woman" and it was my child inside of her. Yet those feelings were tempered because Beth's striking beauty and her obvious pregnancy caused such looks of desire and longing from the local men that I could never relax in public with her – I had to constantly fend off the rest of the male world.

Our log home was starting to look like a home. We designed a south-facing nursery room that would be warm and cheerful for our child. One afternoon, returning from town with some sharpened saw blades, I sensed that the house was empty. Inside, fastened to the wall of the nursery, was a note. It was forthright: "I don't want a baby and I don't want to stay here anymore. I want to have fun. I'm sorry." There was nothing else, no idea of where Beth had gone. I rushed back to town but she had not bought any bus tickets, which was the only public transportation out of town. She must have hitched a ride, but I had no idea where.

Three days later I received a telegram from a hospital in Berkeley. Beth had gone in for an abortion but now she was asking for me. Could I come immediately?

The psychiatrist at the hospital told me that Beth hadn't been able to cope with the responsibility of having a child and, at the same time, she couldn't bear the thought of killing our child by an abortion – so she had taken an overdose of some potent drug as a way out. Now the abortion was scheduled again. Because we were not legally married, the choice was solely Beth's, and she refused to let me see her.

In spite of sedatives, when it was time for the abortion to be performed, Beth was hysterical and was calling for me again. This time, they put me through some cursory sterilization routine and ushered me into what looked like a small operating room. Beth was crying and she grabbed my hand and kept repeating, "Hold me, hold me."

I stood there, holding Beth's hand, tears overflowing down my cheeks, comforting her and watching the child I had helped create, through this woman I loved so deeply, removed and destroyed.

We sold the Oregon property and Beth and I took up residence again in Berkeley. But Beth had changed. She still wanted drugs and fun, and she now realized she couldn't have them with me. So she would leave and stay away for a month or so, then, without warning, come back and beg me to forgive her. She loved me, would always love me, and would never leave again. Until the next time. And I, wanting her so much, missing her so much, would take her back in each time, knowing full well that I was prolonging our mutual misery.

One day, when Beth had been home for a week, we decided to drive out to the ocean. It was magnificent, as the Northern California coast always is, and we seemed to recapture some of our early togetherness. But then another argument over drugs erupted, and there was no more room for tolerance or compromise. Beth told me to stop the car and, independent spirit that she was, announced that she was leaving me forever, right then and there. She was so strikingly beautiful that, almost before she had lifted her thumb to hitch a ride, a car had stopped, let her in, and whisked her away.

I sat there, numb, not quite realizing what had happened. After a half hour or so, I looked up and noticed my surroundings. A whispered "Oh, no" came from my lips. The car was parked at a beach near Half Moon Bay – the same spot where, four years ago, I had stopped to tell my wife *I* was leaving *her*.

In the year after losing Beth, I had, I think twenty-two lovers, seeking solace in their warmth. I won't say it didn't help – it did, a little. I had taken some beautiful photographs of Beth, close-ups of her eyes, with a double-exposure of billowing clouds as background; silhouettes of her dancing at dusk on a beach; nudes in the pose of classic Greek statuary that outshone, by her beauty, the originals in our art books. I hung them all on my bedroom wall, to better wallow in my misery and savor my loss.

We had had a big dog named Claude who had loved Beth very much and had been fed by her all of those years. When I put down his bowl of dog food in the evening, instead of starting to eat it, the dog would sadly look around the room from side to side, and I knew he was thinking, "Where's Beth?" Simple things like that tore me up.

At night I cried for hours at a time. Great sobs shook me and I felt as though dozens of knives were piercing my guts, tearing my innards apart. These feelings increased over the months and, if possible, grew more intense. Finally, one night, I knew I had hit rock bottom – I hurt so very much there was no room for more.

The realization that I had experienced grief to its ultimate was, in itself, a comfort. There was nothing more the grief could do to me – it had done its all. And that became a turning point for recovery. Gradually, ever so slowly, I came back to near-normalcy.

Now, many years later, I am remarried and have beautiful children and a loving wife. I know that my experience with Beth can never be repeated; that feelings that intense will never occur again, for any reason – neither the great highs nor the terrible lows. A very small place inside me still yearns for intense romance, and a very small voice in this very small place tells me that I will have to wait until the next life to experience it again.

Beth helped make me into a man in the full sense of the word. When she left, that feeling stayed with me and is with me still. It's amusing to look at the women's magazines at the supermarket counters, and to read the seductive, illusory headlines about romance. They make me want to say to someone that I know what romance really is. You see, I've had a man's romance.

CHAPTER XI

Music of The Soul

. . . the soul's messages have been clear from the beginning and given to man through his feelings which are the music of the soul, through the impulses which impel you to act. It is your feelings and your impulses that you trust and those will lead you to whatever you want, to what you think of as esoteric truth; to physical exploration; to the creation of the arts or to an excellent relationship.

Seth

An Allegiance With Feelings

The conversation you are about to read took place between myself and Bob Trowbridge. Bob is a dear friend with whom I share a common philosophical and spiritual perspective. Among other things, Bob has an avid interest in dreams, the creative and therapeutic value of symbolism, and has published what for me is the finest piece on channeling I've come across. I love his line, "Just 'cause you're dead, don't mean you're smart." This is in reference to channeling "spooks" (Bob's term for non-physical beings/entities). His insights come from one who is actively involved with studying and understanding psychological processes from a variety of fascinating perspectives.

193

Here are just a few of the ideas from Seth that Bob and I used as creative material for the conversation that follows:

Be thankful for whatever feelings you have. They are a signal that you are alive, that you are reacting to the environment and to each other. They are a badge of physical authenticity. They are the fire of your existence whether they flame or smolder. And they are lovely in any case.

Now, when you trust your feelings and your impulses; when you learn to trust, something strange happens. They turn quite trustworthy. Your feelings and your impulses are your own private messengers from the inner self – whatever term you want to use. Each impulse, to one extent or another, carries within it the initial power of the will to be that gave you birth.

You have been taught not to trust your feelings and not to trust yourself. But if I tell you or if you are told to trust yourself, and at the same time, you do not trust your own feelings or your own impulses, then where is a self in which you can put any trust? You must look instead for some elusive inner self; some elusive, cold, impeccable and distant soul that seems to send you no messages. A soul that you can only reach through the most esoteric of methods.

But the soul's messages have been clear from the beginning and given to man through his feelings which are the music of the soul, through the impulses which impel you to act. It is your feelings and your impulses that you trust and those will lead you to whatever you want, to what you think of as esoteric truth; to physical exploration; to the creation of the arts or to an excellent relationship.

. . . feelings will move you psychologically to new places when you think of feelings and impulses as motion that can lead you where you want to go.

A Conversation with Bob Trowbridge

Yevrah: Let's talk about the Seth quotes in terms of trusting and expressing our feelings. What are your thoughts on your own experience, and some observations on the relationship between men and women and the issue of trust? Speak about it in terms of your feelings, trusting your feelings – externally and inside.

Bob: When you look at the external, it's true for me that my relationship with my mother was the main thing that influenced my sense of trust in relation to women. I don't think I created a sense of not trusting women from my mother, although I did come out with a sense of not trusting emotions from my mother. She had nervous breakdowns which were like outbreaks of emotion – uncontrolled emotion – so I had the idea that emotions were dangerous and really needed to be kept under control. I got the message from my mother, unconsciously, that sexuality was dangerous or being male was essentially dangerous and needed to be suppressed. It may be that I got the idea that all emotions need to be suppressed.

Y: You had a very extreme situation.

B: Yes, an extreme picture of emotions; not in the sense of a home where there was a lot of anger, but rather a situation in which emotions were so out of control.

Y: Through your counseling experience, friends and observations of society as a whole, what do you think is the common experience and dilemma in terms of men trusting women? Is the core issue related to emotions?

B: Men are a little bit afraid of the power of women's emotions. In this culture, in the past, a woman would cry when she wanted something from a man or if she wanted to stop him from doing or saying anything that was hurtful to her. She'd cry, and the man couldn't deal with it. There may be some feelings about women's emotions because they have been used in the past as a weapon against men. Women didn't feel they had any other means of dealing with the man, so they'd use their emotions as a weapon or a shield. So there may be a mistrust . . .

Y: In the ability of men to deal with it?

B: Yes, to deal with women's emotions and therefore an inability to deal with his own emotions. Because the man comes to mistrust the woman's emotions, and therefore his own, he disavows all emotion and uses rationality as his weapon. The woman, then, disavows her rationality and gets more and more emotional. At the end, both will probably be angry but the woman is not in touch with her rational self and the man is not in touch with his emotions (not the final feeling of anger, but the initial emotion which was probably hurt or fear).

When the man disavows emotions and the woman disavows rationality you create a false polarity in which the woman becomes more emotional than she really is and the man becomes more rational.

Let me give you an example. There's a man and a woman that have three kids. Two of them have grown up and left home. The last one is about to leave home – a 19-year-old boy. Mother is falling apart. She's crying, "My baby – he's leaving!" She's an emotional wreck over it. And father is Mr. Cool. He's walking around saying things like, "Now I'll know where all my tools are." So he's real calm. He's handling it and she's falling apart.

The wonderful thing about this story is that the man has a dream and in the dream his son is leaving home. But in the dream the man breaks down and sobs. Dreams often allow us to express emotions and take actions that we're unable to carry out in waking life. The man was not able to allow himself to experience the emotions he had over his son's leaving. But emotions *will* come out. There's also a good chance that his wife was incorporating his feelings into her own, making her reaction more intense.

Y: Is this a way of achieving balance or restoring equilibrium to the relationship?

B: It's part of our belief system. We expect women to act a certain way and men to act a certain way. If a man is not free to be emotional, he still has to express it somehow. Jung spoke of projection as a psychological defense mechanism whereby we deny certain aspects of ourselves, project them onto others, and then react against those others. Psychologists primarily focus on negative projection, but I believe projection is pervasive and it includes the denial of positive aspects as well. The emotions that the man projects onto the woman are not bad. The man just believes they're bad because of the stereotypes of his upbringing.

The man will either project his emotions onto the woman or distort them and express them in his driving or in an inappropriate emotion such as anger.

Y: Is his projecting it onto the woman a statement of his own denial?

B: Yes, but she denies her masculine self as well, and projects that onto the man so that he acts sort of super-masculine. If it were more natural, they'd both be upset, but they'd be balanced about it.

We don't trust females and their emotions, and therefore we don't trust our own emotions because we see them as feminine and potentially controlling, and dangerous. A lot of the anger and inappropriate actions of men may be the result of an inability to express emotions, especially love.

So the whole thing is that false division between what's a woman and what's a man, and the idea that, still, it's not okay for men to be emotional, or at least not emotional in what we call "soft" ways. It's not okay for men to be sad or hurt. It's okay for them to be angry. So you may actually be feeling sad or hurt, but your response is to get angry.

Y: Which reminds me of the last time I visited my dad. The first thing that I zeroed in on was the loss of my father's role as father with my being the last son to marry, which was compounded by him struggling with his retirement. Now his role of father, as I'm getting married, was coming to an end, but rather than being able to express the sadness or express loss about that, he got angry. He was in one shitty, antagonistic mood. He was itching for a fight.

B: Didn't your father do the same thing when you went into the Peace Corps? He was concerned about you and he was a little scared about that but he simply couldn't express it, so he got angry.

Y: Do you see that as what's condoned, viewed as appropriate for men in our society? Or is it simply the frustration of not being able to express it?

B: Yes, it's both. He's frustrated because he's not able to express what he's really feeling, and anger, if not exactly acceptable, is at least expected of men. Emotions don't ever go away. Unexpressed emotions, in both men and women, will get expressed through inappropriate emotions or behavior or, over time, as illness in the body.

Y: Do you mean that the sheer energy of the emotions manifests as sickness if we express them inappropriately?

B: It's real energy. It doesn't go away. It either gets expressed or it stays in the body and causes problems. And it either gets expressed appropriately or inappropriately. What I'm saying about men in the past – my father and your father's generation – is that it was very definite what men did and what they didn't do, and what was appropriate and what wasn't.

Actually, men getting angry wasn't actually condoned. It was simply more acceptable than the showing of tenderness. That made it a no win situation for the man. He didn't know how to express himself appropriately, so he either swallowed it or expressed it inappropriately.

And even if the man expressed his feelings inappropriately through anger, that didn't totally satisfy the need for expression. That energy release didn't totally satisfy his need to express feelings because they were the wrong feelings. So the energy still gets turned back on the man, whether he expresses that energy inappropriately or just swallows it.

The irony, of course, is that it was primarily the mothers, the women, who taught men this. I think it's important to note that. There was no big conspiracy among men to hold women down and keep them in their place. It's something the whole culture bought as the image of women and men.

Y: So you think that women have actually done that?

B: Yes!

Y: Teaching men what's "appropriate?"

B: It was the mothers who were the primary teachers, especially when the men started going away to work and women became the primary parent. Mothers passed on the images and roles of men and women. If you went back and looked at the media, at radio and early TV family shows, you'd find mothers as well as fathers putting that gender message out; even kids saying it to each other. "Boys don't cry. Boys don't play with dolls." It really permeated the culture, but I think it came from the mothers quite a bit because the mothers were the ones raising us. I don't know if I ever got that kind of message from my mother, but it wasn't uncommon. The mother would be as concerned about her son being a sissy as the father, and would be as concerned about her daughter being a tomboy.

The gender separation was pretty much accepted by the whole culture and it wasn't something men were trying to put on women. It permeated our culture.

Y: It might be enlightening to review the TV shows we grew up with. I used to watch "Leave it to Beaver," which might be interesting to watch for its family dynamics. Perhaps we could draw parallels to the role models we've attempted to emulate in our own lives. Let's face it – Ward Cleaver was a knight-in-shining-armor, spic-and-span type guy. Perfect teeth, forever happy and always on top of it. The kind of man who's kaka doesn't smell. (We never did see these folks go to the head.) Boy meets girl, and they live happily ever after in emaculate suburbia with 2.4 children. This is the Hollywood version of the ideal family many of us grew up with. "Father Knows Best," "The Donna Reed Show," and others of a similar ilk, were carbon copies of one another. This set us up in some pretty sticky ways.

B: And some other shows, especially if there were sons and daughters in the family so you could look at the contrast.

So there was a real rigidity in the male and female roles, and that meant that men were learning the limited ways in which they could express emotions and, at the same time, not to trust women and their excessive emotions. In some ways men saw women as being more powerful because of their emotions. I think men felt a little impotent in relation to that. They didn't really know how to deal with it.

If you watch those old family shows, you'll see that the woman is manipulating the man. He's a total idiot and she butters up his ego. She makes it look as if he's in charge, but it is really her. She's the brains behind it and he's just this incompetent guy walking around and making a living. But as far as dealing with interpersonal relationships in the family, he doesn't know what to do. The mother was the wise one and she would make it all right, but she'd kind of make it look like he was the one who done it.

Y: She'd orchestrate it.

B: Yes. She'd manipulate him. He was just sort of stupid; and not just stupid, but stupid and egotistical. He needed to keep his manhood intact. He couldn't be seen as making a mistake or doing something foolish, so the woman would help to maintain his image while, at the same time, she would really be dealing with things.

So he's really stupid and doesn't know that he's stupid. That was a time when men were supposedly really running things – the 40's and 50's – but in the media they were portrayed as incompetents.

Y: I've seen a part of what you're saying in other cultures – Third World cultures – which are often matriarchal, but the facade is that men are in charge. He's the head of the household. It's simply not true. That's not the way it is.

B: So the issue of trusting others' emotions has to do with not trusting their emotional power, and not trusting our own emotions.

Y: Therefore, we don't trust women with their emotional power because we aren't able to control it and because we aren't able to respond.

B: Not being able to respond. Look at the cliches of the culture. The woman wraps you around her little finger; the whole idea of the ability of women to manipulate men, partly emotionally and partly sexually, because she can withhold her "favors." But a lot of it's just emotional. The man crumbles when the woman gets emotional. He's lost. He doesn't know how to deal with it.

Let me share with you an exaggeration of that experience. The exaggeration of emotional power is someone who's crazy. My number two wife was crazy, but not crazy all the time. Most of the time everything was fine, but when some issue would come up that disturbed her, she'd get crazy; and when she was crazy, she was really emotional and irrational, and I was totally incapable of talking to her. As a male trying to be rational, I couldn't do it. She's on one level. I'm on another level. She's being emotional. I'm trying to be reasonable and rational. It's just not working.

One time I got to the point with her that I was so incredibly frustrated, in trying to deal with her rationally, that I stepped over some line and I became irrational. I went crazy, for a very short period of time, and I did an almost classic crazy action. I just walked into a corner and started wringing my hands. And part of me observed myself doing it. Part of me watched me do that and knew I was doing it. Part of me was just doing it.

She immediately snapped out of being crazy and became rational. She came over, took me by the hand, led me into the bedroom, laid me down and started trying to comfort me and help me. She was completely rational.

We flipped, just like that. In that experience, I realized the seductiveness of emotions, the power of emotions to manipulate. Although I didn't do it consciously, I still realized, as I did it, "Wow, look at what just happened!" I experienced the power of going out of control emotionally and using that power to manipulate another human being.

Y: The way you manipulated your wife?

B: Yes. She changed immediately. When I went irrational, she changed and played the role, the masculine role, of taking care of me.

Y: I get more the image of mothering you.

B: Sure, it's a mothering kind of thing, but she became the rational one.

Y: So there's the fix-it mentality.

B: Yes. The man will take care of it. The woman's all overwrought and emotional and doesn't know what to do, and the man comes in and says, "Relax, calm down. I'll take care of it." You've got a flat tire – whatever it is – the woman can't deal with it. She gets all emotional. The man comes in. He's calm, and he'll take care of it.

So I do see it, in some ways, as a masculine-feminine flip, at least in that exaggeration of what a man and woman are. But I experienced the seductiveness of the ability to control another human being with emotions.

Y: When you say seductiveness you mean . . .

B: There was an attraction to it. I felt the power of being able to control another human being by simply going out of control. There's the irony. By going out of control, you control.

Y: I have experienced being manipulated by women when I felt that they were attempting to manipulate me through crying.

B: You're disarmed, unless you get angry. You have responses you can make, but it's a very disarming kind of thing. She acts helpless, but in reality you become helpless.

In terms of emotional expression, it doesn't mean that every time there's emotion in an interaction between a man and a woman, manipulation is going on. Obviously if you're sensitive, you have spontaneous emotional expressions, but they can be used as manipulation and I think, in the power struggle between men and women in the past, they certainly have been used a weapons. Because women felt they didn't have other ways of dealing with men, because men were seen as being in the dominant position, women had to use other ways of getting what they wanted. They didn't have the option to just come straight at it.

Y: And are not able to match a man physically. So what other alternatives are there?

B: Man manipulated with his position and his strength, and woman manipulated with emotions. But the result is, interestingly, that the man comes to distrust emotions; to distrust the woman's emotions; to distrust his own. The woman comes to distrust strength and directness and the masculine mode.

Y: In our time, I think that's become equated with violence, for good reason, because it often is used in violent ways.

B: If it's really blocked. If there's some sense of expression being blocked in any way, it can come out violently. Women, through the women's movement, have been trying to express more of the aggressive male energy. They've been trying to be more direct and not be quite so emotional. In some cases they went overboard.

Y: Occasionally I see women mimicking or attempting to mimic male aggression. It appears to me as a woman's imitation of what she and society perceive as strength and directness in the male, which I think is a perversion of sorts. Ruth Anne is one of the best examples of feminine, womanly strength that I've known. She was strong and direct at times, and yet it felt different than our version of those same qualities. It's as though there was a unique tone to it. It's reminiscent of what I've felt when I've done Tai Chi – a yielding, flexible, graceful strength that moves with the energies around us in a purposeful way, rather than resisting, standing up to, pushing against an opposing force or energy which is a mode more typical of us as men when we feel in disagreement, or threatened, or assertive. I don't mean this in absolute ways, but in terms of tendencies.

The masculine in her wasn't an imitation of what she saw in men but was an expression of an energy we label masculine but which resides within her innately, strong, direct and different from ours.

B: Because there's female aggressiveness, and there's masculine aggressiveness. It's not that the woman needs to develop her masculine side so much as to develop the full range of what it means to be a female. The same with the man. So there's a sort of softness and tenderness in men that's innate. It's not feminine, it's masculine. That is the mistake we've made in seeing women and men as polarities rather than seeing women having this whole range of expression and men having this whole range of expression.

Y: Then the screw-up is when we try to imitate each other, rather than be our natural, spontaneous selves. This is a central question for me. What is the difference? Do you think there is an innate difference between masculine and feminine energy? Or are these behaviors learned and passed along? Is the whole thing primarily a process of acculturation?

B: I'm not sure about that. I think there has to be a difference. We wouldn't bother to have masculine and feminine if there wasn't something different to learn from it. Even if I get totally in touch with my whole self and still remain physical, it will make a difference that I'm physically a male.

Y: We're so far removed from natural, unimpeded expressions of these energies that we don't really know what they would look like free of our neuroses. Our conditioning is so intense and limiting, I don't think we can see the forest for the trees on this one. I'm convinced that so much of what we consider to be factual, isn't. Very often we think of opinions as truth, rather than what they really are most of the time, which are beliefs and learned behaviors.

B: Margaret Mead's book, *Sex and Temperament in Three Primitive Societies*, dealt with this question. She has since been criticized for her work, but the traditional masculine and feminine characteristics were quite different in these three societies.

I also remember reading about a particular culture where the man goes through all of the symptoms of childbirth. He has morning sickness and has to take it easy. The woman works in the field. When the baby is due, the man takes to his bed. The woman delivers the baby alone in the field and then takes it to the man to care for. The cultural factors in our ideas of masculine and feminine are probably much stronger than we suspect. Seth says that in primitive societies women were as much hunters as men. The differentiation was not as great. I suspect that the more we become our "natural" selves, the less differences there will be between men and women.

It's certainly unbalanced, so I think that distrusting others' emotions really does come down to not trusting those other parts of ourselves. I also have beliefs that I'm trying to overcome, and they're quite conscious; for example, thinking that women are more intuitive than men or that women are more psychic than men. There are certain qualities that I would like to develop and I (mistakenly) believe that it's easier for women, or that women are better at those than men.

Y: It's the part of you that has accepted the cultural belief that the division is real.

B: Yes, I stop myself from developing fully because of those attitudes. Until I become aware of them and recognize them as simply beliefs, I'm going to continue to act them out and limit my abilities. I'm not as intuitive as a woman or as psychic as a woman or emotional as a woman. Even that – we were talking about emotions – that's a belief too. Or even my belief that emotions are dangerous. That's just an attitude I have from my past experiences.

Y: So what's the way out of this mess?

B: What I'm working on is trusting myself. That's of real overall importance. That's the core. I'm not going to have a problem trusting other people, whether it's women or men, if I come into a place of trusting myself.

Whatever I'm experiencing in the world out there in terms of trust or lack of trust is an internal issue with me. It may have come from my family experience, but it's my issue. When I learn to trust myself, it's going to be okay to express myself in a lot of different ways and feel safe.

It's going to be safe to express myself emotionally. It's going to be safe and okay for me to be intuitive and all this other stuff because I'll simply feel safe being who I am. I'll trust myself. It's not easy. It's like self-love. That's a lifelong issue. That's where we're going. It has nothing to do with men and women and trusting men and trusting women. It's trusting ourselves, but it means trusting ourselves in that whole range that we were talking about; trusting ourselves from the most aggressive, so-called masculine part of ourselves to that most receptive, most soft, most sensitive side of ourselves; and trusting all of those equally.

Y: What about anger?

B: First of all, you have to acknowledge that anger as an emotion is a legitimate, appropriate and necessary one. It's not bad all the time. There are times when being angry is the most appropriate and most loving way to respond to a situation. So we have to start out by not labeling anger as a negative emotion. It's just an emotion.

Y: What do you mean when you say that sometimes it's the most loving response?

B: Because if someone you love is acting inappropriately toward you or someone else or in a way that might be harmful to them, sometimes the most loving thing is to get angry with them because sometimes that's the only thing they're going to respond to. You get angry at your child when they go out in the street because you're really concerned that they're going to hurt themselves, and anger is appropriate. Later you explain to them why you're angry, but the anger is a legitimate response because you need to get their attention and you need to get it with some strong emotion because there's real danger there. You're not going to walk out calmly and say, "Now dear, you really shouldn't walk out in the street like that because you're going to get run over."

If you love your country, and you see it doing things that you consider harmful, it's appropriate to get angry because the anger comes from love. I guess that's what I'm getting at. When anger is appropriately expressed it comes from love. It's not a distortion of love. We've talked about anger as a distortion, but anger is often an expression of love. It's saying, "I love you and it really makes me angry when I see you doing this, because my love knows that you can do better than that."

So you can get angry at your country. You can get angry at your mate or your child because you see them doing something that's harmful to themselves.

Y: There's another aspect of this. I agree with what you're saying. I think it's a good point because I think we need to make a case for the appropriateness of anger and I think some of my own discomfort is because I'm off-center about it. I've got too generalized an attitude that says anger is bad, that anger is wrong.

B: Oh, I have a big problem with it.

Y: There's definitely a case to be made for the validity of anger. A variation on the theme – and I think it's a major issue for both of us – is when we project onto another person a model of how we think they're supposed to be, and if they deviate from that image we get angry.

Another variation is feeling disappointed in terms of the potential we may sense in another, as well as in ourselves. You know what you're capable of doing. You know what another person is capable of, the heights they're capable of reaching, and yet they're blocked, frightened, stuck. And sometimes that disappointment may go into anger or frustration.

I was reading a book the other day and there was a quote from Leo Buscaglia. He said something about appreciating who you are in the moment and being excited about what your potential is; self-acceptance. I like what he says about being excited about your own potential rather than looking at what you're not. That's a healthy, productive reframing of that issue. Many times in my life I felt like my self-anger came out of a sense of disappointment and frustration about where I was and what I was capable of doing, or how I was capable of responding to a given situation. Sometimes I've felt disappointed in myself in that way. Like when I've responded in anger to somebody, sensing that my anger wasn't truthful. There was something underneath that. There was a deeper feeling that wasn't getting expressed. If your kid walks out in the street, anger may be appropriate in that situation. And my father feeling concerned, afraid something might happen to me 6,000 miles from home and there's nothing he can do to help – in that case, his anger was masking a loving concern.

B: It's a bypassing of the initial impulse. In order to do that you've got to jump the impulse, because the impulse is to express concern. Maybe that's the key. If the anger is the first impulse, then it's appropriate. If it's not, if you jump the impulse, which might have been just showing concern, then the anger's not appropriate. One of the things I've thought a lot about lately is the idea that basically we are loving beings. In terms of impulses, the fundamental impulse is to love. So the issues we've spoken of, in one way or another, are distortions of love or inability to express love. Anger, violence and war are distortions of our ability to either experience or express love in some way.

Y: Yes, I think that's absolutely fundamental to our existence. Our most primal need is to love and be loved and, as you say, there are distortions of those basic needs and desires. These distortions occur when we're out of touch with our feelings.

B: If certain feelings are inappropriate, you get into a habit of skipping over them. You don't even know that you felt them. You go right to the expression that's safe or familiar. You don't even know that you've bypassed the initial feeling.

Y: As I was saying before, it's the potential that's not being realized, and anger is the emotion that's forefront.

B: It's lack of acceptance. Here's another issue that's ultimately going to come back to the individual and is a major life issue – self-acceptance. If you fully accept yourself it seems to me that you'd have to be pretty accepting of other people as they are.

So the judgment on other people always ultimately comes back to a self-judgment. It's one of those difficult things for us. It's very difficult for me to accept myself as I am because of my perception of my abilities. That's also very cultural, especially for men in the past. Men have been judged primarily by what they produce, what they create, what they do. The message behind that is, if you don't produce, then you're nothing.

Y: Yes. Two years after retirement, on the average, men die.

B: Retiring and dying, because their whole self-image is so tied up in what they produce. What does that mean? That means that there is not an acceptance of themselves, basically, for just being, for being who they are.

Y: Once again, because emotions are intangible entities they don't have value in the male scheme of things.

B: No, and it also has to do with love being conditional. As very small children, as infants, we're loved unconditionally in the sense that nothing's expected of us. We just lay there and we cry and we shit and we eat, and nobody's expecting us to go out and get a job or go to school – but we're loved. We're genuinely loved, at that point in our existence, without producing anything. We smile once in a while and everybody's thrilled to pieces.

But at some point, and it happens pretty early, expectations come in and the child perceives that now love is no longer unconditional. It may not be true. The parent may really continue to love unconditionally but they begin to put conditions on the child. And so performance starts to become important and at some point what you produce and create starts to become important as a child.

At a very young age, we begin to get the message that we are loved depending on what we produce and what we create. We are not loved just because we exist.

We have a built-in impetus toward value fulfillment. The very cells in your body have a desire for growth and value fulfillment. The quickest way to fulfill ourselves and move toward value fulfillment is through self-acceptance. When I'm in a place of not accepting myself, it creates a block in my movement. It's a vicious circle. I want to grow. I want to move. I'm no good now because I'm not doing it. I feel scared about where it's going, or how fast it's going, or the unfamiliarity of it. Who am I becoming?

A lack of self-acceptance protects us from rapid growth and whatever may be fearful about it. There are fearful aspects to growth and change, and to a large extent the problems that I work on protect me from changing too fast. It keeps it manageable.

If we were able to relax about ourselves, accept ourselves, trust ourselves, we'd grow really quickly without a lot of effort. We'd grow at our own natural pace, whatever that is. And it's only when we don't trust or accept ourselves; when we have ideas about what we should be doing that we're not doing; it's when we judge ourselves critically that we actually slow down our growth. And that's real ironic.

The environment that encourages growth is one of acceptance. The child that really feels loved and accepted is going to grow like crazy, but if the parents are really on them and saying, "You should do this and you should do that," or "Why aren't you doing better?" they're going to stunt them. Here's the irony for the parents. The environment for growth is one of acceptance.

Y: What you're saying echoes my feeling about the universal tendency to distrust strangers or people of different cultures.

I heard an interesting thing the first time I was in Australia. A well-known founder of a community there was interviewed on the radio, and he talked about being in the United States. What he observed in his travels throughout the States was how much men and women mistrusted one another. He said that the problem goes back to the origin of man and woman. Immediately, there was an innate biological difference, and differences are mistrusted. His vision for the world, of our evolution, is an appreciation of differences.

I went to hear the Reverend Cecil Williams last weekend. Differences are one of the things he talked about. Right in the middle of his sermon he said, "Isn't it wonderful how different we are!" It was infectious the way he said it because at that moment I think a lot of us there had an intense appreciation for what he was celebrating. He also said, "Just think how boring it would be if we didn't have that. Not only boring, but isn't it wonderful that we're different?"

But the cultural beliefs about gender are quite distinct; women are intuitive, men are not; men are unfeeling, women are not, etc. One of the reasons I enjoy going to other cultures is to expose myself to differences, to help me appreciate them. But even in foreign cultures there are very rigid ideas about right and wrong, appropriate and inappropriate, male and female.

B: You only have to protect what isn't secure. A lack of self-acceptance leads to non-acceptance of others.

Y: There is a very high level of self-acceptance in those cultures, far more than we enjoy here in our own country. They don't put themselves through the ministrations and self-judgment we place upon ourselves – our constant analyzing and judging . . .

B: As nations.

Y: I believe self-acceptance is related to the evolution of our species. I'm thinking in terms of the evolution of consciousness, where we as a species, as a race, evolved from tribal communities to nations. We're on the cusp of realizing a global consciousness. The evolution of our species is moving from a narrow concept of self towards something more expansive and inclusive. Our boundaries are expanding. Our sense of identity has evolved from caveman, tribe, community, state, nation, national alliances, to – what's next? Look at our progression.

Here we are with two superpowers and enormous schisms in the global community. But you can see the beginning. The edges are becoming a little fuzzy now. We've had some arms agreements; more are on the way. We're increasing cooperation with the Russians. McDonald's is selling hamburgers in Moscow. I think this progression is indicative of our evolution. The lack of acceptance we've been talking about has been a part of our collective learning experience.

B: My understanding from our talk is that feelings and impulses lead to motion. If they don't lead to motion, then there's blockage, and that blockage, if it lasts long enough, leads to inappropriate motion, whether it's internal, physical or some other way. It leads to some distortion.

There's something important about following feelings and impulses and not blocking, because somehow they're going to come out anyway. We were talking about the rational minds of the politicians and generals denying that their feelings are involved. But through their rationality they're still expressing feelings, but in a really distorted way. They become irrational. While on the surface acting rationally, they're acting out feelings that they're denying, and therefore the outcome of their rational decisions is incredibly irrational.

Y: A predominant aspect of life on earth, one of the primary motivations we know, is fear. Fear has produced massive armies and weaponry.

You're talking about not dealing with feelings, being super-rational. The reason we don't deal with feelings is fear of discomfort.

B: You don't need protection if you're not afraid. I also think that our whole cause-and-effect idea is backwards. The assumption is you build weapon systems because you're afraid, and you're afraid because there's some real danger. What actually happens is you're afraid because you build weapon systems.

On a psychological basis we don't run because we're afraid; we're afraid because we run. That's a physiological fact. If something threatens you, what happens is that adrenalin rushes through your body. That adrenalin is neutral. The feeling of the adrenalin does not get labeled until you decide what to do. If you decide to stay and fight, the adrenalin becomes anger. If you decide to run, the adrenalin becomes fear. It's not fear until you run. There was a study conducted in which people were "shot up" with adrenalin. They were then introduced into different rooms where different emotions were being expressed. The adrenalin caused bodily sensations but had no reference (anxiety is adrenalin without action). So when these people went into a room where someone was laughing, they translated their adrenalin sensations into happiness and laughter. If they went into a room where someone was angry they picked that up and became angry.

I knew a woman who became terribly anxious when she was going to go to a party. She was a teacher and didn't have any trouble standing up in front of a group of adults and speaking, but parties just did her in. A friend of hers suggested that she call that energy "excitement" instead of anxiety. As soon as the woman changed the label from anxiety to excitement, that's what she experienced.

This gets back to your father jumping the initial feeling and impulse. That initial impulse represents the most "correct" response to a situation, but if that response is uncomfortable, we can simply change the label – from loving concern to anger – and we experience it as we label it. Of course, in your father's case and in most cases this re-labeling is quite unconscious.

Y: It's the labeling?

B: Yes. The weapons represent fear. They don't provide safety. The idea is you're safe because you have weapons, but the weapons, themselves, represent the fear.

Y: Because the fear's not being dealt with? The feeling is not being felt?

B: The weapons don't work. They don't have the effect they're supposed to have which is to make us feel safe. We're not safe because we have all these weapons in the world.

Y: Yes, many people have been trying to point out that these weapons are destabilizing, that they don't create security. A male dilemma is to fear feelings. Do we have an equation in our psyches of fear of feelings? Are feelings fearful?

B: What we said before is that men had a very narrow band of feelings that were okay for them to express or even feel.

Y: Certain feelings are permissible; others aren't.

B: So men's range has been narrowed down in terms of what it means to be a man and what kind of feelings a man can express and experience. If a man feels feelings that are not within that range, they still have to be translated either into rational stuff or anger. If you're feeling sad or hurt, you can't express that. It's not within the range. It's like having a limited emotional vocabulary. You either get rational or you get angry or, as you suggested, you go numb. The range of expression is real narrow, and yet the actual range of feelings is no more narrow than what women experience. The natural motion is simply stopped.

Y: Feelings hide in my depths. A wall comes down and I go numb. But it's not that I don't feel. It's just that my feelings are so deep and perhaps "unmanly" that I don't allow myself to feel them.

B: And you get into a pattern of not feeling them. So, they don't go away. They're being built. Those feelings are building and stockpiling, so the armament gets bigger and bigger and the danger, as with two nations, gets greater and greater. The more there are, the greater the possibility that something is going to trigger them.

Y: So, emotionally, you have explosions; mini or maxi explosions. The energy has to go somewhere, manifest somehow; it doesn't just evaporate, vanish. As Bly writes in his poem:

> "... If a man, cautious
> hides his limp, Somebody has to limp it! Things
> do it; the surroundings limp.
> House walls get scars,
> the car breaks down; matter, in drudgery, takes it up."

B: And you may just do it in traffic, but it's there.

Y: And possibly one could see illness as an internalized version of these kinds of explosions – cancer, for example.

B: Or the heart. Look at the incidence, among men, of heart trouble. Our diseases are meaningful. They're not accidental. Men's illnesses, in some ways, tend to be feeling-related illnesses – lots of heart trouble, heart attacks – broken hearts or injured hearts, wounded hearts. Those are the kinds of illnesses men have. These illnesses are stress-related. Heart trouble's very high for men. Cancer's high in this society in general.

Y: Some cancer being an example of this internalized blockage. The energy gets internalized, goes inward, is stockpiled, and eventually erupts into a deviant cellular pattern.

B: Cancer is growth. It's very interesting. Because growth isn't directed out into the world, because creativity isn't directed out into the world, it stays internalized and is destructive.

Y: You mean that creativity, if frustrated, can be life threatening creativity.

B: It's a growth disease. You're threatened by your growth because it's held in rather than expressed. It's a good image for non-expression. It's growth that's not expressed, for men and women.

Y: I wonder if cancer's more prevalent amongst men than women?
B: I don't know. I do know that in terms of those who have the most success in overcoming cancer, it's the ones who are the worst patients. They're the most angry. They're the fighters. The ones who are successful with cancer do not lay down and say, "This is it." They're pissed. They're terrible patients because they're demanding, and they fight. They're angry. And they're the ones that are successful.
Y: They re-direct their anger to overcome their illness, is that what you're saying?
B: Maybe they didn't do that before. Maybe they weren't expressing themselves. The ones who are successful are the ones who are angry and fight, not the ones who submit.
Y: In military jargon, to mobilize one's energy to defeat the illness.
B: The ones who mobilize or begin expressing themselves emotionally have a better chance.
Y: In that case the anger's appropriate. Which brings me to the point you made before of anger being appropriate when it comes from love, that being a valid and useful form of that energy.
B: And inappropriate when it takes the place of love. When anger is the first impulse, it's correct. It comes from love and it's correct. When you skip the impulse – when the impulse is love and you skip it, or the impulse is concern and you skip that and go to anger, then the anger is inappropriate.
Y: In the early days of the *Journal*, I felt some anxiety about how the *Journal* was being received and judged by others.

Pretty early on, I started getting letters of appreciation from men grateful for the support they were deriving from the *Journal*. I began to feel more and more comfortable, less fearful about being critiqued, ridiculed, misunderstood or put down. I was so richly encouraged by the response that I started feeling more loving, empathetic and compassionate about men's issues and men's struggles. This enhanced the time I spent in support groups, men's gatherings and of course it enhanced my personal friendships.

All of this led to an impulse to sign my editorials, "With Love." That was the impulse I felt after writing one of my editorials, and yet I felt inhibited. I was concerned about being judged and ridiculed for doing that. I went through a little dance over that one. I looked at it and I said, "Okay, this is what my concern is," and what I came back to was: "This is a very genuine feeling for me. I'm being true to myself and it serves as an example or model for other people to express their true feelings." I really felt very loving towards the subscribers. So I signed it that way. It was a stretch for me to do that, to make the decision that I was going to stay with it. As a man, I chose to let people know that this is what I had to say; an expression of love, and screw the ridicule if it should come.

B: And it never came.

Y: No. But isn't it interesting that I actually felt fearful of being criticized for expressing love to a community of men? I still come up against it. It came up in the letter that I wrote to "Beyond War," because I signed it, "With Love," and that same thing came up again; the same feelings of inhibition in putting out this expression of love. Odd to be fearful that I would be seen as weak or wimpish – things that would challenge my masculinity or my integrity, my wholeness.

B: So the identification is, feelings equal weakness.

Y: Absolutely. And that I would be judged. There would be some kind of put down. And so it was a personal challenge to say, "This is how I feel and I'm putting it out there." I also think it would be inspirational for other people who may go through a similar process as myself, and come up against similar walls. I know when other people do things like that, it inspires me. I become strengthened by somebody else's willingness to expose themselves, to express themselves in a clean, true way, and that includes clean anger.

It's amazing that that kind of dilemma comes up for me. I don't think I'm strange for going through these kinds of concerns in a society that doesn't encourage a broad range of feeling and expression, free expression. I'm sort of out of my range, I guess, applying it to the model we're talking about – what gets the nod of approval and what gets frowned upon, the collective thumbs down.

I felt vulnerable. I think that's the shyness I feel. That's the inhibition for me. And to do it publicly like that was a public exposure. I am putting out something highly emotional to a lot of people, and it's like opening myself up. I could have closed with, "Sincerely," and there would have been no problem with that.

B: It's like placing a weapon in their hands.

Y: Yes, I suppose so, you could say that. The antidote for me, when I do express my feelings, is that when I'm in a more expanded state of mind, I'll see it as their problem and not mine. If their reaction is critical and I'm feeling good about myself, I know their negativity usually comes from their own woundedness, their own fears, their own unlovingness.

B: And don't you think, since we're talking about impulses, when you do express an impulse, you usually don't get any negativity back, and if you do, you'll be able to deal with it in just the way you said? You feel right enough and good enough about following that impulse that even negative feedback is not going to affect you because you're clean about it; you know you're okay.

Y: Yes, but it will still touch upon some of my insecurities because they're still here. I'm still feeling vulnerable. So it's a sign that there are insecurities present, but the criticism and its effects are like diminishing ripples. They'll sort of pass through me without me being sorry that I did it, or having second thoughts. I can withstand it because it's minor. Someone strikes an insecurity chord; it still affects me, but in varying degrees.

B: I was very surprised when I was doing a group in a church in Vallejo and the church essentially threw me out and stopped the group. The people who were opposed to the group were wrong in what they were doing and they were wrong in their assessments of what I was doing. I felt okay about what I was doing. And it still hurt me that they wanted to stop my group. It wasn't a matter of me thinking that they had some justification, but it still hurt. I felt okay about what I was doing, but just the fact that somebody thought that I was doing something harmful was hurtful to me.

So I guess we're always vulnerable to other people's opinions, even when we're clear that we're okay about what we're doing and those other people's opinions are in error.

Y: I think vulnerability is a very important issue. I remember a friend saying something like, to be alive is to be vulnerable. And we want to feel connected to others, but I think we often judge our sense of closeness in terms of our being in agreement with each other.

B: Being vulnerable is associated with feelings. There's some connection between feeling and being alive.

Y: "Whether they flame or smolder, [feelings] are a signal of your aliveness in this reality, and they're lovely in any case" – that's Seth speaking.

For me, that's easier said than done, because when I feel shitty, I don't feel lovely about it – I feel shitty. From Seth's perspective, feelings are a badge of your existence, your aliveness in this reality. So it's the judgment, which reminds me of what you were saying about adrenalin. The adrenalin is neutral. It's the judgment that determines the nature of the experience.

It's a judgement that we call a certain kind of plant in our garden a weed; it's a determination that has nothing do with truth, although we'll tend to see it in those terms.

B: This may be a real key. It isn't so much our experiences which determine our feelings, but our judgement of those experiences. A quote from a lady who just gave me her book to read: "It is never what we look at, but always what we see, that determines our experience."

So you feel bad about feeling bad. Instead of simply feeling bad, you judge yourself for feeling bad.

Y: So one of the main points is that we often feel ashamed and guilty about feelings, and that is the major obstacle to change and self-acceptance.

B: Men deal with shame and guilt and they're in a sort of no-win situation.

Y: I think that is the crux of our dilemma. I had a talk with a friend today, and that was one of the things he had to say to me that really clicked. It's useful to have somebody hear what you have to say, to be truly present. You know they're empathetic and they feel for you. One comment to me was, "I think where you're getting tripped up is that there's a part of you that says it's not okay feeling these things, or you should be feeling differently. Look, you just got married. You've got a kid on the way and this is all happening in a very short period of time. You've taken a lot on very quickly. It's understandable that you're going to be going through these kinds of feelings."

I think what this friend helped me see was that there was a voice inside of me saying that I shouldn't be feeling this. I would add to that "shouldn't be" that I "don't want to be" feeling these things. They're unpleasant, troubling and draining.

B: It's the nature of the resistance and the judgement, I think, that makes them draining. If we were able to accept those feelings I think they would flow through much more quickly and naturally. It's the nature of the resistance and the judgement that makes them worse and makes them last longer. It's a real bind. To resist them and say, " I shouldn't feel this way," is to feed them and to make them bigger.

So let the feelings flow through and follow the impulses. It's okay to feel bad for a while, but the more you resist it the longer it lasts and the bigger it gets.

Y: Talking about this reminds me of one of the good things that I've gotten out of being in men's groups; being in the company of other men who can relate to the kinds of experiences you're talking about in a very intimate way without being defensive. There isn't the male/female polarization.

B: And they're not judging your feelings.

Y: They're not judging my feelings at all. If anything, there's identification which usually translates into empathy and compassion. It's a very rich empathy, a profound empathy, which says, "Yeah, I know what that's like," and the comfort that comes from somebody voicing feelings most of us ignore or make believe don't exist and usually judge as bad.

So there's the shift from judgement into acceptance, and you can use that acceptance from others. You can be energized. You're supported by others in that way.

B: And the feelings can be healed then. It's almost as if they can't be healed until they're accepted as okay.

Y: I want to get into talking about anger versus natural aggression and how that relates to men, war and androgyny. It seems to me that men's groups aid one's sense of self, and that increasing sense of self can be a stepping stone in one's development. So if our movement as a species is toward androgyny, and I think that is humanity's direction, what's the importance of a men's movement in the grander scheme of things?

B: I look at things as outside and inside. If, as you say, we're moving toward androgyny, "male" and "female" is very strongly there on the outside. In terms of knowing the self, the movement must be toward the inside, where we're more alike than we are different. In terms of knowing ourselves and moving toward androgyny, that's what it means. Knowing ourselves moves toward androgyny and knowing ourselves means moving inward and finding out who we are inside because that's where we're more alike. It's on the outside that we're more different.

I'm not sure how that movement comes about, but in terms

of things we've talked about already, that's been one of the problems for men. Men have been mostly on the outside. It hasn't been acceptable for men to look inside.

Y: What does that mean to you?

B: It means for me to be in touch with my feelings, to question my self, my motives, to question my behavior, to go inside and look at myself.

Y: To have a sense of yourself.

B: Yes. To have a sense of yourself. A lot of men in the past kept busy in order not to look at themselves. For a man to be alone would be frightening because he would naturally begin to ask questions and look inside. As a dreamworker, I know that men don't remember dreams as much as women. There's nothing biological about that. That's the inside. That's the interior. I think men assume that they're not going to like what they see if they look inside.

I've talked to men, including my own father, who tend to only remember bad dreams and so they assume that's what's there.

Y: That's quite prevalent isn't it, for a lot of people, both men and women, not to have vivid dream recall?

B: People who don't have good recall tend to remember the emotional dreams which are either frightening or sad. And then they come to assume that that's what all dreams are about, and so they consciously don't want to remember their dreams.

Maybe this has something to do with retirement. We talked last time about men dying after retirement. Part of it was that their role in life was gone, but the other part may be that men don't know how to go inside. In older cultures, in oriental cultures, in India and others, there are stages of life, and the last stage is the seeker stage, the spiritual stage. When you finish your work in the world and have raised your family, the last stage is the spiritual seeking.

In American culture defined stages in life don't exist and aren't supported. They're not even believed in. And yet they may be a natural process. If you're blocked in that process, there you are again with physical problems, lack of expression. The man only knows how to work. He only knows how to create.

Y: I believe there is a psychic acceleration later in life, it is experienced by everyone. This state of mind is revered in other cultures: the medicine man, the shaman, the grandfather seer, but what happens here is that we put many of our elders into senior citizens' homes. I believe much of what we label as pathological in later life is actually a natural psychic acceleration, an expansion of consciousness, and at times, an appropriate preparation for death and the afterlife.

B: An inner exploration that's not acknowledged and is interpreted as crazy.

Y: It's a biological, as well as a spiritual process. Or another way of saying it is, the body is divine.

B: Yes. But men in our culture are never rewarded for going inside at any point in their lives.

Y: From the beginning we are taught not to trust our feelings. We're taught not to trust our impulses, so naturally, within our experience . . .

B: We don't trust ourselves.

Y: Here's an appropriate quote from Seth: ". . . when you trust your feelings and your impulses; when you learn to trust, then something strange happens. They turn quite trustworthy."

B: As a man, when you get to the end of your work career, you can't all of a sudden start doing something you haven't done for your whole life. But there may be an impulse, as you say – I think you're right – there's probably an actual biological clock there. There's an impulse to go inside, become contemplative. If a man has no idea how to follow that impulse, it's going to get distorted.

I suspect that a lot of men worry about themselves at that age if they find themselves starting to question things and go inside and look at their lives. It may be quite upsetting.

Y: We need a break from this lengthy conversation. Here's a poem I'd like to share with you.

Comes The Dawn

After awhile you learn the subtle difference
between holding a hand and chaining a soul,
and you learn that love doesn't mean leaning
And company doesn't mean security,
And you begin to learn that kisses aren't contracts
And presents aren't promises
And you begin to accept your defeats
With your head up and your eyes open
With the grace of a woman,

not the grief of a child,
And learn to build all your roads
on today because tomorrow's ground
is too uncertain for plans,
and futures have a way
of falling down in mid-flight.
After awhile you learn that even sunshine
Burns if you get too much.
So you plant your own garden
and decorate your own soul,
instead of waiting
For someone to bring you flowers.
And you learn that you really can endure . . .
That you really are strong
And you really do have worth.
And you learn and learn
with every goodbye you learn.

Anonymous

Let's get onto the topic of war. I think it's a natural progression. You've got anger versus natural aggression, and violence on a mass scale, exploding perhaps into war; and war perhaps being an ultimate expression of the denial of Man's inner feelings. The antithesis of that would be a fully integrated male or what we would call an androgynous male. Rape, warfare, and environmental violations; these things would begin to dissipate if we began to come to terms with our feeling side and our impulsive nature, if we began to trust ourselves. Do you see that progression?

B: There is a denial of portions of the self. In the one case we're saying it's the feminine self that's being denied. I think an argument can also be made for a denial of the shadow or, in Robert Bly's terms, the Wild Man. The denial of the shadow emphasizes differences, which we talked about before. It makes them more extreme than they really are. What else?

Y: Well, if you talk about the denial of the shadow, you're talking about something that you perceive in yourself which is so uncomfortable that you don't want to admit to it. Therefore the barriers and denial are so intense that they get displaced onto someone else, and that becomes the hated one, the feared one, the enemy; as when Reagan labeled the Russians the "Evil Empire."

We all do this in our private lives in varying degrees. The place where we have to begin is in our own, private backyards. Perhaps it's more fitting in the context of our conversation to say, going inside to do our personal housecleaning.

B: The irony is that the shadow, itself, represents positive impulses not expressed. In almost every case, when you're working with dreams, when someone confronts some frightening character in the dream, they almost always transform. They almost always end up being a friend, a guide, a helper or even creative energy that's been suppressed. So the shadow itself is ultimately an impulse or a feeling denied.

Y: There's a wonderful saying from Jung. He said that 90% of the shadow is gold.

B: I had a lady who had invasion of the house and rape dreams, and then it actually happened to her. Someone did break into her house. But even after that she continued to have the dream, so I suggested a confrontation. She had a dream about this big white alien kind of scary looking man. She ran into the bedroom and closed the door and then remembered what we had talked about. She remembered she was supposed to fight this guy.

So she opened the door and he came in and she starts beating on him with her fists. He grabs her hands and then he takes one hand, which is still in a fist, and he pries her fingers open and places a gold coin in her hand. What an incredible image of just what you're talking about. And I think that's always true. The things that we're afraid of always contain our energy and that energy is gold, or at least it's neutral and we can use it for anything we want.

Y: I had a dream once about Jesus. I was at a party and everyone there was standing in a circle. I knew that the man standing across from me was Jesus. He wasn't special in any notable way – appearance-wise. He was and he wasn't ordinary. He was one of the group; not separate, apart or superior to the rest of us. I knew, in looking at him, that this was Jesus Christ. I also knew that this was one of the most extraordinary individuals to have ever lived.

I realized as I looked at him that he was the only one who wasn't wearing shoes, he was barefoot. I had an association with non-materiality, spirituality, in that moment. I looked at him and wondered, "What is it that makes him so special? Why is he who he is and why is he revered and remembered? Why has he had such a profound impact on humanity?"

I heard an answer inside of me, and it was very simple: "Because he accepted all parts of himself." The dream ended. When I awoke and reflected on its meaning, I knew that we don't accept all aspects of who we are. That was what distinguished him – simply – distinguised him from us; total integration, total acceptance of all aspects of himself as opposed to the denial, the projection, the shadow and all those things that we have.

B: A saying in the Bible, which is pretty radical and is not taken very seriously, is to love your enemy. People see that as some kind of high ideal. The fact is it's not a high ideal. It has to do with loving all the parts of yourself. Because there isn't any enemy out there. The only enemy is in here. It's more radical than it seems. To love your enemy means to love all parts of yourself. When you do that, then there aren't any enemies out there to love or to not love. There just aren't any. I think that's really powerful, and that's exactly what it's all about.

War and violence are the result of men, in this case, not accepting parts of themselves. It's the feminine and it's the shadow, and if we thought about it we could probably come up with some other aspects that men don't accept.

Jesus, according to Edgar Cayce, went through initiation in Egypt. I don't know whether he did or not, but in the temple initiation, men were buried in the tomb. You were put in the sarcophagus for three days and three nights and what happened there was that you confronted all of your demons. You were alone.

We were talking earlier about a man retiring, and perhaps being in a position where he's going to have to start looking at his demons because his mind's not as busy. And maybe he really is afraid of that because he knows that he might have to confront his demons. But that was the initiation for Jesus – confronting his shadows and demons. If you survived that you were transformed.

Y: It's strange you say that. It reminds me of another dream. I was reading the book *Initiation* at the time, and it affected me.

In the dream I was placed in an opening in one of the chambers inside a pyramid, but it was very, very small. A stone sealed me in. It was pitch black, no sounds . . . a void. I couldn't move. I was that person in that dream, and I became extremely anxious as I thought about spending three days entombed, unable to move. I felt like I was suffocating. I was acutely aware of the potential to go insane. I bailed out of the dream. I awoke. The growing terror I felt in the dream was still very vivid, very intense. I ejected, mentally, from that tomb. I sensed that this was a potential rite of passage. And I knew, intuitively, that the juncture, the option, was either insanity or spiritual transcendence and mastery of out-of-body.

B: We do that a little bit at a time if we're growing at all. We face our demons a little bit at a time.

Y: That individual in the dream, the individual was me, was a candidate for the priesthood, the Egyptian priesthood.

B: It's a real nice way of weeding folks out. I feel that violence and war are all the result of individuals not accepting the full range of who they are; not accepting all the parts of themselves, and therefore projecting parts out there and reacting to them. They're the result of inner divisions, not outer divisions. They're the result of inner divisions, inner battles and inner enemies.

That's a very powerful kind of insight, to look at the mass reality. Think about it! All the killing, all the fighting, all the fear, all the mistrust; ultimately, it's an individual situation. It's individuals not trusting themselves, not being aware of their own multiplicity, not being aware of the enemies inside, not being willing to look inside. And the masculine model of the rational male has been to suspect the inner self.

We can go back to Freud, and Freud said, "The inner self is where all your craziness is. That's where all your negative impulses are."

Y: What Freud believed to be dark impulses.

B: According to Freud, negative impulses are the only kind of impulses that really exist; all your darkness. Basically, you're an animal. The id only wants to have what it wants. It wants food, it wants sex. It doesn't care. It's totally immoral. And that's basically the view of the inner self. So civilization and civilized man controls that inner self. He's certainly not going to cultivate it. He's certainly not going to go exploring in there unless he's got problems, and then he'll go get psychoanalyzed. But his problems had better be real severe or he's not going to do that.

Modern man is trained not to look inside, not to trust what's there; or to assume that what's there are negative impulses and that's why we have all this protection. I'll put my cause-and-effect thing in a different way. Think about this. We don't have police and laws because we have criminals. We have criminals because we have police.

I read something about that recently. It's almost as if the lawless society would be a safe and just society. Because laws come from the belief that we can't be trusted. It isn't safe. That's the origin of laws. Police and criminals need one another. In fact I'll bet if you looked at times when there were police strikes, you'd find that the crime rate went down. And when hospitals go on strike there are fewer people who get sick. During a hospital strike in New York City, the death rate decreased 15%. Our whole cause and effect is backwards.

So all the stuff we're talking about, violence and war, is the result of lack of self-awareness and an unwillingness to look inside, and a fear of what we're going to find there; the assumption that what we're going to find there is negative. When you boil it down, then, war and all of the negative expressions of energy in the world are based on an assumption that human beings are fundamentally bad.

I think we finally can get to that. Certainly in Jane Roberts' books – the William James book and a couple of others – she talks about science, religion and psychology, and the fact that all of those are based on the assumption that we're bad, that we're basically flawed. And so we act that out. Wars act out that assumption, as do all forms of violence.

In a sense you can say, "It's not my fault, I'm just human." That's one of our excuses for doing rotten things. The assumption is that being human means that you're basically flawed and you're basically not good. And if it weren't for the fact that we have laws and civilization to keep us in order, we would be crazy. We'd all be out there raping and pillaging because that's really the way we are.

Star Trek has played that out a couple of times, when people have lost their inhibitions because of a virus. They always end up having sex or punching each other out. They're totally animals, and that's an insult to the animals because we assume that animals are like that.

Seth talked about the lack of guilt in animals. They simply do what they feel like doing and don't feel apologetic for it or feel they should be doing something else.

Y: As if there's some moral wrong.

B: Right. You're a dog and you're lying in the sun. But the rest of the dogs in the town are out running around the neighborhood. Shouldn't you be with them and not sun bathing?

Y: I'd like to get back to the men's movement. What about the role of the men's movement in our evolutionary process?

B: At its best, the men's movement is helping men to express a wider range of feelings. It is helping men to break out of some of those restricting ideas about what it means to be a man. It is offering the possibility of men coming to their own conclusions about who they are. I think there was a problem in the women's movement early on, and the same problem in the men's movement. In reaction to the old image, you created a new image which was just as limiting. So in the case of women, the new image was: you went out and you had a career, and now it was not okay to just be a mother and a wife and raise kids. In the men's movement, in the early days, in reaction to or in sympathy with the women's movement, you became tender and soft and you could cry and have feelings; it wasn't okay to be energetic and aggressive. So you changed one restrictive image for another restrictive image.

If the men's movement is going to mature and become what it can potentially become, it will come to the point where the message is that you need to find out who you are and to express that. There are lots of models, but essentially each of us is going to have to create his own version completely from scratch. We need to find out who we really are and act that out in terms of our feelings.

Socrates said it a long time ago: Know yourself and be true to yourself. That's the message. And that's where the androgyny comes in, because when men and women are true to themselves, then there's not going to be these incredible restrictions between men and women. And nobody's going to raise an eyebrow if a woman is out there being aggressive and strong and getting things done. And nobody's going to raise an eyebrow if another woman is staying at home and raising children and loving it. The range of what we can be is going to be expressed more, by individuals. And the range of what's okay for a man and what's okay for a woman is going to expand tremendously. That's the ideal.

One of the main focuses for the men's movement, in the beginning, is to create safe places, as you suggested, where men can share their wounds. That's got to be done before something new can be created.

Y: That's primarily what has happened in the men's group I've been a part of. When you get together in a setting of mutual trust and profound feelings, talking goes toward where you are struggling, feeling frustrated, feeling blocked, and what you're angry about. It's predominantly the feelings of grief and anger. It's a place where judgements are lifted, left at the door, and authenticity is honored.

B: And hopefully, in terms of what we started out talking about, the healing is not just in being able to express that old grief and get support for it, but the healing is in learning a new way of being.

So the men's movement, hopefully, will teach men to feel their feelings, to legitimize them and express them in a healthier way.

Y: And it's easier when people around you are saying it's okay. Because most men feel extremely alone. Most men feel very isolated, weak and less than whole in having those kinds of feelings. That's why men's groups are called support groups. You can be who you are and be true to yourself.

B: In the business world there's a real facade, almost an expectation, a necessity for men to create some kind of facade with each other in business relationships. You just don't express anything that isn't strictly business.

Y: There's a term I like that I made a note of: the natural self. I think I actually prefer that to the term androgyny. Androgyny's a little stiff.

B: There's something I thought about earlier in relation to the natural self and to talking about animals. Another reason for the things you named – war and aggression and especially the rape of the environment – is the disconnection from nature. That's a significant factor because, symbolically, disconnection from nature means disconnection from the natural self.

So I think the whole rational scientific attitude has been extremely harmful. Control nature, use it; the whole exploitation of nature.

Y: In our society, everything has a utilitarian purpose. Earlier we were talking about unconditional love being free of utilitarian qualities where things are not viewed from a functional perspective or value scheme.

B: Society looks at a forest in terms of board-feet. It's not distorted just because of the destruction to nature which it causes, but also because it represents a cutting off of our natural selves.

Y: On the other hand, I think of Zen and its eloquently essential philosophy of, "What is, is." The natural self is non-judgemental; expression in the moment, and a non-functional point of view. Do you see the associations? At a very early age we become acculturated to think in functional terms; production, and the values equated to production rather than simple beingness. Results become the standards by which we justify our existence.

B: Ultimately, it's a lack of self-love. We do not love ourselves for being. We love ourselves for what we do.

Y: It's real hard to learn that. That's one of the things you're struggling with. You want to produce, you want to be productive, you want to be creative. You've got all those impulses. You've got those abilities. And you don't want to sit around and be a blob and say, "I'm into my beingness."

B: The irony is that you are most creative and productive when you accept your beingness – that is, when you're not judgemental. When you accept your beingness, you're free to be in that kind of flow, that natural impulsive flow, and you are at your height. You talked about that before. Your relationship was going best when you were in what you called a state of grace, and things flowed. When you accept your beingness, it is the most creative time. The bind is that when you don't accept your being, then you also block yourself in terms of doing.

When I'm most uptight about not doing and not producing, it's most difficult for me to do and produce. It's a terrible bind. Whereas if I can relax and accept myself, it flows. It's easy. It's not that you would stop being productive, but that production would be a natural outgrowth of who you are rather than an attempt to make you into something. I like that!

In our culture, we make ourselves into something by what we do instead of doing because of who we are. And so our productions, themselves, become distorted. And maybe that's why nature is being destroyed, because production itself becomes a distortion rather than a natural expression of who we are.

Y: In terms of evolution of the species, what is the overview? Where have we been, where are we now and where are we going? The parable of the Garden of Eden represented living in harmony with nature – total identification of self with nature – a spiritual, womb-like existence. Being evicted from the garden represented the development and individuation of ego consciousness, of individual selfhood that knowingly stepped out of nature; divorcing ourselves from nature to have a heightened experience of individuality. It was the gift of self-responsibility, not a violation as the church interprets it, but a gift from our creator, our source, or whatever term you want to use.

This is such a long conversation that I want to give you a break with this limerick:

> *In the Garden Of Eden lay Adam*
> *Patting the twat of his Madam.*
> *He chuckled with mirth*
> *For he knew on the Earth*
> *There were only two balls,*
> *And he had 'em.*

[Uproarious laughter] Getting back to our conversation, where was I. . . this separation from nature, as necessary as it was, is now threatening our very survival. We're at a crossroads in terms of our evolutionary development. The environmental issues are pointing out, very dramatically, our interdependence. Our next step is conscious awareness of the interconnectedness with all life and that step is becoming more and more urgent.

B: Yes. First, unconscious connection to nature and then consciousness with separation from nature. The next step is conscious connection *with* nature. There's a cycle. We come back to nature but we do it now with awareness.

Y: So we see the natural self, the androgynous self as beginning to flourish, as really coming to its full expression, its full fruition.

B: Part of what you were saying earlier about Jesus accepting all parts of himself is that nature is part of him too. It's not just all people as parts of himself or ourselves, but all life, all being, all nature. That's the direction. The direction is not just recognizing that the Americans and Russians are connected but that we're all connected to the whole thing. All of nature is part of who I am. It totally changes our responsibility. It's the difference between seeing nature as a resource, as something to be utilized and even plundered, seeing it as an extension of ourselves.

Y: To sustain us.

B: It sustains us. We have to sustain it. There's a relationship.

Y: Right. A few years ago there was a minor change in wording in Catholic scripture, the biblical mandate that man had dominion over nature. The change in wording was minor in its brevity, but monumental in its scope. It came out of Rome, where the church redefined Man's relationship to nature in its biblical writings. Previously, the word "dominion" dictated our relationship to the world, to life, to nature. This word represented and sanctioned our relationship of controlling, or attempting to control nature. It permitted us to view nature in the utilitarian terms you've spoken of – forests as board-feet. In the traditional interpretation that has reigned for two thousand years Man had dominion over nature. Dominion was a synonym for control.

B: It's related to dominance, dominating.

Y: Essentially, one word was changed. The word "dominion" was changed to "stewardship." Man has stewardship of nature. That means that we have a responsibility and a role and an interrelationship. We have to act responsibly. We're caretakers. Nature caretakes us and we caretake nature. We have a responsibility in that we're care-taking life's bounty, and therefore we must use it wisely, in a sensitive, conscious way.

B: And when we change from dominion to stewardship, we give up a measure of control.

Y: You can almost see stewardship as another kind of relationship. Seth said, "Spontaneity knows its own order." It's not that spontaneity is out of order – it's a different kind of order. Impulsiveness is, within its own framework, a highly intelligent form of organization and association. And impulse is very energetic – it has a lot of juice behind it.

B: The word control seems to come from a place of fear. You don't need to control something unless there's some danger if it's out of control. So the whole idea of controlling nature or controlling ourselves says that if we don't, something bad's going to happen. It comes from a basic mistrust of nature. The whole Darwinian view of nature is survival of the fittest, tooth and claw.

Y: Dog eat dog.

B: So society believes we humans need to control ourselves because our impulses are dangerous; we're basically not trustworthy.

When we come to the place of trusting our own natures and therefore our impulses, we will find them to be trustworthy. We will also find that we will be able to trust other people and trust nature. If we trust ourselves enough, we will not need to control ourselves. If we trust nature enough, we will not need to control nature.

We project our views about ourselves onto nature rather than the other way around. We see nature as the survival of the fittest, tooth and claw, dog eat dog, because that's the way we see ourselves. When we no longer see ourselves that way, we will no longer see nature that way.

Y: Bob, we've covered a huge amount of material here. I hope the reader is still awake. We have been talking about men and we have been talking about self-acceptance – trusting ourselves and our feelings, and trusting our spontaneous impulses. I think we've shown how these not only encompass individuals, but lead to a new relationship with nature; an evolution from dominion to stewardship. We've suggested movement toward a natural self that transcends the cultural restrictions of male and female and honors the finest qualities of both; a natural self that recognizes spirituality, in its broadest sense, as the ultimate goal. Thank you, Bobaloo.

CHAPTER XII

ANGER AND VIOLENCE

The Shame Of Anger

Yevrah Ornstein

This may be the most arduous section of the book for me because of how uneasy and judgemental I can be with myself when I feel angry.

Plain and simple, it's just damn unpleasant; and more often than not, I hold myself back from saying my anger when it's there. Fortunately, this is beginning to change as I become less judgemental, more spontaneous and less inhibited in the moment. What I notice time and time again is that when I handle my upset in the moment, it's said and gone. It passes through and out and I feel freer for its expression and release. I like what a friend says: "Sometimes anger is the most effective and loving form of communication."

The mulling over, the rehearsals in my mind of what I should have said and done, the loss of self-respect I place upon myself for "chickening out" . . . these things don't haunt me when I'm clean and honest in the moment. I'm glad to say it gets easier with practice.

I think the main point in letting this stuff out has to do with respecting the validity of feelings. All too often we equate our opinion of ourselves with feelings. If big boys don't cry, then perhaps we may recognize something in the messages we've gotten that good people don't get angry. And when I think of that training and the damage its done in my own life and collectively, well, that pisses me off.

What has helped me has been to re-evaluate my attitudes and to authentically express myself in the moment.

I have seen how being present and true to myself and my feelings in non-judgemental ways allows me to get through them and not get stuck in them. This kind of flow provides motion and stepping stones, in most cases, to feelings of caring and affection, which seem to be what usually motivates me.

I know that anger is a signal of a deeper connection. There's juice there – energy – and we just don't get hooked on things that don't have meaning and value to our lives.

Of course, there are those occasional situations of someone drag racing up and down my street on his motorbike. In this case, I feel no inner connection, just plain old pissed off with that inconsiderate bastard and that damn piercing noise that sounds like a 500-pound mosquito buzzing around my head.

But I'm talking about anger in relationships that count for something.

So once again, the keys, for me, are my judgments about my own feelings and the inhibition I place upon myself at times, in expressing myself in the moment.

I think I have some model in my mind that invalidates anger. (And I love the words from a Paul Simon song: "I think I think too much.")

I also know that at times my anger arises from an idealized version I may place upon someone else. This was beautifully expressed by a friend:

> *When you do not feel guilty about your feelings, you can discuss them. You can decide to make compromises. You can decide because then you are free to let your natural feelings express themselves; your feelings of love, for they are there and they motivate much of your behavior. And when you are angry at someone you love, it is because you love an idealized version to which the other can never live up to. So they must always behave as you think they should. So you do not see the other person clearly but only the person that exists in an idealized version in your mind. And that idealized version may or may not have anything to do with the real person that you know.*

> *You must approve of the self that you have with all
> your characteristics so that both of you can honestly
> say, "I feel thus and so, I feel this way or that way."
> Then the other has the same right and when it is all out
> in the open, you can compromise when you want to.
> There really is no problem except the problem of shame
> and guilt. And that is A PAPER DRAGON!"*

I get chills every time I read the above, and I read it from time to time because I definitely need the reminders. This is what I call a life-long issue; something I will spend the rest of my days coming to terms with, hopefully incorporating its wisdom into the fabric of who I am.

Sometimes I feel I've made good progress, and there are times I feel I'm slipping back into forgetfulness, habit and unawareness. To be honest, I have been pleased with being more spontaneous, present and expressive in the moment these past few years.

When it's all said and done, I come back to the advice above and I recognize so much of myself and my struggles within those words.

When I go to the heart of the matter – go for the guts – it does indeed come down to my own feelings of shame and guilt over what I'm feeling. He says so accurately, *they are a paper dragon!*

Letting It Out
Yevrah Ornstein

Here's a story about what I would call my first conscious encounter with anger:

After my two years in the Peace Corps I traveled through South America for three months.

From Ecuador, I flew south, directly to Lima, Peru. I had heard wonderful stories about the Incan ruins of Machu Pichu and wanted to see them firsthand.

There are no roads to Machu Pichu. You've got to go to Cuzco first and then take a train to the ruins or hike the trail, which takes five days. The trail is supposed to be spectacular and many people opt for the pedestrian route.

Cuzco is a wonderful town. The streets are cobblestone and the character of the place is a mixture of Indian, Peruvian and European flavors. There are many travelers from all over the world, and unlike many other popular places that are descended upon in this way, Cuzco has retained its individualistic flair. At least it did when I was there in 1976.

I met a man, a Peruvian, whose home was Cuzco. I'll call him Carlos (to protect the innocent).

After breakfast, in an out-of-the-way place that the locals enjoy, Carlos took me on a tour of some ruins outside of town. Machu Pichu's grandeur and renown eclipsed these ruins, making this site virtually unknown and devoid of tourists.

I really enjoyed our time together. Being fluent in Spanish made all the difference in the world in terms of being able to spend time with locals.

Having just completed two years in the Peace Corps, I was feeling very content, fulfilled, happy and at peace with myself.

On our way back to town, Carlos and I made plans to meet at a local bar after dinner, a place made popular by the *gringos*.

I had mentioned to Carlos during the day that I wanted to exchange currencies before going on to Bolivia because I had heard that I could get a better rate on the black market for my American dollars outside of Bolivia. This may sound shady but it's common practice – a secondary economy that official eyes simply turn away from.

American dollars are prized in certain countries because of their resale value. In countries like Argentina and Chile the official exchange rate at banks is considerably lower than what you can get on the street.

Anyway, Carlos knew I wanted to change monies but he didn't get the details quite right. He had gotten to the bar before me and had met an American woman who was traveling north to Ecuador and Columbia and wanted to exchange most of her remaining Peruvian money.

Carlos told her I, too, wanted to change money and that I'd trade money with her, giving her dollars for her Peruvian pesos.

WRONG!

The details are kind of fuzzy at this point, but the essence of the problem was Carlos said I'd do something without consulting me, without understanding I'd lose a fair bit of bucks in the transaction. This was especially unacceptable with my being on a very limited budget. You don't get to put aside a whole lot on a Peace Corps salary of $200/month. He didn't understand that I was saving my dollars for elsewhere where they'd fetch their highest value.

So what would be a dumb deal for me would be a jackpot for her.

When I got to the bar, Carlos told me what he had set up. I explained the situation to him and said I'd simply tell the woman there was a misunderstanding – no big deal.

She walked over to our table and proceeded to pull out a wad of pesos letting me know what I owed her in dollars.

I explained to her that Carlos meant well, had misunderstood, hadn't consulted me about this; sorry for the inconvenience, no thanks, *adios*.

She immediately got indignant and said, "Your friend here said you were going to buy my pesos for dollars."

At first I thought this whole thing kind of silly and overly melodramatic for such a simple miscommunication. I was also mildly entertained by her theatrics; I repeat, *mildly*.

I went through the explanation again and she fired back even more vehemently, "But he said you would!"

Now let's take a break at this part of the story because just the day before something important happened.

I had come across some writing on the subject of anger that had a big impact on me. I recognized how off I'd been when it came to my feeling angry and how sensible the author's advice sounded. I realized, with his help, that I had indeed considered anger to be a moral issue of sorts and had consequently judged my own feelings of anger as bad – wrong. I knew I had a lot of discomfort in this area, and I felt changes were certainly warranted.

Yep, that does it, enough of this b.s., it's time for a change!

Have you ever noticed that when you make a definitive decision to change something about yourself, you're usually presented with the worse case scenario afterwards; an opportunity, a challenge to put the change into effect? I see experiences like this as representing all the stuff we've been repressing for however long . . . along the lines of, "Be careful what you wish for, you just might get it."

If you're serious about making the change, the opportunity is just around the corner.

Richard Alpert, best known as Ram Dass (depending on his latest whim), has a great way of describing the way the universe cooperates and orchestrates perfectly just what we need to learn, at the most opportune moment and dished out with culinary expertise. He calls it, "Being sent by Central Casting."

I love that one.

Back to our story.

So, here I was, freshly out of a decision to stop sitting on my anger, and Central Casting had fulfilled my wish by sending me an obstinate, pushy, rude character.

It would have taken a lobotomized saint to turn the other cheek after a while.

I tried to explain to her in the clearest, most sensible logic I could muster that it would be *very* foolish for me to trade off my dollars at this time and that I had never said what she claimed I had said to Carlos – period.

As you've probably sensed by now, we are not at the "period" part of the story yet. Central Casting had other things in mind.

After impatiently hearing me out, she berated me with some off the wall comments.

(Stage left, enters, Jackie Gleason's *to the moon Alice* . . .)

Patience was no longer in the cards, reason had just dropped dead, and what was a slow burn had just crossed over the line into major anger.

In a flash, I recalled what I had read the morning before, my reflections on the subject and my decision. This all arrived in a prepackaged holographic bolt of a reminder.

With her next verbal shove, I snapped . . .

You stupid, fucking fool! What does it take for you to get it through that fucking dense skull of yours that I'm not interested in selling you my dollars and I never promised you, Carlos or anyone else that I would! Now get the fuck out of my face!

No doubt the crew at Central Casting was rolling in the aisles with this outburst. It all happened in a public place and the decibel level of my message brought the entire bar to a deafening silence.

After she slinked away, I turned to Carlos, who had the most incredulous, stunned look on his face; one that conveyed his shock of – are you the same *tranquilo* guy I spent the day with?

I took one look at his expression, felt completely and utterly relieved and "exorcised" of the anger I felt, flashed back on the whole scene and burst out laughing – I roared. I was so outrageous I thought it hysterical, all of which probably created the impression of me being doubly crazy.

Well, I must say, Central Casting presented me with an important lesson here. I had gone from theory to reality and back again.

The most interesting part of it all was I felt GREAT afterwards. I felt no shame, no guilt for having gotten pissed off. I felt completely justified in my reaction and with my feelings. I felt that I had bent over backwards far more than most under the circumstances, and when the time came, I didn't censor, repress or self-judge.

Really, the most fascinating and telling part of this whole thing was how I felt *afterwards*. I thought the whole melodrama was just that, and it struck me as really funny. I thought my display was outrageous. The most interesting thing, when it was over, was that I felt not the slightest bit of hostility or anger towards this woman – none – and *that* was the really incredible and novel part of it all. A first.

I got to see firsthand that when I stuff my anger, I all too often harbor a grudge afterwards, often plagued by imaginary scenarios that become exaggerated and increasingly ugly. I feel a loss of self-respect for not dealing with the situation, and that contributes to the aftermath of negativity.

Does any of this sound familiar?

I felt so cleansed and revitalized by the experience that I could have easily been open to a friendship with this lady afterwards, although, understandably, the feeling wasn't mutual.

Anyway, interestingly enough, I felt grateful to her later for being a part of what was a valuable lesson.

This certainly was an exaggerated situation, one that was in direct proportion to the years of repression behind it. I have found that this getting over the hump has resulted in fewer and less intense similar situations, if I stick with my spontaneity and with getting off my judgements. When we begin to incorporate change, the lessons and situations we attract to ourselves change, too.

❄   ❄   ❄

I was angry with my friend;
I told my wrath, my wrath did end.
I was angry with my foe:
I told it not, my wrath did grow.

And I watered it in fears,
Night and morning with my tears;
And I sunned it with smiles,
And soft deceitful wiles.

And it grew both day and night.
'Til it bore an apple bright.
And my foe beheld it shine,
And he knew it was mine.

And into the garden stole,
When the night had veiled the pole:
In the morning glad I see
My foe outstretched beneath the tree.

William Blake/*The Poison Tree*

There's another face to anger in my life that I struggle with. There are times when anger is camouflaging pain or hurt. It seems that anger is somehow "manly," perhaps, or the conditioned, appropriate male response. Sometimes going with the anger leads me directly to the deeper feeling, if I give myself permission to do so.

Sometimes I simply don't know what I'm feeling. There's a numbness. I've found something very useful here, and that is to once again go with what's on board and, if it's numbness, then that's what's going on. Be honest about that. It opens the way for the feelings to come in their own time, and they will. The key seems to be to pull off the judgements and the messages of: *I should be feeling this or that*, or the internal pressure to *know* what I'm feeling.

Yes, it's the shame and guilt that impede the flow. No doubt about it.

Here's a wonderful excerpt from the keynote address, delivered by Shepherd Bliss at a men's gathering attended by 110 men. There were many fine points in Shepherd's talk. The following comment stood out as an especially meaningful one for me. It is something I respected immensely when I first heard it and I have brought it back from time to time as a guiding light:

I want to recommend the book, *Holding on or Letting Go*, by Sam Osherson. I like his metaphor, "holding on or letting go." What is it about the old masculinity that I want to hold onto? Define that: bravery, courage, loyalty, being with other men in the wilderness, being rowdy sometimes; doing a lot of those male things. And what are some of the things I want to let go of? What are some of the ways in which I have felt numbness, as a man? And how can I let go of that? Some people think that men don't feel as deeply as women. That's bullshit as far as I'm concerned. I know that I feel very deeply. At times a barrier comes down and I can't get in touch with that feeling and I go numb. I know that. But part of that's because I feel so deeply down there.

. . . listen deeply to the stories of others, to the stories that men and women tell. Listen without judgment. Listen without criticism, so that when anger comes your way, strong anger from a from a woman or a man, think what's beyond and beneath that anger. It's often fear or sadness. It may come out as anger in its protective armor coat. But you know what I've noticed? If a man comes at me and I'm afraid (he's even putting up his dukes), but I touch him in a certain way, sometimes around the waist, or sometimes just put my hand right here on his chest – it's a very important place to put your hand, not to keep him away, but softly put your hand right here. Sometimes the anger just falls off and a man will start crying. I've been scared to death of anger coming my way and the potential violence, and I put my hand there and it comes out as crying. It's amazing how you can turn it around. As far as it's gone, you can always turn it around to get back to some of that deeper stuff. I don't think we're basically violent. Men are basically loving at the deepest level, and there are ways of getting back to that, through listening and connecting. [45]

Is it any wonder that there's a crisis in masculinity? Is it any wonder that many men are confused and some go into violence? They go into self-abuse or other-abuse, child abuse and spouse abuse. Or they go into passivity. They go into that soft man that's just so passive.

Alternatives to this violence or passivity exist. It's very important that we explore these alternatives. It's also important that we be cautious of what happens politically in that vacuum I spoke of earlier. Because, you see, in that vacuum certain political leaders rise and project themselves as the solution to our problems. For example, in a recent presidential election, the candidate who won ran as much on sexual politics as he did on foreign policy. He projected himself as a cowboy, able to solve our problems with the old masculinity, and he projected the other candidate as an incompetent man, unable to be forceful. And he won! Then that candidate projected himself as the good father. He stepped into that vacuum with a lack of a good father and he said, "Look, I will take care of everything. I'm in charge." Nice soft voice. "And I have the power to prove it: nuclear weapons. And I'll invade Central America."

So the issues of masculinity are not only individual issues, as we each work toward being the best possible man. They have to do with our world and our nation. I want to bring those two – the personal and the political – together here from the beginning. [46]

❋ ❋ ❋

The material and articles that follow, develop further what is perhaps an introduction to the subject of anger as relayed by me, a somewhat confused author on the topic.

I like the different angles these other men shed on such an important subject; for anger unattended can lead to violence, and violence unabated can lead to war.

And if there is going to be change, a re-crafting of the rampant violence in our lives and world, we need to talk about it honestly.

Impotent Rage, And The Myth Of Attis
Jim Moyers

Several years ago, in a class on Hellenistic religions, I encountered the strange myth of Attis. This is a complex myth, existing in several versions. To simplify it somewhat, Attis was a young man who was desired by Cybele, the Great Mother goddess. Ignoring Cybele's desire for him, Attis attempted to take a mortal woman as his bride. Enraged by the snub, Cybele disrupted the wedding, driving Attis into a mad frenzy in which he castrated himself. His intended bride was killed by Cybele.

While most of the people in the class viewed this story as another bizarre example of ancient religious belief, I was fascinated, though not quite sure why. Only later did I realize that Attis represents a kind of impotent male rage which I know from firsthand experience. I also suspect this kind of rage may be involved in many instances of domestic violence.

Since early adolescence, if not before, I have experienced periodic outbursts of uncontrollable rage which seemed to have their origin somewhere outside myself. In what seemed a possession state, I would feel something which was not me, taking control.

After I married, my wife was the usual object of my outbursts. While I usually felt a great deal of love for her, when in one of my rages I felt only hatred. Several times I came close to physically injuring her. I had no idea where this terrible thing came from or what I could do about it. I only knew I seemed unable to control it and was very ashamed of my inability to do so, which rendered me less of a man.

I eventually began psychotherapy – not specifically to deal with my rages, but they of course did come up. As I worked on them, it became apparent that they were triggered by something, often a critical remark made by my wife, which I construed as an attack on my competency as a male. I would then try to defend my image of myself as my masculine ideal, denying what I seemed to identify as feminine weakness (because it was not part of my idealized male image). But since my wife's observations were usually accurate, refuting them was difficult. My sense of powerlessness would increase, further threatening the illusion of myself as a strong, competent male, making my attempts to defend that false self-image all the more frantic. Unable to either win or give up my defense, I would suddenly find "something else" in control.

According to my wife, I would behave "like a hysterical woman" during these episodes. This did nothing to improve the masculine self-image I had been trying to maintain! My refusal to admit the existence of "feminine weakness" within myself paradoxically made me into an embodiment of the very traits I sought to deny. Attis was driven to castrate himself; I was certainly rendered impotent.

My therapist, who had a Jungian orientation, introduced me to the idea of the Anima, the feminine element within a man's psyche. When a man refuses to acknowledge his feminine side, it begins to act as if it were an autonomous entity, capable of actually taking control of him against his will. The "anima possessed" man, according to Jung, behaves like "a second-rate woman," unconsciously acting out all the negative characteristics he associates with the feminine from which he has tried to dis-associate himself. So I acted the part of "a hysterical woman." It is interesting to note that the priests of Cybele, who followed Attis' example of self-castration, were called "counterfeit women."

In exploring the reasons for my rage, I realized that the idealized image I had been trying to live up to had little to do with who I really was. My masculine ideal was the rugged American frontiersman who always knew what to do, and did it without letting his feelings show. There was little room for "womanly weakness" in such a figure. If I was going to be Davy Crockett (my childhood hero), I certainly couldn't put up with such shortcomings in myself. Actually, I do have many personality traits traditionally thought of as feminine. I tried to deny them, only to be reminded of their existence in a most forceful way.

As I began to consciously acknowledge my other, feminine, side, my "anima attacks" became less frequent and finally virtually disappeared. When I stopped attacking my inner woman she stopped her counterattack. We became partners instead of opponents. Giving up my need to live up to my idealized male image, I actually became more of a real man, as opposed to the illusory ideal I had sought to maintain before, able to use both my masculine and feminine sides without being overpowered by either.

Conscious recognition of the feminine is not the same thing as an unthinking surrender to the power it represents. Attis' mistake was not one of failing to follow Cybele's demands; it was rather a failure to consciously deal with them. According to the myth, he didn't say no; he just tried to ignore her. If one is to truly become a man, free from being unconsciously controlled by the anima, he must consciously face and deal with the demands made on him by the feminine, especially those of the mother, the first representative of the feminine he encounters.

Attis' father was unknown to him. This is often the case in myths of the hero (Attis is a type of failed hero). From observations of myself, of male friends and men with whom I have worked as a therapist, I believe men tend to form their identity as men more in relation to their mothers than their fathers. As others have pointed out, fathers are typically not as close to their sons as their mothers are. In order for a boy to identify himself as a male, he must first realize he is radically different from his mother. At the same time it is his mother who tells him what he must do to be her "little man."

In order to be a "real man" then, a boy must somehow form an identity for himself as someone distinctly different from his mother while at the same time winning her approval by living up to her image of the ideal male, something his father, being only human, probably failed to do. A mother overly-involved with her son may attempt to elevate him to what is actually a semi-divine status, a danger reflected in myths of the divine son-lover (Attis was one) who never achieves full manhood. Caught between the need to be other than mother and the need to win her approval, it is no wonder so many men are confused about their relation to the feminine, both within their own psyches and as embodied in the women in their lives.

In commenting on the Grimm Brothers' tale of "Iron John," Robert Bly (in Chapter IX) stresses the necessity of a man taking back the power he has given his mother. As the fairytale puts it, the key to unlock the primal male energy is to be found under the mother's pillow.

It was very important for me to be a "good boy" for my mother. I was told I should "be like Jesus" (another divine son/lover figure), an impossible ideal if there ever was one. I thought I escaped this demand when I married someone from a very different religious background, with whom I could do things my mother's "good boy" would never do. But at times I still heard my mother's disapproving voice, often mistakenly thinking it came from my wife.

I had never consciously faced and dealt with my mother's expectations of me. I tried to ignore them as Attis tried to ignore Cybele. But, again, like Attis, I found myself overwhelmed and reduced to impotence, helpless before the power of the unacknowledged mother whose voice remained within me.

Cybele was the Great Mother goddess, an archetypal, non-human entity. We often make our mothers into goddesses (and goddesses are not always benevolent beings!), giving them an importance and power which does not belong to the human beings they really are. If we are to reclaim the power we have given to them, we must see through the images of the Great Mother, in both her nurturing and devouring aspects, which we have projected onto our mothers and quite often onto other women in our lives. *It is impossible for a mere mortal man to have a sense of his own power if he believes he is in a relationship with a goddess.*

As I have tried to come to terms with my mother issues, I have been surprised to find that my mother is actually quite different from the image I had of her. She does not really demand that I remain forever under her power, threatening to withhold her love if I do not do so. She is simply another human being, with her good and bad points like all other human beings. I must admit I do not always see it this way, but I do manage to see through my projections to my real mother more often than I used to.

I often projected the disapproving maternal voice, the trigger for my rages, onto my wife. But I hear that voice much less these days. When I am angry with her now, it is more clearly related to what is actually happening between us than with what I imagine is happening. In withdrawing my image of the archetypal mother from my real mother, I also withdraw it from the other women in my life. My relationship with my wife, a relation Attis was unable to establish, is more real. By taking back the power I had given up to my mother, I am able to have a relationship as a real man to a real woman who is my equal. **[47]**

Encountering Rape: Not For Women Only
David Seeley

Joel, a married Dallas professional in his late 20's, still finds it hard to talk about what happened to him months ago. He doesn't want his real name used for this story, but he wants other male victims to know they are not alone.

"It was a Friday evening," Joel says. "I was getting in my car in a parking lot, near a not-very-well-lighted street. As I was getting into the car, I was attacked, and the man had a knife.

"I was scared. I was caught off guard. He was big. I had no idea what he wanted – I thought he was going to rob me, or take my car. I had no idea at that point what was going to happen."

Then the man pressed the knife against Joel's throat.

"He told me he was going to . . ." Joel pauses. "He was very graphic in his description in saying that he was going to show me what it felt like. He was very angry, very hostile. I didn't think about it then, but looking back, he was angry. And he verbalized that a lot, about what was going to happen.

"I think I was still in disbelief at that point, but I was more frightened that he was going to kill me. I would have done anything. I didn't try to resist him. I did what he told me to do. He told me he'd hurt me, he'd cut me. He held the knife to my throat."

The assault was over quickly. The assailant didn't threaten Joel again – he just shoved him to the ground and ran away.

"I think it was probably the most frightening moment of my life," Joel says, "I'm not a small guy. I've always felt like I could take care of myself. But I had lost control of everything. I didn't control what was going to happen to me for the next five minutes, and I'd never had that feeling before."

Joel drove home and tried to act as if nothing had happened. He didn't call the police. He didn't tell his wife.

"Later in the evening I was in pain and upset," he recalls, "and I called the Rape Crisis Center. I had no idea whether a male had ever reported a sexual assault or not. But I felt like I had to find somebody who could help me."

Sue James recalls what Joel was going through when she first saw him. "The first few weeks he came in here, he would just shake; he couldn't stay still, he had so much anxiety," she says. "Then he reached out for some help and support."

Most people didn't believe him, Joel says. The ones who did believe him thought Joel somehow had caused it, "that I either picked the guy up or made him mad."

Sue James says, "People stopped joking about women (rape victims) when they believed it was really rape. As a lot of people began to realize that rape wasn't sexual, that it was really violence against women, that it hurt them, then they stopped joking. But what we see now is when they hear about a man being sexually assaulted, they don't believe it. They often believe that he wanted to have sex with another man, that it's just sex, it's not violence. Or it didn't really happen and he's crazy, he's making this stuff up.

"Men don't report sexual assaults now for the same reason that women didn't report them ten years ago," Sue James says. "They don't believe anybody will support them. What can be done now is the same thing that was done for women: convince people that (male rape) is a violent act committed against another human being." **[48]**

Tarzan Must Weep
Toward A Fuller Manhood
Robert Masters

Sometime ago, I dreamt that Gail (my life-partner) and I were in a large room with many men. The men were talking and smoking, wandering about, looking tough. Gail and I were waiting for a meal to begin, feeling quite uncomfortable. Finally, she left to take a shower in the women's shower room. The men near me wore black leather jackets, and didn't let their sneers stray too far from their faces. One of them was sprawled on top of my possessions; when I asked him to move, he growled unintelligibly. I pushed him aside, and he immediately attacked me. We fought, and I pinned him, threatening to break his arms if he didn't leave my stuff alone. Eventually, he muttered agreement. His buddies encircled me, menacingly; the air quivered with violence. Suddenly, I felt present. Waves of compassion poured through me. Looking into the eyes of the man who'd attacked me, I saw not just his carefully cultivated toughness, but his faraway sadness, his fear; a bewildered little boy seemed to crouch behind his defiant stare. I directly and honestly told him what I saw, and what I felt. I spoke of my own violence, and my fear of it, and of how acknowledging its presence helped me to express it in non-violent ways. As I spoke, I sensed that the man and his cohorts didn't really understand what I was saying, but that they liked, or respected, the way in which I was speaking. After I finished speaking, I went to get Gail, and told her I missed her during the encounter with the men. She and I left the room, and the building of which it was a part.

In the dream, as in my life, Gail reflects the woman in me. She leaves early because there's no place for her in such an unfeeling, hard space. She takes a shower in the women's shower to cleanse and nurture herself with the feminine. The males' toughness is my toughness. At first, I'm polite, as I was when I was the obedient son of my father. Then I fight, as I chronically sought to best the other males, including my father. My winning only makes things worse. As I see that I'm literally encircled by the situation, penned in by it, I break through my context of either giving in to or fighting against the other men, and come present.

My attacker is a blend of all the boys and men I've known, including myself, who wouldn't befriend their own vulnerability. I see what he won't see – his pain, his lovelessness, his isolation, his darkness. What I see is the barrenness of a world characterized by excessive self-control, hardness, and unillumined power. And I see this and speak this only because I know another world, one in which I am intimate with the woman in me.

That I speak with power impresses the men, though I only do so to reach them, and to protect from them what is tender and soft in me, for they are at war with what is tender and soft in them. Their attitude toward women, which is either degradingly obscene or exaggeratedly sentimental, guarantees their isolation. I only go to Gail when I've left the men, for she, the woman in me, could not find healthy expression among such people, except perhaps as an intuitive guiding of my speaking. I could not share her with them, for they wouldn't see her, but only sissy-ness, only something to exploit or fear.

Without the woman in me, without her unrestrained aliveness, I'm crippled, lost in a wasteland populated by shadows of mind, marooned from love. With her comes the integration of love and joy; all I need do is make room for her. As I become strong in my softness, finding in my vulnerability the strength to be myself, I'm less and less concerned with proving myself, with demonstrating my manliness to the dark inner sanctums of "male" unfeelingness, the black leather jackets of my dream. And . . . I'm tempted to stop here, to close out this essay, to leave the men of my dream behind. But . . .

I'm disgusted by them, and yet my heart goes out to them, even as I turn from them. They loiter in me, dark and hard. I've struggled to discard them, to finish with them, to transcend them, especially as I've more and more deeply reclaimed my more tender feelings. My competitiveness and forcefulness have often seemed to be in the way of the expression of my vulnerability. But these qualities, these "male" attributes, are as much me as my tenderness or softness. I have abused them, kept them in the dark, dressing them up in black leather jackets. I have been ashamed to reveal them in their full potency to the woman in me. Lately, I've been enjoying undressing them, letting them wander about naked, permitting them to energize the man in me. Gracefully and passionately, he comes alive, delighting in his forcefulness, exulting in his full-bodied wildness, celebrating the play of his power, even as he remains sensitive to his impact on his environment. At such times, competitiveness is not junked, but is stripped of its seriousness and infused with loving playfulness, without diluting its intensity and excitement one bit, so that it becomes for me a way of sharing myself, of revealing myself, of saying an unqualified yes to my maleness, to my humanity.

When I lose touch with my love and my power, my maleness contracts, tightens up, shrinks into the black leather jackets, into a caricature of manliness. In the very recognition and undoing of such contraction, male and female meet in me, spurring each other's ripening. In their embrace, I feel the strength to be myself, to see myself, to love myself, to let myself leap for joy, full of shining boy. [49]

The Roots Of Male Violence
Ian M. Harris

Violence in this world is often attributed to males. Men wage war. Men commit the majority of crimes and are the major perpetrators of domestic abuse. More men than women serve in the armed forces. Men developed and used the atomic bomb.

Male violence creates terrible problems in this world. Millions of people are killed by male armies. Human beings throughout the world are held captive to the nightmare of nuclear winter, which represents the ultimate male fantasy of destruction. Women cringe before the musculature and anger of their male lovers. Children bear the scars of father's temper.

What is your image of an angry man? Mine is Clint Eastwood with a 357 magnum in his hand, blowing away all those close to him.

If we are to address the enormity of the problems caused by violent masculine behavior, we must understand it. Male violence is a response to aggressive urges. Some argue that male aggression is either inherited or has an instinctual status passed through the culture in our collective unconscious minds. I deny both these approaches.

The argument for genetically inherited aggression comes from the existence of the Y-chromosome in male sperm. Men have this chromosome and women don't. The Y-chromosome is said to help produce testosterone, a hormone that stimulates aggression. But many men are gentle. Men with double Y-chromosomes have been shown upon occasion to exhibit anti-social, violent behavior. But many individuals with the double Y-chromosome are nonviolent; therefore, these genetic or inherited factors by themselves, do not always cause violence.

Men and women who are provoked get angry, and hence anger does seem to be rooted deeply in human behavior, even at a level that could be called instinctual. However, responses to angry-making situations vary from individual to individual and from culture to culture. The sources of male violence come from the cultures men inhabit. Anthropologists have discovered some cultures, such as the Eskimos and Navahos, where men aren't violent. Men learn violent behavior from their surroundings.

What does belong to our collective unconscious minds is a strong aversion to violence deeply rooted in what Jung referred to as our shadow side. Such is the source of nightmares and anxieties. Men fear being beaten up. If we have been physically violated, we are resentful. Demoniac images of violence, which may be seductive to some, cause anxieties which feed a violent beast deep within all human beings that represents our destructive urges. As Freud stated, "War is the expression of the unconscious barbarity of man."

Male Messages

My curiosity about the roots of male violence has led me to explore masculine messages in the United States. These messages are scripts that men receive from the culture that help determine what behaviors are appropriate for men. After five years of researching this issue, I have concluded that violent messages like "Tough Guy," where a man has to protect himself, and "Warrior," where he takes death defying risks, are not so important in the overall scheme of things. Each man in this country hears violent messages all the time. These messages form part of the picture he carries around in his mind of what it means to be a man. He is pulled toward acting like a Rambo or a John Wayne – messages that belong to his culture. Boys want to be men. I wanted to hunt when I was younger. All the men around me did, and it was expected of me by all my peers.

However, not all men act in those ways. Not all of us use our fists when we get angry. Some of us are devoted fathers and passionate lovers, capable of the deep enriching tenderness that builds good relationships. Messages like "Be the Best You Can" and "Nurturer" rank higher with the over 500 men I have been studying. Most writers tend to prefer to discuss the violent aspects of male behavior and not dwell on the gentle aspects of the male species. But after all, each of you readers has a father. Is he violent? The violent messages that promote male aggression form an important part of the monster that is male violence, but they aren't this monster's heart and guts. They represent the outer shell, the collective images of violence we all have learned and carry around on our shoulders like epaulets from the army.

The Angry Monster Within

The brain and vital organs of male violence come deep from the shadow side of human existence. Deep down in our psyches exist repressed hostilities that represent our destructive urges and feelings of hatred that feed the angry monster within. When our fathers spanked us; when our mothers abandoned us; when our teachers humiliated us; when our friends mocked us; when our drill sergeants yelled at us; when our bosses fired us; when the opposition beat us; when our lovers left us; when our children hate us – millions of angry-making moments that create an explosive force that has to be released.

Some of us play sports to burn off this anger energy. Others have learned to release anger in ways that don't hurt others. But the vast majority of us – whether it be a commander ordering forces into peasant villages in Nicaragua, a father spanking his child, Clint Eastwood destroying the enemy (that we project out from our shadow side), a husband beating his wife, or Ronald Reagan ordering a Star Wars system to destroy his fantasy of the evil Soviet empire – let that monster power our muscles as we strike out at our enemies, imagined and real.

Some of us resent social messages that teach us to kill. I remember with great anger my father making me destroy animals on our farm. Men returning from Vietnam hate the country that forced them into jungle platoons. These resentments build up inside us, sometimes exploding like hot lava from a volcano, emitting poisonous, life-destroying gasses.

Don't Be Emotional

Although anger and fear are eager to get out into the world to wreak carnage, the ways in which they are able to express themselves are severely limited by the cultures men inhabit. Men are told to not be emotional or expressive. They can't express their feelings because that would be a sign of weakness for strong heroes; it would be feminine. Rather than encouraging this repressed anger to come out of its dark hole and enter the sunlight of public scrutiny, the culture puts a cork on top of the genie and drives the cork home with a sledge hammer. "If you are a man, I don't want to hear your problems. You are supposed to be in control of your emotions. Crying and acting like a girl doesn't fit you!" Given that the pressures build up and normal expressive ways of releasing tensions are denied most men, the frustrations often become explosive, resulting in violent outbursts that hurt others.

Adding to the repressive nature of these messages which block feelings, are expectations to compete. The social institutions for which we work and within which we play, contribute to our violent behavior. If we serve in the armed forces, we are systematically instructed in the killing of others. The companies we work for thrive on competition. Leaders are supposed to be tough, make hard decisions, and destroy other people's lives – all in the name of profit. Parents praise their boys for "gutsing it out." Football players are applauded for hurting others, and Lieutenant Calley did a good job at My Lai.

We are supposed to be self-reliant. We are not to become dependent on others. We are told to excel in a competitive society. In the unending scramble to the top, even our friends put us down. These put-downs are supposed to toughen our skins so we can compete in Corporate America. Instead, they feed that monster inside us.

It has been shown by Hannah Arendt and others, that the greater the bureaucratization of public life, the greater the attraction of violence. When we turn on our televisions, we are surrounded by violent images. Our frustrations about not being men of action are played upon by huge advertising companies that glorify violence and allow us to play out some of our fantasies of destruction. (Can you feel the monster tugging at his leash?)

What Can Be Done About This?

In order to solve some of the problems created by male violence, men should explore the roots of their own violent behavior. In addition to finding out about the impact of these messages and who perpetrates them, each man should take time out in therapy, at bars, among family members, with trusted loved ones, in encounter groups, and at men's conferences to explore how he learned to express his aggressive tendencies.

Men get in trouble because of their violence. Some men, profoundly confused by the violent tendencies within them and estranged from the ones they love, grow to appreciate how their violent behavior pains others. In the violent milieu in which most men live, it is not easy to talk to others about their fears. The guys on the street corner are too busy putting up a tough front. Fellow workers in the corporation don't want to let down their guard. Teammates are too busy winning. And spouses are terrified. Men need to talk through the violent tendencies they feel within. I have found that the most potent format is a men's group specifically focused on violence. In a trusting environment, these "mean guys" can let their monsters out, put them on a table and describe their horrible features. Understanding their ugliness is an important part of remodeling their features into a more tender and cuddly beast.

All people on this planet can adopt the goal of creating an environment where men can express their emotions nonviolently.

Male aggressiveness need not be destructive. Men can learn nonviolent ways to express their aggressive urges and channel their energies towards the peaceful resolution of conflict. Male gentleness can be taught and nurtured in schools, workplaces, and families. We need to think through child-rearing practices, opposing all forms of physical abuse and not using force with children. We can construct environments where others can exercise their free will and freedom of choice.

Unfortunately, human behavior seldom changes by trying to expunge a set of behaviors. Individuals resent others telling them what to do, so perhaps the best way to make the world less violent is to become a model of nonviolent behavior, each individual searching within his soul to find new nonviolent ways of dealing with situations that raise our ire.

The kingdom of the male mind is not all ugly. Within each man are positive messages – scripts that expect men to be nurturing, to love nature, to worship, to take risks, to be faithful, to work for social justice and to care for others. In order to change male behavior away from violence we have to enforce those life supporting and affirming tendencies that also exist within the male kingdom.

We don't have to teach young boys violence. When I was a young boy I did not want to slaughter pigs. In fact, I was seven the first time I saw hogs being butchered, and threw up. My stepson did not want, at age ten, to dissect frogs. Young boys don't want to kill and eat the fish they catch.

Each individual on this planet wages a Faustian dialogue between the devil of violence and the God of love. Women are trained in the ways of love. Men hear both messages and can also learn to love. They can learn to balance their aggressive energy with the life forces that sustain this planet.

All individuals on this planet can also use a good dose of morality, where they are taught to think through carefully the effects of their actions upon others. Men can learn not to distance themselves from the consequences of their decisions and challenge organizations that demand dehumanizing behavior from them. Males can pull themselves out of bureaucratic quagmires and accept the consequences of their actions. They can neither continue to build nuclear weapons nor rape their mother, the Earth.

They can channel their aggressive tendencies into political campaigns that directly challenge the predominantly violent mode of conducting human affairs. Men can use their strength to take risks to change the goals of societies that promote violence.

And they can nourish the gentle flowers within. [50]

From: *The Prince Of Tides*
Pat Conroy

It was still raining when we went to bed that night. My father put out the lights in the house and smoked a pipe on the screened-in porch before he retired. He seemed uncomfortable with us when my mother was not orchestrating the tenor of household life. Several times during the evening, he had yelled at us when something minor and insignificant had irritated him. My father was an easy read. When there was real danger, you knew instinctively to avoid him; he had a genuine gift for tyranny but no coherent strategies. He was both brutal and ineffectual as a man who would always be a stranger in his own house. As his children, we were treated as some species of migrant worker who happened to be passing through. My father was the only person I ever knew who looked upon childhood as a dishonorable vocation one grew out of as quickly as possible. He would have been lovable for his fecklessness and his blustering eccentricities if he had not been born a violent and unpredictable man. I think my father loved us, but there has never been a more awkward or deviant love. He considered a slap to the face a valentine delivered. As a child, he had felt neglected and abandoned and neither of his parents had ever laid a hand on him. He never noticed us except to scold us; he never touched us unless in anger. At night, surrounded by his family, my father looked trapped, and he taught me a great deal about the self-made loneliness of mankind. I began my life by being taken prisoner in my father's house. I would begin my manhood by walking over him on my way out the door.

My life did not really begin until I summoned the power to forgive my father for making my childhood a long march of terror. Larceny is not a difficult crime to condone unless your childhood was the item stolen. Without equivocation, I will tell you he was a terrible and destructive father. Yet it will always remain one of life's most ineluctable mysteries that I would one day come to feel an unabiding compassion for the man, and a frayed, nervous love. His fists were the argosies of his rule and empowerment. But his eyes were the eyes of my father, and something in those eyes always loved me even when his hands could not. He brought no natural talent to the dilemma of loving his family properly. He had developed none of the soft gifts of fatherhood. We mistook his love songs for battle hymns. His attempts at reconciliation were mistaken for brief and insincere cease-fires in a ferocious war of attrition. He lacked all finesse and tenderness; he had mined all harbors, all approaches to his heart. Only when the world brought him to his knees could I reach up and touch my father's face without him bloodying mine. By the time I was eighteen I knew everything there was to know about a police state, and it was only when I left his house that the long state of siege was ended.

Though I hated my father, I expressed that hatred eloquently by imitating his life and becoming more and more ineffectual daily; and by ratifying all the cheerless prophecies my mother made for both my father and me. I thought I had succeeded in not becoming a violent man, but even that collapsed. My violence was subterranean, unbeheld. It was my silence, my long withdrawals, that I had turned into dangerous things. My viciousness manifested itself in the terrible winter of blue eyes. My wounded stare could bring an ice age into the sunniest, balmiest afternoon. I was about to be thirty-seven years old, and with some aptitude and a little natural ability, I had figured out how to live a perfectly meaningless life, but one that could imperceptibly and inevitably destroy the lives of those around me.

So I looked to this summer as a last chance to take my full measure as a man, a troubled interregnum before I ventured into the pitfalls and ceremonials of middle age. I wanted, by an act of conscious will, to make it a time of reckoning and, if I was lucky, a time of healing and reconstitution of an eclipsed spirit.

Through the procedure of remembrance, I would try to heal myself . . . **[51]**

❃   ❃   ❃

Who are these men with the overwhelming experience of relationships with their fathers; this group of men who, when they become fathers, spend an average of 10 minutes a day with their children? They are men who find that underneath their fear lies a deep seated anger and outrage at the pain that has been inflicted upon them – on their lives. Accompanying this outrage resides the presence of real guilt, guilt for the ways in which, rather than accept the pain, they have projected and passed it on to others. Beyond this anger and guilt lies the passion and power of a deep-seated, erotic, unleashed force that holds out the promise of a full expression of manhood – an expression of manhood that finds its source in the heartbeat, its sound in the drum and its expression in the prophetic influence of transformative male energy on the culture. **[52]**

Much of *From The Hearts of Men* is autobiographical. I've shared with you experiences I've had along the way and those of other men whose stories have developed and enhanced a particular topic or theme. My guiding light has been to delve into subjects that I think have a high degree of universality for men. I don't presume to speak for other men. Simply, I hope you, the reader, see something of yourself within these pages that stimulates insights that may shed light on issues of importance in your own life.

I have grown by hearing others' stories and others' reflections. Sometimes, something that is foggy and perplexing gets a little clearer in the sharing. And sometimes, actually many-a-time, I've felt comforted simply by hearing that I'm not alone,

I'm not the only one who thinks, feels, and reacts the way I do. I'm not the only one who has this kind of feeling or problem.

The following poem captured a feeling that became a collective yearning and realization at the first men's retreat I attended. We periodically chanted this poem, joining 90 voices with our soul's desire.

Love Come Quietly
by Robert Creely

Love comes quietly,
finally, drops
about me, on me,
in the old ways.

What did I know
thinking myself
able to go
alone all the way. [53]

CHAPTER XIII

WAR

I recall something a friend once said: "The purpose of suffering is to teach one how not to suffer anymore." Perhaps by facing what impels men to go to war we will discover and unhinge these kinds of tragic heroics, in hopes of ending the abysmal suffering endured by all humankind. As far back as our recorded history extends, our stay on this earth has been a violent time indeed. All too often, people espouse the belief that war is an inviolate part of Man's nature. I strongly reject such a notion in spite of our past.

Patricia Sun tells of a conversation she had with an Israeli soldier. She asked him if he thought there'd ever be peace between the Arabs and Israelis. He firmly replied, "No." She asked if he thought peace *could* ever be a possibility. Once again he said, "No." She went on to say, "If people don't ever *consider* the possibility, isn't it reasonable to say that there will never be openings for peace to be created? If everyone flatly rejects any chance for peace negotiations because of such pessimism, then doesn't it make sense that peace will never become a reality?"

He was silent.

She closed the conversation with: "Years ago, did you ever think there'd be peace between Israel and Egypt?" To that, he once again replied, "No."

In his book *Journey To Brotherhood – Awakening, Healing and Connecting Men's Hearts,* Frank Cardelle paraphrases Fritz Perls:

> *Fritz Perls, the father of gestalt therapy, wrote in*
> *the 50's that 'repression of aggression' and not·*

repression as Freud and others believed, is at the core of our personal and social conflicts. When we dam the opening of our instincts and true aggressive urges, we are setting the pattern for development of social neurosis and eventual psychosis. This repressed urge simmers in our unconscious and if the lid is held on long enough, it will boil over. A society that is repressed and passes this training on to its youth is a walking time bomb. An inbred hostile pattern develops and the people continue to be increasingly frustrated. The most devastating result of the extreme misuse of aggression is 'war.'

As long as war is the outlet for pent-up, frustrated, and blocked aggressive urges, history will repeat itself, complete with all the agony and insanity. If we believe that due to men's aggressive natures, war will be inevitable, we are perpetuating a terrible falsehood, a deadly myth and a self-fulfilling prophecy. We must realize that war is acceptable if we believe it so. If we change our beliefs and our thoughts we can create fresh and healthy ways to vent our aggression. **[54]**

One Bullet Too Many
Mike Felker

Big Man was over six feet six. His shoulders were broad. His chest deep. His arms well muscled. He had once lifted me with all my gear over a tangle of barbed wire. His legs and thighs were sturdy from a boyhood on an Indiana farm. His large rough hands were stained yellow from cupping joints, his nails embedded with the dirt of rice paddies and jungle. A fine downy coat of hair covered his body, shining like a faint corona when he stood naked in the sun. His blond hair was short and a wisp of a moustache was barely visible on his lip. His clear blue eyes did not reflect the pain and death he had seen. He was and will be the only romance of my life. I was in love with him then and I love him more now. He haunts my dreams and strides through my fantasies.

Big Man had survived eleven months in Viet Nam in the bush, untouched by bullets, booby-traps or malaria. He had been drafted into the Marine Corps and sixteen months later he was a corporal, Alpha Squad leader, First Platoon, Bravo One/One. Before he was drafted he had finished his freshman year at the University of Indiana, where he had met the girl he was engaged to. Now that his time in the Marines was almost over he wanted to go back to school, that girl, and home. His application for re-admission to the University included a two page medical exam which I, a hospital corpsman, a medic, the closest thing to a doctor in the bush, completed. We sent the application with the medical exam back to the World in the mailbag on the resupply helicopter.

Word filtered down that we were going on a company-size search and destroy operation in the mountains near the Laotian border, Charlie Ridge. We humped the six kilometers back to the battalion rear area to lighten ourselves of excess gear before we went on the op, have a hot meal in the mess hall, take a shower, and get a clean set of fatigues. After the shower, we stood naked searching through ammo boxes piled with clean fatigues. Our first change of cloths in over four weeks. His body glistening in the sun, Big Man smiled in pleasure from the hot food and the shower, unconcerned in the swarming mass of naked men.

Flak jackets and helmets were discarded, a few K-rations went into our flaccid packs. I filled my medical bag with battle dressings and slid a thin yellow book of T.S. Eliot's poems in with the intravenous bottles of plasma and sterile saline. The holster of my web belt held a pair of surgical scissors and a small box of morphine syrettes, but no weapon.

That evening mail call was held; a letter from my father included a newspaper clipping and a picture of a screaming woman crouched over the slain protesters at Kent State.

At five the next morning, the company assembled by the landing zone, waiting for the choppers to come and take us to the mountains. As the sun rose through the mist we could see villagers squatting into the rice paddies near the LZ, shitting, while their water buffalo waited placidly. An hour later the choppers landed and I ran aboard one with the Alpha Squad, choking on the dust and wind from the deafening blades. The chopper took off and beneath us passed the gray geometric precision of the rice paddies and the green lushness of the jungle, pocked with the barren brown of bomb craters. We came to Charlie Ridge and landed in a clearing surrounded by tall trees tilted at impossible angles. A dull, not too distant bombing of B-52's could be felt more than heard. The ground was steep, the foliage dense and difficult to get through. For four days we humped the mountains, using knives, machetes, and ropes to make our way. At night we would set up a base camp, and before it got too dark I would squat on the ground, eating my reconstituted K-rat chili, reading "The Wasteland" or "The Hollow Men." The fourth night I sat with Big Man. We shared a joint and we talked of how "short" he was and how soon he would be back in the World with his woman. I tried to explain "April is the cruelest month . . ." to him, but his eyes were glazed and uncomprehending. Beyond our muffled voices was the mountain dusk and the silent jungle.

On the fifth morning I went on a patrol with Alpha Squad; Big Man walked point. After about two hours we reached a small valley between a hill and a cliff. Big Man started up the cliff alone, to find the best route for the patrol. The rest of us were scattered along the floor of the valley and on the hill. On the slope of the hill I was sitting, waiting with a Black Marine from Atlanta named Flynne. There was a short, sudden spurt of an "ack-ack." Flynne and the rest of the Marines opened up with their M-16's, spraying the side of the cliff. V.C. had been sighted; they had shot Big Man. People were yelling "Corpsman" and "Doc" as I stumbled down the hill. While the rest of the patrol went after the V.C., Flynne, another Marine, and I searched the side of the hill for Big Man. For twenty minutes we searched among the rocks and crevices. We found him wedged in a deep cleft between two rocks, eyes closed, his head at an absurd angle. As we dragged him from the hole, a rasping sigh came from his chest. There were three bullet holes in his back. Big Man couldn't be dead. I knew he was still alive. I searched for a pulse and thought I felt one in his neck. I put an S-curved plastic airway down his throat and tried artificial resuscitation. My mouth filled with his blood. I tried to start his heart beating with cardiac massage, pounding his chest. I tried to pray and beg him back to life.

By this time another patrol had come to the side of the cliff. Chuck, a hospital corpsman from Third Platoon saw my hysteria, that my frantic efforts were futile. He shook me hard and when I started crying that Big Man was alive, Chuck slapped me. I stopped. Big Man was dead.

The men of Alpha Squad put Big Man on a poncho and tried to carry him, stretcher style, but he was too awkward and heavy. They found a strong, straight tree branch and tied him to it by his hands and feet. He swung like a slaughtered animal as they carried the branch through the jungle to the LZ.

Big Man lay in the clearing surrounded by the tilting trees, covered with a dusty poncho. The chopper landed, and his squad carried him aboard, laying him on the vibrating metal floor, leaving him alone on his trip back to the World. The tree tops whispered as the chopper took off. I watched, as I will always watch, until it disappeared.

Jungle Action
Bob Mertz

Into this jungle like a cat stalking his prey,
We hear a muffled curse or stumble,
As we take to our machete
To try and hack a simple path
Thru this growth so thick
Where no man has ever strayed.
But never can we leave our thoughts
To wander on their way.
For this is when we are very alert,
To make contact with them now
Would be worse than the other day –
When for a moment or so
It seemed as if hell found its way;
And with a multitude of cracking sounds
That sent green tracers sweeping the ground
Until all I could see were the bodies –
Of my brothers who had been shot down,
Never to see another day
Unless we could signal a medivac

But I knew the priority
That's been requested
Will be answered in the usual way –
"There's too much contact
To set a chopper on the ground;"
And this is when I found my thoughts
With words I hoped I'd never say,
As all we can do is watch a young life
Slowly letting death have its way,
And we finally learn to accept what is known
Among the ranks that fight on the ground.
We're just another number and
can be replaced
By someone else, who'll continue to
hack away –

Recommendations For A Rambo Doll

Mike Felker

Ms. Barbara C. Wruck, Vice President
        Corporate Communications
Coleco Industries, Inc.
West Hartford, Ct 06091

Dear Ms. Wruck:

In a recent *New York Times* article reprinted in the *San Francisco Chronicle* of August 1, you stated that Coleco Industries planned to manufacture and market a line of "action figure, action figure accessories, and other play items" based on the Viet Nam veteran portrayed by Sylvester Stallone in the very popular film *Rambo: First Blood Part II.* Having served as a hospital corpsman with the Marines in Viet Nam, I would like to offer the following suggestions to help Coleco produce an authentic "action figure, action figure accessories, and other play items."

The Rambo doll should have removable hands, feet, legs, and arms to be interchangeable with miniature prostheses – tiny mechanical hooks and limbs; as a "play item," Coleco should also manufacture a little electric wheelchair to move the Rambo doll from one room to another after he's been paralyzed from the waist down by a piece of "play" shrapnel from "friendly fire." In fact, as an offshoot item, a Rambo inspired board game could be developed called *Friendly Fire* – instead of landing on "Boardwalk" or "Go To Jail" the player could "Step on a Booby Trap" or be "Hit By Sniper Fire" – this would provide hours of fun for the entire family. To provide a realistic setting for the Rambo "action figure," Coleco in conjunction with Dow Chemical, could produce aerosol spray cans of Agent Orange, enabling children to make any American backyard look like a little bit of Viet Nam in a matter of minutes. I'm sure you would have a real "winner" in the development of a "Battered Barbie" doll, the Rambo "action figure's" significant other, who must suffer the consequences of his flashbacks and his bouts of rage resulting from Post Traumatic Stress.

And finally, Ms. Wruck, as Coleco wants to aim the Rambo "action figure" for the Christmas season, you should have the doll and accessories hit the stores (with appropriate promotional advertising) on November 26; that will be the sixteenth anniversary of the death of Staff Sergeant Arthur John RAMBO, in combat in Viet Nam. I'm sure Coleco's advertising department could develop a really strong campaign around this date, and it would provide you almost a month of merchandising of the Rambo doll before Christmas.

I do hope that Coleco Industries will find the above suggestions useful in the manufacture and marketing of the Rambo "action figure, action figure accessories, and other play items."

Sincerely,
Michael Felker

This letter was reprinted in the San Francisco Examiner and resulted in a local television station producing a half hour documentary on Staff Sgt. John Arthur Rambo in December. **[55]**

Emotional Scars Of War
John Macchietto

Twelve years ago this March, the last U.S. troops left Vietnam. With 3.8 million servicemen and 15,000 servicewomen in Indochina, which includes the 2.6 million servicemen and 8,000 servicewomen who served in Vietnam, there are at least as many U.S. stories of the war. Over 59,000 U.S. male soldiers' and eight female service nurses' stories will never be told from their own perspective. They died in the war. Not all who served in Indochina saw combat. For each land soldier fighting firsthand, there were approximately five other service personnel in support positions. An estimated 1.5 million men were exposed to combat on a repeated basis. I say men, because of the 8,000 women who served in Vietnam and of all the estimated 15,000 women who served in Indochina, 83.5% were nurses and though their jobs were not pretty, they were not assigned to combat. I state this to emphasize the point that men fight wars; rarely do women. But even more importantly, the psychological costs of fighting a war are barely visible except to those survivors who remember, yet almost never talk about it. That is my goal in this article; to examine war as an issue of masculinity in terms of the emotional costs that men endure because they are men.

Although as of September 1984, there are still over 3.4 million present-day U.S. survivors of the Vietnam theatre, I can safely predict that very few of their stories will ever really be told by them or heard by most of us. As in Vietnam, Korea, WWI, WWII and all other American wars, veterans rarely talk about their experiences.

I remember that less than five years ago, my wife interviewed my father for a class she was taking concerning WWII. My father served in Patton's army in Europe and seemed somewhat flattered to be asked. What impressed me the most was my father's comment at the conclusion of the interview that although he was treated like a hero when he returned to the U.S., he said no one ever asked him about (until my wife's three-hour interview) nor had he ever told anyone his story, except for a few fragmented portions told to different people at different times. I further recall that whenever I asked him in my childhood, what happened to him in the war, I only heard "War is hell!" and little more than that. It makes sense to me now that the only time I saw my father cry, is when I was 18 and leaving on a plane for basic training during the Vietnam war.

I believe I understand that more clearly now, because I have had the good fortune to have worked for two years as a psychological clinician at an inpatient Vietnam Post-Traumatic Stress Unit at the V.A. Medical Center in Topeka, Kansas. During my V.A. work, I witnessed approximately 180 men suffer in torment and agony as they relived their memories of a war they fought and were spending the balance of their lives trying to forget. Thus, my emotional understanding of war comes from these men, to whom I am greatly indebted. I will share, to the best of my ability, what I have learned from their experiences.

Presently, 14% of the U.S. population are veterans, and 97% of them are men. I am amazed at how our society's attitude towards victims of violent crimes and tragedies is one of great sympathy and understanding while the trauma men suffer in war is, at best, ignored. For example, two aerial skywalks spanning the lobby of the Hotel Hyatt Regency in Kansas City collapsed killing 114 people and severely injuring 200 others. That incident gave me the opportunity to interview a few who were there and suffered the physical and emotional pain of that tragedy. The horrible task of emergency crews, who had to use chain saws to cut off the crushed limbs of screaming victims trapped under tons of steel and concrete, will be etched on the minds of both rescuers and victims forever. The public's hearts leapt out to those who suffered that trauma.

I recall one veteran's comments when asked by a non-veteran hospital visitor how Vietnam could be any worse than such a tragedy, and his response is paraphrased as follows: "If those people caught in the Hyatt were trapped for 365 days, and the skywalk fell only a few pieces at a time over that period, killing and maiming people slowly before their eyes, and they knew that someone was responsible for each piece of concrete dropped, but they could only get an occasional glance at who it was, then I guess that would be similar to what I experienced in Vietnam."

I have learned in my work with veterans, that it does not matter whether a man was drafted or enlisted in the army, the anxiety of landing on an airstrip in Vietnam seemed to be the same:

fear of being killed, and wondering if they would pass the ultimate test of manhood: "Will I be able to kill and perform under fire or will I freeze and be a coward?" Perhaps the similarity I have seen most amongst the men, was that regardless of the number of registered kills or missions a veteran was on, the fear of not measuring up to the masculine standard was most basic. This aspect fits with the humble-like response of most of the decorated American heroes in wartime: "I'm not a hero. I was just doing my job."

Most veterans experienced an initiation test by their peers who were also wondering if this FNG (Fucking New Guy) would be a trustworthy soldier. Although the initiation took many informal forms, one typical example is of a veteran with the tatoos and disposition of a stereotypical "biker." He described his experience as being told to move a pile of V.C. corpses which had been rotting for three to five days. While he lifted the first corpse, the chest and abdomen burst open and drenched his body with the greasy liquid of human intestines. Then he shared the feeling of humiliation, hearing his squad laughing at him as he vomited a few paces from the scattered corpse. In his gruff tone of voice, this veteran defended his squad's actions, saying it helped him prepare for his first kill and the rest of his tour of duty.

Perhaps what I have learned most from these veterans, no matter how tough, emotionally reserved and macho they strived to be, is that their sensitivity and compassion for life was the strongest I have ever witnessed in human beings. This was evident to me many times in my work, but was most obvious when I told my psychotherapy group of six veterans of my decision to resign and take a university position in Texas. Men who were routinely hostile towards me for helping them remember what they wanted to forget, were suddenly crying along with me, sharing our deep sense of loss. It is difficult to explain this sense of closeness and compassion from men that from all outside appearances are too macho to love. I know they have the capability to love and care deeply. Otherwise, they would not have their nightmares and memories, or their guilt, and they would not hurt like they do. Yet, because they are men, they have learned, like all war veterans, to suffer alone and in silence.

It is easy to see the costs of war in terms of death statistics. Since 1941, well over one-half million men have lost their lives protecting American society. The emotional scars of war are not as clearly visible. The point of this article is to examine war as an issue of masculinity in terms of the emotional costs that men endure because they are men.

My work at the Vietnam Post-Traumatic Stress Unit has helped me understand the emotional costs of fighting and surviving a war. Now I should explain that I am not a Vietnam combat veteran. My tour in the Air Force was stateside, so I never saw combat. This makes this article difficult for me to write because I know I can never fully do justice in explaining what it is like to be in combat; nor am I attempting to glorify or exploit any soldier's experience. I only write with the deepest sincerity because I believe that we as a society have to face the fact that war is not like the image we hold and what the media perpetuates. Thus, my understanding of war comes chiefly from those Vietnam combat veterans who have shared the emotional scars of their war experiences while in treatment in the Stress Unit.

It is difficult to imagine the sense of helplessness at not knowing if, when, or how your death could occur. Add to that, how it could be endured in that intensity for a full year, as in Vietnam (Marines' tour of duty lasted 13 months). I believe that under those circumstances, severe psychological changes took place. The change that I saw in my work, was to down-play the meaning of life. "It don't mean nothin'" was a very common expression in Vietnam as well as on the ward. Think about it. If life was seen as being so valuable, wouldn't its sudden loss be much more terrifying and frightening? So much of the behavior of combat soldiers was to psychologically convince themselves that life was meaningless. If losing a close friend is difficult to endure, realize that death in Vietnam was not experienced by crying at a hospital and then viewing the cleansed loved one at a wake. Many veteran's first encounter with the death of a friend was graphically viewed at the time it happened and during the confusion of battle.

One veteran's most traumatic event, which took weeks of painfully remembering it piece by piece, occurred when he and 13 others were on a secret mission in Cambodia, which made it impossible for them to have air support. His squad was ambushed. His best friend took an RPG (Rocket Propelled Grenade) in his upper chest, and his head came off. It is difficult to portray the fear and terror in this veteran's eyes during group psychotherapy, as he described his sensation of seeing the whole firefight in slow-motion and experiencing the head of his buddy fly slowly toward his own face, making whistling and gurgling noises as it passed by. And further memories of how another one of his buddies reacted to the ambush by picking up the dismembered arm of another soldier and using it as an imagined rifle; the thumb being the trigger.

In therapy, this veteran discussed with glassy eyes and shaking legs and arms, his recollection of hiding after the ambush and watching the laughing enemy dissect ten of his fellow soldiers' bodies (some while still alive) and placing the body parts in the middle of a circle of ten stakes; each stake with the head of each of his comrades. For this veteran, it took his great courage at being able to relive this memory dozens of times before he could see that a large piece of his life's rage was really his intense survival guilt, for not charging the enemy like a "real man" would have done, to avenge the slaughter of his squad. He felt less of a man for not doing so, and consequently very angry and ashamed for the 15 years between the event and his treatment. Fortunately, he came to realize that his attacking the enemy would have only resulted in 11 instead of 10 stakes in Cambodia, and though the memory is vivid and will haunt him forever, at least it is more bearable now.

Unfortunately, if this soldier's story seems too graphic or extreme, I have learned that stories like these are more the rule than the exception. There are many other stories that are similar, and many more that I believe most would consider more brutal. Therefore I emphasize my learning from those events that most of war is not portrayed in movies as accurately as I would like to see.

Almost every war movie has at least one scene where a rocket or bomb explodes close to one or two soldiers upon which they fly in the air several feet and land unconscious. In reality, the soldiers would lose their arms, legs and/or head, and the parts would be scattered across the battlefield and on other soldiers. The largest remains would be a torso that looks more like a blob of hamburger. Add the heavy smell of gunpowder and burning human flesh, the sight of blood and internal organs, and the sounds of screaming wounded, and the scene becomes a more accurate image of combat.

In a firefight, some soldiers would be panicking or frozen in fear (usually depending on how much combat experience they had) while others had learned from other firefights to effectively suppress their fear and grief to meet the task of battle. Usually after the firefight, survivors would place tourniquets around the stumps of the soldiers who lost their legs or arms, while lying to them, saying they were going to be okay and the choppers would come for them soon. That masculine training of repressing feelings certainly had it's utility there, while gathering the dead and body parts, putting them in body bags, and placing them in the chopper – moving like zombies and in silence.

Other realities of war encompass entering a village or clearing and finding the remains of other G.I.'s tied and hanging upside down by their ankles with their heads in baskets filled with rats, and others that died from strangling on their own dismembered genitalia. I recall a veteran, who was a dentist, report that his first week in Vietnam, he was given 20 bodies and 20 separate heads, with the task of matching the correct bodies with their appropriate heads through the use of dental records. He claims he and his men were somewhat successful, with this task taking only a few days and several trips to the bathroom to vomit.

It is not surprising, then, with the many hideous sights, sounds, and events in war, that retaliation occurred on both sides; soldiers feeling the grief and rage of personal loss desperately looking for revenge. This is nothing new. All the tortures and beheadings in Vietnam occurred in Korea, WWII and all previous wars. Yet, the shame of the experiences is a part of the psychological cost men pay for fighting wars. Studies indicate a large proportion of WWII veterans continue to suffer nightmares of their war experiences. Most WWII veterans report that they have learned after 40 years to live with their horrible memories. Yet these psychological costs men pay for fighting a war go unnoticed and unspoken. I have recently learned that Israeli strategists have removed their women combatants from the front lines, because their enemies feel it a disgrace to lose to a woman soldier and consequently would rather fight to the death. Wars continue to be fought by men, and the survivors pay the emotional costs for the rest of their lives.

Perhaps the best way to conclude is with a poem written by a veteran who posted his poem publicly on the ward; but protecting his anonymity will only allow me to list, as he has done, his initials – J.W.

A Warrior's Dream

Quiet jungle sounds, the gentle sway of palm fronds. Heat – so
tepid – so hot it's hard to breathe.
As I listen to the soft buzzing of the insects
Reality is shattered by the explosion of a
Bosch's hell
only this is a hell that is reality
and here, and now
The burning powder smell of screaming steel, and blood filled whiz
of jagged flesh ripping metal. Smashes against us – into us.
Ten yards ahead lie the pathetic bleeding remains of Rich &
Smokey amongst the rice stalks and larvae filled water

The cries of agony and pleas for death or mercy – I confuse the two
fall on ears that no longer hear,
and are seen by eyes that will never know again
the faces of those they loved.
Yet they are heard by me . . .
and are seen by me . . .
and still another night.
Ten years have only made the sounds and sights more clear, and if
possible more painful yet.
This is the freedom we so unknowingly fought for . . . and still
another night . . . I cry. **[56]**

Any man that
doesn't cry,
scares me a little bit.

General Norman Schwarzkopf

The Psychology Of War

Shepherd Bliss

The following is the second half of a keynote address delivered by Shepherd Bliss. The gathering was entitled: *"In Celebration of The New Emerging Male – Looking At Men's Roles And Men's Lives."*

I teach a course called the "Psychology of War." It's a course on war, not peace. Much of great art came from war: Tolstoy's *War and Peace*, Picasso's "Guernica," all those beautiful Greek statues. I just love them – the statues of the warriors, the male bodies. I was concerned when I taught this course that I'd only get peace activists. I was glad that they came and they were an important part of the class, but I also wanted to get some men who understood themselves as warriors. So I went on the radio and I talked about this course. Sure enough, the first time I taught it I got six veterans in the class. One man was currently in the United States Marine Corps. One guy had been an Israeli paratrooper. He introduced himself by saying, "I was very good at my work. I killed about a hundred men in combat." The woman next to him responded, "Gee, I couldn't even watch the Three Stooges on TV. They were too violent, and you're telling me that you killed other human beings."

One thing that was beautiful about the class was that we all told our stories. Through the telling of our stories we were healed. We did it in a non-judgemental way – no judgement at all. That was the ground rule. If you had some feeling about this man killing someone, go outside the class and deal with it. It was very important that safety for everybody be there. What happened was the stories began to change as we went into the class. They got more intimate.

For example, I remember a drill instructor in the class. For those of you who have seen the movie *An Officer and a Gentleman*, you remember that drill instructor, the black man; very strong. I liked him a lot. I thought he had a lot of heart. He was really there. Well, I had such a drill instructor in my class. I wasn't sure how I was going to handle him, 'cause he was used to being in charge. He'd gone from the Marines to being a professional baseball player. Then about the fourth day of class he talked about leaving the Marines after 15 years. He said, "The last group of men that I sent to 'Nam – 80% casualities." He said, "No, no – 80% fatalities." He said, "No, no. What I mean is that 80% of my boys died."

He just went into his heart and you could tell it by the language change. He loved those boys. The military was his family. There was strength in what he was saying that everybody in class understood. This man wasn't a killer. This was a man caught in an historical moment. Listen to the war stories, when they come up, and don't judge the man. Our storytelling was not in the bravado way. We didn't do that. We weren't cheering. Recontextualize the stories and reframe them. Perhaps you were beaten by your father – tell that story. Find someone to tell it to. Perhaps you killed somebody. Surely there are men here who have killed somebody, perhaps with their own hands. Don't judge that man. Understand what it is that got him to that moment of violence. And know that deep down in that man, at the base of that man and all men, is the love that connects us as brothers and to our sisters. How do we get back to that love?

On the last day of our "Psychology of War" class, the veterans came in uniform. I asked them to do that. I brought my uniform back. And we took a picture. For her class project, instead of doing a paper, one woman did a death costume. She took a death mask and she put it on and she wove – this beautiful weaver woman – wove into herself this death. Then we took a picture. There was so much harmony between these peace activists and these warriors. There was a sense of connection. That's what I'm calling for: a coming back together of the male community and a linking together with women. [57]

Where Are The Fathers?
Robert Nixon

"Where are the fathers?" That haunting question rang through my soul as I stood in the middle of the night over my little girl's bed after waking up from a nuclear nightmare. In the dream I had clearly seen the missiles releasing from the silos, was momentarily intrigued by their metallic power, and was clear that their leaving the earth was the end. I wondered quickly where my two girls were – at school or at the babysitter's. I was also clear that I was not wondering where they could be that would be safe, because I knew there was no such place. I just wanted to know where they were, and I knew that they would die. I did not have much feeling in the dream about them or their death; I was numb emotionally. But when I woke up I was sweating. I walked into their dark bedrooms – one is nine and the other is eleven – and gazed at them for a long, long time. One was uncovered and though it felt like a nearly absurd gesture after the helpless feelings of the dream, I pulled the cover up around her to warm her for the rest of the night. I knew that in the time it took me to have the dream, the reality could have happened. I felt unspeakably alone. Out of my mouth came the plea and the question, "Where are the fathers?" It was as if the question was not coming from me but rather through me.

I did not want to be standing there alone. Where are the men who will help me and put their arms out to protect my children? Where is the father in all of us men who will look at the death machine that we are building in the name of power, security and strength, and help to rip it down? What is happening to that archetypal energy that resides in the soul of us that is strong enough to face the forces that run against our children and families and enables us to stand up to them and truly protect our children against them? "Where are the fathers?" There is much written about the new male and rightly so, for the old models that may have worked before are not sufficient to meet the challenges of today. I propose that part of the new male is the new father. I am reminded of the section in *A Choice of Heroes* on fatherhood, describing the difference in bonding between the men who participated in their children's birth and those – most fathers before the 70's – who were not interested and not allowed to participate. Perhaps that is one of the basic differences; the older fathers, the current decision-makers, were not bonded to their children.

"*. . . studies documented that fathers who were involved in childbirth classes and childbirth itself felt more positive about the* *experience; . . . by the age of four weeks, infants respond differently to their fathers than to people outside the family. In other words, social science began to discover that a father-infant bond did exist – if only men would let it.*

"Fatherhood is moving back from the periphery to the center of many men's lives."

The new father has to be willing to enter into the world wherever he finds himself, and work to ensure that that world is giving his children the space to breathe, to choose to live. He has to look around the edges of the world in which his children find themselves and ask not only, is it good, but is it safe? And the answer he is going to come up with is no!

There is no community in this world, certainly not in the Northern Hemisphere, that is safe. Observe what happens when I say "because of the nuclear threat." Most of us turn off because it is too hard to look at on that level. But the news media keep me aware of it. Every day I see my children, and on some level am aware that their lives are in jeopardy because of the unwillingness of fathers to be fathers and to let our fury erupt at the system that so threatens the lives of our children.

I do not know the tactical answer. I do not know what organizational approaches to take to turn things around. I do feel that it will be the work of many years, perhaps the rest of our lives.

But the current call to manhood also is a call to stand and look at the apocalyptic straight on, and it may actually be in the looking that we attain our stature as men and as fathers. In the book *No Bar to Manhood*, Daniel Berrigan poses the question:

". . . whether or not the apocalyptic consciousness may . . . not bring an old man to his true greatness? May not such responsibility bring on a crisis, in which his soul . . . may stand purified and vindicated?"

So the potential holocaust, in this case seen in dream form, serves to deepen consciousness and call to fuller and more responsive and responsible life. The key is to look into and grasp the apocalypse rather than turn in terror from it.

I am also confident that if we as men, whether we have biological children or not, decide to act consistently as fathers/protectors, the course of aggression and particularly the nuclear arms madness will be turned around. What I, as a father, need is to know that there are other men whom I can depend on to help look after my children. I am committed to the best of my ability to look out for theirs. A man acting alone in the nuclear world cannot father effectively.

The image that comes to me is from the pioneer myth we got from watching cowboy and Indian movies as boys. When the attack on the wagon train was imminent, the shout would go out and the men would circle the wagons, both to fight off the attack, and to protect their families. Within the circles were campfires, cooking and the kids playing games, confident that although there were dangers without, the adults would take care of them. Putting aside the negative images of the various Indian nations, the image of circling the wagons against a common enemy and supporting each other in the effort to survive is the type of image that comes to me in the current frontier we are on. All nations are within the circle now and the enemy is not so easy to define. It's more complex but not less threatening. Though the territory and enemy are new, we do have the ability to circle to meet them. We have rich imagery to pull from. We have deep power that we can draw from to protect our most precious cargo. We can do it in unison, probably with many circles.

The threat of nuclear destruction is so imminent – a computer error away – that it demands our attention no matter what other important commitments we all have. What if, when a child asked the question, "Where are our fathers?" the child could say without hesitation that they are working to protect us? What if they were clear that men – fathers – were there as a buffer between them and the threat? What if they knew that their providers were also their protectors?

Fathers have always had the role of protectors to their children. This has not always been carried out. But now with the nuclear threat, even those who want to provide the safe space for children to grow up feel inadequate. And alone we are. Safety is not something that we can provide within the walls of our homes. And the children know that.

As Thomas Merton writes in *Raids on the Unspeakable*:

"It is supremely important for us not to yield to despair, abandon ourselves to the 'inevitable' and identify ourselves with 'them.' Our duty is to refuse to believe that their way is 'inevitable' . . .

"When we 'stand by' we try to think of ourselves as independent, as standing on our own two feet. It is true that as an intellectual (having the consciousness) we ought to stand on our two feet – but one cannot learn to do this unless he has first recognized to what extent he requires the support of others. And it is our business to support one another . . ."

As I read in the morning paper of the Senate approving the MX system, I wonder again, "Where are the fathers?" The games they are playing have repercussions in the lives of our children. Is it a surprise to anyone that teen suicides are rising at what health statisticians consider epidemic rates?

When the question came through me, "Where are our fathers?" I, myself, was also being asked the question, and it continues to rise in me. I share the question with you. Let yourself be asked (whether you have biological children or not). As long as children and nuclear threat remain, so will the question.

It is helpful for me to identify the era in which we are raising our children. It is the era of survivors. The fact that I dreamt the dream, rather than suffered it, makes me a survivor. We all are. We are survivors of miscalculation, radar misreadings, computer error, nuclear accidents and political stupidities. We are all survivors, and there are certain patterns we share with survivors who have gone before us on smaller scale holocausts, and from whom we can learn. In the *Life of the Self*, Robert Jay Lifton describes five psychological patterns that characterize the survivor:

1. *An indelible death image and death anxiety. It often includes a loss of a sense of invulnerability.*
2. *Death guilt – why I survive and they didn't.*
3. *Desensitization or psychic numbing.*
4. *Suspicion of nurturance.*
5. *Struggle for inner form or formulation, the quest for significance in one's death encounter and remaining life experience."*

Dismal as the first four elements are, Lifton concludes this section, writing:

"The painful wisdom of the survivor can, at least potentially, become universal wisdom . . . . What I am suggesting is that to 'touch death' and then rejoin the living can be a source of insight and power."

Most of us cannot hold the image of nuclear holocaust before our consciousness for long. We try to avoid it. As fathers, what we cannot forget is that our children have sixty plus years ahead of them that should be full and joyful. So the response to the nightmare is not the denying of it, nor is it the observing of it, but in some degree, the mastery of it, giving it a place in our imagination from where it can evoke choices on our part. We need the potential of the final holocaust to deepen and free the imagination for the leap it must make.

It is with trust and deep hope that I write this and stand as a father among fathers, a man among men, and a brother among brothers.

Additional Reading

Daniel Berrigan, *No Bar to Manhood*, Bantam Books, New York, New York, 1970.

Mark Gerzon, *A Choice of Heroes*, Houghton Mifflin Co., Boston, Massachusetts, 1982.

Robert Jay Lifton, *The Life of the Self*, Simon & Schuster, New York, New York, 1976.

Thomas Merton, *Raids on the Unspeakable*, New Directions, New York, New York, 1966. **[58]**

FATHERS

You have rich milk
For your children's soul
Feed them
That the earth might become
A more compassionate place
For all of us.

From: *Realm of Nurturing Men*
Jane Evershed

CHAPTER XIV

THE NEW FATHERS

My Child's Heart, written after Mencius:
The great man is he who does not lose his child's heart.
Steve Grubman

My childhood heart was full of innocence and love,
Wonderment and excitement and enthusiasm
About the world.
I loved the silent dance of butterflies
And the cushion of tall grass beneath my head.
I dreamed under blue sky and green tree.
I kicked along the beach
And knew the earth was really flat,
that England stood just beyond the horizon.
Just go beyond, you'll see,
The waves would bring me there.
Angels visited me for my afternoon nap
On the arm of sun-rays.
I read of dinosaurs and said
I'll be an archeologist
Between dreams of dancing, singing, playing,
Riding, Hoping, Loving.
My heart swelled as my mind grew with dreams and plans.
Even now.

I marvel at her being,
Simply:
At how she touches me when I begin to think

What life was before her.
She shows me life again – sometimes for the first time –
When we feed the ducks and gulls and sparrows at the cove.
Her hug is as a rainbow-cloud must be:
She is brightness and light,
Holding me with no strings.
Her laugh is easy, fluid and catching:
Oh, to keep hold!
I learn from her question-answers of the poetry that is pre-literate:
When I pick a flower, does it hurt?

When my old cat-friend died,
And I wept again as I walked in to tell her,
She held my moist cheeks in her hands, and advised:
"Let her go now, Daddy."
A note in her lunch box is cause for a chuckle,
And a piggy back the wrong way is a lesson
in navigation over art work, blocks, and other stuff.
When she aches, I hurt.
The threat of harm charges me with dread and anger.
A fever burns my throat.
Her sadness too.

Last December,
Among the crowds of hurried, harried shoppers,
I danced along Market Street with her.
Understand: I love to dance.
I dance everywhere I can.
I've danced in Washington Square
At Tufts
On the sixty-third floor in front of Detroit,
And on the steps of the Art Institute
Under a Chicago autumn moon.
But:
On that special day, on Market Street,
As she and I polka-waltzed through the crowds,
Chanting our new song,
I knew this was an original for me.
Never before had I taken so much

> *Pleasure and happiness to others.*
> *On that cold and dreary day,*
> *She and I put on a show for the tired-still,*
> *Now smiling, shoppers of Philadelphia.*
> *As I watched her grin*
> *And felt her bounce in my arms,*
> *As I heard her repeat my silly-song lyrics and tune,*
> *I knew:*
> *If Mencius had met her, he might have written:*
> *The fortunate father is he*
> *Whose child's heart finds his open.* **[59]**

❋   ❋   ❋

The latest commentary I've gotten on first-time dadhood came from a friend after he heard the news from his wife.

"Be prepared to have your patience taxed as its never been taxed before; know that you're not going to sleep much for six months; get used to having your hands in baby shit, *a lot . . .*"

He then went on to gloat about what's it's like to be recognized and responded to by your baby, how fascinating it is to watch the changes that come weekly. And then he said something I've never heard a dad say in quite this way: "It's the most creative thing you'll ever do in your life."

I was really touched by that. Isn't that a fabulous thing to say?

Let's turn to others who have some wonderful things to say on the subject. These men are the "new fathers" – the light at the end of the tunnel.

The Birth Of A Father
Martin Greenberg, M.D.

Companionship: Union of the Spirits

As a new father I felt preoccupied and absorbed in my own infant, buffeted by emotions and forces over which I had no control. My son had a powerful impact on me, and I found myself acutely sensitive to him as well as to what I imagined was expected of me as a father. What really shocked me was the realization that I had never completely understood parents until I became a parent myself.

The event of fatherhood is a momentous occurrence in the life cycle of a man. It inevitably triggers off strong emotions – emotions that are multifaceted and often tumultuous. I want to emphasize the importance of the human response – the far-reaching ramifications of the father's interaction with his newborn and the impact this has on his feelings about his infant, his wife, and perhaps most significantly, about himself. The process of becoming a father is a gradually unfolding phenomenon, similar to the pregnancy but running on its own timetable. At times there is chaos, at times anger, and at times joy. But the process continues ever forward and in the end reaps a bountiful harvest. The birth of a child can be a process of reawakening for all fathers, increasing the breadth and depth with which we view the world.

Viewing my infant son's birth was an overwhelming experience for me. But it was when he first began to smile, and shortly thereafter to coo, at around two months of age, that I really felt he was beginning to respond to me as a person. As his face brightened when he saw me, I felt my own world light up. If I was feeling dejected and in the doldrums, his smile illuminated my mood and washed away the gloom. It compelled me to reach out to him, to hug and hold him. The realization that he was reacting specifically to my face even at this early age was very exciting to me. It was at this point that our relationship became more and more a two-way stream, and our companionship began to grow and flourish.

I began taking Jonathan for strolls when he was very young. Using a modified baby sling, I carried him against my chest and abdomen until he was four months old and thereafter carried him on my shoulders in a backpack. Our walks together became treasured moments during which I shared my thoughts and feelings with him, a process that bound us ever closer together. Jonathan became my "confidante." I talked to him about things we saw – about the sky, the ocean, the trees, the birds. And I told him what I was feeling, when I was happy and when I was sad. When Jonathan smiled and cooed in return, I felt that he somehow understood and accepted me in spite of my faults; and I felt elated by this unique sharing. At times like these I knew that he was very much aware of my presence.

In the hushed still of the forest where we walked, the regular resonance of his breathing resembled a drum beating in time to the sounds of life around us. The rustling of leaves, stirred by an occasional puff of wind; the song of a robin overhead; and the distant murmur of a brook as it wound its way over impeding rocks coalesced to form an all-embracing presence. Everything enveloping us reflected the rhythm of my walk with Jonathan, and I felt in tune with him and with the beauty of nature about us. It was on these occasions that I felt an unusual sense of peace and tranquility. I experienced an overwhelming love for my newborn son, and I felt that we were linked by a bond that was strong enough to transcend the ages. It was as if our companionship had entered into another plane, and there was now a union of our spirits.

At this point I would feel rejuvenated. I had become exquisitely sensitive to the world around us – to the natural ambience – to colors, smells, sights, and sounds. Although I might have taken that path many times in the past, my sensations now revealed things I never knew existed.

Sometimes as I talked to Jonathan it seemed that I was really talking to myself, and I would feel in touch with my own center. His presence helped me break out of my adult world in which everything was ordered and set, and allowed me to experience the world of childhood, where everything is free and spontaneous. Past memories, long since forgotten, of earlier years and relationships with my own family would surface, effortlessly, to my awareness. It was as if Jonathan was the door, the entryway, to my experiencing a new and different aspect of myself. At the same time, I felt even more intimately connected with him.

The Hospital: Asserting Your Needs

An increasing number of hospitals have become sensitive to the needs of the parents and encourage father participation in labor and delivery. However, there are still hospitals that, without realizing it, encourage fathers to blunt their feelings toward their babies. They do this by denying that the father exists. Would you believe that even now, in our enlightened age, there are still many hospitals in the Western World that regard the notion of a father's presence in the delivery room with disapproval? Even when the father is present, he may be ignored or treated as an intruder, and the newborn may not be offered to him. The notion of the family bonding and the opportunity for the whole family to be together for several hours immediately after the birth may be entirely neglected.

An outsider looking in might readily assume that this hospital policy is designed to isolate the father from his wife and child, to encourage him to deny the birth experience and the existence of his baby and thus gradually become detached from the family unit. If the destruction of the family was the hospital's goal, it would be hard to imagine its being accomplished more effectively.

Five hours after the birth, Jonathan was brought into Claudia's room for the first time. But the nurse became alarmed when she saw me and asked me to leave. She said that fathers were not allowed in the same room with the babies on the first night after the birth – hospital policy.

It was only after I made a special request of the head nurse that I was allowed to stay with them for twenty minutes. It wasn't as much time as we wanted, but at least it was something.

I was happy that I had not given up when the nurse told me to leave, and I felt grateful to the supervisor for granting my request. It was only later that I asked myself why it should have been so difficult to spend a small period of time with my wife and child. Why should it be such a big deal for us to be together as a family? [60]

Hints And Guesses
Kent Hoffman

"There are only hints and guesses, hints followed by guesses."
T.S. Eloit

I used to think I was right. But I was wrong. Then I changed. I got right. Which, it turns out was wrong. Also. So then I figured it all out and finally got it right.

That was five years ago; I've changed a lot since then.

"If it ain't fun, it's the wrong revolution."
Bumper Sticker

One cannot hope to right this world until one has learned to enjoy it."
Garrison Keillor

For one thing, I've taken the "I'd rather be suffering" bumper sticker off my Volkswagen. Now don't get me wrong. I'm still an easy mark when it comes to self-seriousness. It's just that "grim" no longer holds quite the appeal that it once did. You know – grim: "As long as there is suffering in the world, I have no right to experience enjoyment." Grim.

"Underneath all his preoccupations with sex, society, religion, etc. (all the staple abstractions which allow the forebrain to chatter), there is, quite simply, one tortured beyond endurance by the lack of tenderness in the world."
Lawrence Durrell

Tenderness. Like the newborn child who miraculously birthed into my arms four weeks ago today. Tiny body – terrified body, screaming at the top of his lungs for someone to hold him close. Tenderly – safely – for the longest time.

I've got a hunch. It's a hunch about the need at the heart of all of us. Each of us. And it's a hunch about why things continue to stay the same the harder we work at making them different. It has to do with being held. Deeply – tenderly – like a baby. Held with arms. Held with laughter. Held with tasty food. Held with song. Held with long walks on this good, good earth. Held with gratitude.

My hunch is that we all need more holding than we currently get – more than we've ever gotten. We. They. Adults. Children. Republicans. Russians. Protestors. Neighbors. Enemies. The whole damn circus. But something gets in the way.

Worry. Worry gets in the way. (By worry I mean activity that has nothing to do with holding. I mean that particular brand of busyness mixed with an often unconscious fear that overextends us, uncenters us . . . so much so that enjoyment seems superfluous and gratitude can wait another day. Tell-tale hints: burn-out, self-righteousness, bitterness, never enough time, "If I don't do it, it won't be done," "If you don't see it my way, we won't get there," laughter that comes at the expense of others . . . or ourselves, etc.). Worry. The more things change, the more they stay the same.

(The new physics teaches us that we can) . . ." experience the cosmos as interconnected. Mind and matter, near and far, small and great – they are all part of a larger unity, and unbreakable bonds join them all. It is as though each entity were linked to all other entities by fine piano wires, and a cause set in motion by the thought, word or deed of any being sent vibrations shuddering through the whole system, leaving nothing quite as it was before."
Robert Ellwood

"The entire ocean is affected by a pebble."
Blaise Pascal

I have yet another hunch. Worry has weight. My guess is that each moment of worry weighs one pound. My guess is that on top of all our good deeds we place our worries, our business, our unheld fears. And my hunch is that without being held (without truly savoring that next beer; without drinking in this moment of sunlight; without walking openfaced into that falling rain; without feeling the force of those eyes across the table; without being rocked like a baby again and again), without a deep and continuous sense of delight in being alive – all of our wonderful and necessary external deeds are weighted down and rendered ineffective.

"There is no way to peace, peace is the way."
A.J. Muste

"Drinking a bowl of green tea, I stopped the war."
Paul Reps

Peace. Not that this is ever easy. But it may be simple. It may be as simple as being held . . . and holding. Perhaps once we are willing to be held, we may begin to hold this world in a new way. We may begin to hold this tiny globe and *everything* upon it with the same tenderness, and even delight, with which we hold a baby. (Sometimes she laughs, sometimes she cries. Sometimes she is sick, sometimes she is healthy.)

I'm only guessing. But I'm not kidding. It may just be that without delight, there is only darkness. It may just be, as the saying goes, that angels are able to fly because they take themselves so lightly.

I don't know what your destiny will be, but one thing I do know: the only ones among you who will be really happy are those who have sought and found how to serve.

Albert Schweitzer **[61]**

Male Parenting: Beyond The Female Agreement
A Psychological Perspective
Robert Sayers

Parenting historically has been the domain of women. And today, even with the great numbers of women entering the work force, the *emotional parent* still is the mother. Society has merely expanded the male's traditional role as teacher and provider to include "mother's helper." This motherhood mentality is the female agreement.

One barrier to achieving balanced emotional parenting is our description of "good" parenting and young children's needs – nurturing, sensitivity, understanding, affection, and sympathy, all "female" qualities. Men are raised to be different, socially, so "good" parenting – mothering – goes against the father's masculinity, objectivity, ambition, forcefulness, competitiveness, dominance and assertiveness. These different expectations create a dilemma for men as they try to stay involved as fathers. As fathers seek greater involvement in childrearing, we must redefine the qualities of a "good" parent so they include those traditionally thought to be male.

We also must reassess what children need in order to develop as complete persons. An imbalance now exists for children raised only by women, or by men trying to exhibit "mothering behavior." The lack of a male parenting perspective deprives these children of half their potential psycho-sexual personality and cognitive development during critical years.

From these formative beginnings, children grow to adulthood. In becoming parents they rely on their own family experiences to develop their own style of parenting. The rigid roles of mothers and fathers, differentiated and highly specialized, have created strong expectations and barriers to sharing and mutual understanding.

As a result, men raised solely by women often experience strong barriers to parenting. They may expect women (mothers) to do the parenting and, more important, may doubt their own parenting skill and defer to the female as the primary parent.

Most men lack the *model* of an involved father in their own childhood, and so mistrust their own involvement to the point of feeling guilty if they "waste" too much time just being with their children.

"When I play, I really play hard – I have a difficult time sharing feelings. I'm really most comfortable when I'm by myself. I feel guilty and restless when I'm not working either at the job or doing something around the house."

A father may feel he is being sensitive and supportive when he lets the mother take charge of critical situations instead of sticking with them himself. He also may have learned that intervening provokes criticism from the more involved mother or causes her discomfort. As a result, fathers often develop a habit of *withdrawing* from situations involving their children. Over time, fathers mistrust their own parenting style as distinct from and complementary to the mother's.

The reason fathers typically are uninvolved in the emotional support of their older children is their lack of skills in this kind of support, never having practiced it when their children were little. Also, as the mother and infant develop greater familiarity, the father becomes more distant, detached and uninvolved.

"I took a week off after the delivery, and my wife and I shared taking care of the baby, and we both felt we were able to

respond to the baby's needs. Now that I'm back at work, I'm feeling somewhat behind in knowing what her cues mean."

This imbalance in parenting roles affects women, too, who are expected to be the knowledgeable, prepared parent. Put in the awkward position of always being involved, the mother is the one who develops the "third ear" and "eyes in back of her head." Even if she isn't there when something happens, she feels she should have anticipated it and prepared in some way. Because of their experience with males in their childhood, women are likely to have a distorted perspective of men's abilities as parents. Female children may see fathers as untouchable, heroic or symbolic figures; as mothers, they may have difficulty trusting males as parents.

Together these situations make *giving* responsibility difficult for women and *taking* responsibility difficult for men. As long as children are raised to be adults by mothers only, we will perpetuate this psychological imbalance that inhibits both men's and women's support of each other as parents.

To understand male parenting, we must begin to accept the fact that males and females are different. We must unlearn what we know and what we trust.

"Because men are traditionally more involved in social and institutional roles and settings, the male's identity is more related to society's rules and rituals. Men as fathers need similar types of settings to validate and support their new parenting roles. Men need male peer support to "buck the social tide" as they become involved fathers. They need male peer involvement in establishing new rules and rituals for male parenting."

Because most of us have been raised by only half this system, we are a society that responds primarily to only half of its human potential. We have learned to trust, love, and depend on the external female myths and qualities, and mistrust and reject the external male myths and qualities. Much of the "crisis" in families today is the result of this imbalance; men and women struggling to express different parts of themselves but lacking the understanding and skills to support each other in their struggles as changing parents.

Research on male parenting to date has only examined the father's relationship to his infant, and suggests that fathers tend to be more arousing, tactile, physical and stimulating in their play than mothers. Playful and physical, the fathers engage their infants in "idiosyncratic" (creative) games that use novel stimuli and settings. Mothers, on the other hand, tend to be more fluid, verbal and containing with their infants, and engage in visual or verbal games that are more "conventional" and smoothly modulated. Mothers also engage infants more often in "attention maintaining" activities.

"Fathers more often pick up the baby and engage in playful interaction. Mothers pick up the baby and hold it."

These different behaviors reflect the differences between male and female parenting. Female nurturing – or what today is called parenting – means *caring* for the child to enhance its security. Activity is secondary to the caring. Holding and rocking are the primary levels of female nurturing; meeting a child's need to explore and learn is at the secondary level of female nurturing. While the female allows the child to feel surrounded and secure in the world and in himself, the male allows the child to see and experience and differentiate himself from the surrounding world. The primary level of male nurturance might be responding, challenging or instructing, and the secondary level of male nurturance holding or merging with the child.

Most mothers and fathers have found themselves in this kind of situation: A child is playing on a jungle-gym set and falls into a sandbox below. The father's first response in this situation would be to run to the child, bend down and say something like, "Wow! That was really scary falling from that bar. Are you all right?" The secondary level of male response would be to merge with the child's experience by holding or physically caring for him. The mother in the same situation might reverse this response. She would first run to the child, bend down, and touch and hold him. As a secondary response she might say something like, "I'll bet that was really scary. Do you want to take a couple of minutes to catch your breath?"

Men and women have within themselves a sense of male nurturance and female nurturance that results in different thoughts, feelings and behavior patterns. These affect the way they perceive, approach, and respond to situations as parents. Exploring these patterns offers parents an opportunity to enhance their relationship, their parenting, and their children's lives. **[62]**

Being A Daddy
Yevrah Ornstein

It's her red hair, her "crowning glory" that turns heads. But it's her spirit that captivates me.

"Tell me about The Three Bears, Daddy," she said after breakfast this morning. She's two and one-half years young and precious and I am a proud fool. She's napping now, pooped out from running through pasture grasses that equal her height, playing hide-and-seek and exploring her still-new, wide-eyed world.

"Where you going to be, Daddy?" she wants to know as I put her down for her nap. She's mastered the art of speaking audibly through a pacifier. "On the porch, Sweetheart, right nearby," I assure her, as I stroke her beautiful hair and kiss her.

Sometimes I can't believe we all started out this way, and I think of all the men who have been denied one of life's greatest joys – being a daddy.

Savannah's mother and I provided her ingredients: a broad range of traits and inclinations, a palette of considerable characteristics. Savannah gets to choose those she wants to explore, highlight and create with. Some are accentuated, some ignored and some hang out on the back burner in the "maybe" department.

As her parents, we have the major say for the first five years or so, and we pay great attention to our decisions about Savannah. It is so easy to hurt a child. Perhaps I'm overly sensitive because my own childhood was so painful. In my childhood home I felt ignored and overshadowed. One repugnant braggart of a brother, another brother a superstar athlete, Dad always pissed off and remote, Mom intimidated. *The dog was the only one with any proprieties or a semblance of balance.* And me – reclusive at home and wild on the outside, a stranger to my own family.

"You're hypersensitive," they kept telling me, over and over, and now, when Savannah feels happy or silly or sad or angry or scared, I am so careful, so very careful not to invalidate her feelings. "Are you hungry, Savannah? Would you like some cereal?" Savannah was discovering her newfound freedom to make decisions. "Yes, Daddy – no, I don't want any cereal. I want a banana. No cereal! No, I'm not hungry! Yes . . . umm, no (angrily)!" Then an outburst of tears. I picked her up and held her close to me. "I understand, Savannah, it's okay . . . I understand . . ."

Robert Bly tells a story about being in church with his wife, children and mother. His son was (understandably) bored and restless. There are some hushed words from grandmother to grandson, the boy replies, "But I'm bored," and grandmother says, "No you're not." That's when Robert sees red. His heart pounds, his eyes flash as he recalls years of invalidation, and he feels a volcanic fury rising as he hears beneath the lines what his mother is really saying to his little boy, "No, you're not feeling what you're feeling."

Robert had another story – even better. There's a fight with his brother, intervention by Mom, and Robert screams, "I hate him!" "You don't hate him," Mom says, "he's your brother." Robert brings the house down with, "I wanted to kill the fucker with a baseball bat!"

What a need there is for our feelings to be validated, and how rarely this is done. So I think about this with Savannah. When she was a little over two, she went through a brief period of the "terrible two's." She cried often and was frequently distraught over little things that hadn't bothered her before. "Savannah," I said, "I know you are feeling bad and that's okay." I tried in every way to let her know that her upsets were okay with me. No judgements, no demands for her to be otherwise. I wanted my message to be that I respected what she was feeling, that I was with her through it all, and that I loved and supported her.

Of course I made some mistakes, too. Perhaps I was too lenient at times. But, by and large, Savannah's mini-storms were traversed in minutes, and departed as quickly as they had come.

How much easier strong feelings are to deal with when they're allowed to be.

*The ultimate test of
humankinds conscience
is our willingness to
sacrifice something
today for a future
generation whose words of
thanks will never be heard.
This is a test we now
must take and pass.*

Gaylord Nelson
Founder of Earth Day

CHAPTER XV

RITES OF PASSAGE

A Vision Quest

Yevrah Ornstein

There is much in this book that focuses upon "the wound." You've heard me and other men write about the pain of absentee fathers, the down side of competition, the need for a clean separation between sons and mothers, the horrors of war, etc.

Along with the revelation and giving voice to the hurt men feel, suffer and endure, I think it equally important to examine where we go from here.

I'm basically a nuts and bolts kind of guy; got a problem, do something about it if I can.

The latter portion of this book pays more attention to the light at the end of the tunnel, our hopes for a brighter today and tomorrow.

A couple of years ago I received a call from Michael saying he wanted to lead an all-male vision quest. He had taken over the reins of an organization called Rites of Passage founded by Steven Foster and Meredith Little.

Michael had heard of my work with *The Men's Journal* and called me in hopes of doing some recruiting/networking. We worked out a trade. I'd put an ad in the *Journal* in exchange for participating in the vision quest.

To be honest, I had heard about vision quests years before, had always been drawn and fascinated by them and also felt hesitant to venture into what I thought would be an ordeal, as in hardship.

The time was ripe, and I told Michael he had a deal.

Rites of passage, as created by Native Americans, served many important functions. Young Indian males began their initiation around the age of thirteen. I'm a bit embarrassed to say, I sampled mine at age 34.

Our small group of men met with Michael and Richard, our guides, several times before our quest. It was through them that we were introduced to the meaning and format of the journey we were about to embark upon.

We went to a privately owned retreat center located on the coast just north of San Francisco. After our morning preparations we were to find our own spot; a location hopefully arrived at intuitively, and there draw a circle, a boundary around ourselves. We were encouraged to stay awake for 24 hours. We had begun our fasts that morning and were to remain in solitude within our circles.

The vision quest is an opportunity to invoke a vision, to ask for inner guidance, to pay heed to nature's wisdom, and to sit with life's meaning and purpose.

It's your quest – your focus.

Upon returning the next morning, we spent time individually with Michael and Richard to ask questions, if there were questions to ask, and to hear from them their sense of who we are and receive counsel. For two men who barely knew me, I was amazed by their intuitiveness and thankful for their advice.

From there we entered a sweat lodge we had built. Glowing red rocks that had been placed in a fire outside were brought in periodically and water sprinkled over them. I have been in sweats, saunas and steam rooms before, but never have I experienced such intense temperatures as in that womb-like enclosure.

There's a term used by fighter pilots called the outer envelope. It's the limit, the edge, the border of endurance of the man and his machine. I was face to face with my outer envelope.

Inside, Michael led us through round after round of traditional ceremonies laden with symbolic meaning. This was a time of purification.

I'm finding it difficult to write about what happened in there because I feel somewhat lost in trying to convey the profundity and dearness of many of the things that happened personally and between us.

Sometimes a voice within whispers, this is not meant to be revealed – contain . . . contain.

> *. . . may I tell them what the stars were saying?*
> *You may, but you won't be able to.*
> *Why not?*
> *Because, before you can, the words must take root inside you.*
> *But I want to tell them – all of them. I want to sing them what*
> *the voices sang. Then everything would come right again,*
> *I think.*
> *If that's what you really want, Momo, you must learn to wait.*
> *I don't mind waiting.*
> *I mean, wait like a seed that must slumber in the earth before*
> *it can sprout. That's how long the words will take to grow*
> *up inside of you. Is that what you want?*
> *Yes, she whispered.*
> *Then sleep, said Professor Hora, gently passing his hand*
> *across her eyes. Sleep!*
> *And Momo heaved a deep, contented sigh and fell asleep.*
> **[63]**

After the sweat, we shared a light meal. All of these experiences, both shared and solitary, enhanced our feelings of brotherhood, friendship and compassion.

The river ran deep, for here were primary ingredients for soulful bonding.

The rite is a two-day experience and the most important thing I can say about that experience is that I have never, ever felt as vulnerable as I did when it was over. The fasting, the fatigue, the extreme temperatures, the psychic components and intentions all contributed to stripping me bare of my day-to-day armor.

I felt a profound sense of brotherhood to the men I was with, and I felt privileged to witness, be present with their most intimate revelations and in some cases, deepest grief. The words are too shallow to express the feelings, the bonding, the humanity I felt.

Yes, that's the closest I can come: feeling our humanity.

In the days that followed, it was with great sadness that I was acutely aware of my armor, my unfortunate, perceived need to protect myself from others, returning, piece by piece by piece. I felt the weight of each shielding as my body resumed its previous stance.

In my time with Michael and Richard I told them of what it was like for me to be devoid of worldly attachments. Late in the evening, perhaps halfway through that sleepless night, I was struggling to fight off sleep. It was extremely difficult. One's movement is restricted and I was quite cold as a thick blanket of fog crept in for its nightly visitation. The boredom was almost unbearable.

And then something happened and I crossed over to the other side.

In talking with my guides, Michael said something quite piercing and true: "All the luxuries and comforts put us to sleep, they deaden us."

Yes, it's true.

I am considering doing a two-week rite come spring, for I remember vividly what it was like to be . . . free.

> *. . . the new seer aims to be free.*
> *And freedom*
> *has the most devastating implications.*
> *Among them is the implication that*
> *warriors must purposely seek change.*

Don Juan/Carlos Castenada

So getting back to the nuts and bolts approach, here's an outstanding step-by-step guideline for creating a rite of passage, by an individual imminently qualified to do so.

Toward An
Adequate Rite Of Passage Into Manhood
Steven Foster

Modern American males possess few meaningful, ceremonial means of formally marking their passage from boyhood to manhood. What our culture does provide (high school commencement, driver's license, the armed services, higher education, voting rights, drinking rights, employment, the age of 21, possible marriage and fatherhood) can hardly be said to comprise a coherent rite of passage.

Now that nearly 50% of American marriages end in divorce, the father and mother must prepare their manchild for adulthood separately, in different homes, with often contradictory values. Sometimes, the influence of the father in the upbringing of his son is negligible or nil. Sometimes, the sexual passage, perhaps the single most important adult initiation, is ignored, avoided, or distorted by the parents. The young man is left to piece together the meaning of his sexuality with his peers and cultural "aids" such as the mass media.

In attempting to remedy this by designing a meaningful rite of passage into manhood, we must be aware that a modern rite of passage does not contain the full social force of a traditional one. At the present time our culture does not validate or focus on such rites. For a modern passage ceremony to gain the full power of an ancient one, the very drift of our culture toward secular materialism would have to be diverted. The young would have to grow up knowing, even as little tads, that they were getting ready for their rite of passage into manhood. But given the reality of our culture, we can only start with what we have and work to create the best model possible under the circumstances.

The Components Of An Adequate Model

Before describing a model rite in detail, I will mention a few key elements whose importance must be understood. The basic dynamic of a rite of passage is described by an anthropological formula that underlies all passage ceremonies. First depicted by Arnold van Gennep, this formula divides such rites into three phases: an end (severance from childhood), a middle (threshold) and a beginning (incorporation into manhood). In other words, a rite of passage begins with an ending and ends with a beginning.

The Heart Of The Experience – The liminal (or threshold) phase, the central experience of the rite, is always performed in a secluded, wild zone, away from the encroachments of other humans. Within the sacred threshold enclosure, the boy becomes acquainted with his real Mother, symbolized by that part of himself known as the goddess. Through her, he senses his true place on earth and his true place in his body. She will show him the image of his own fear of death reflected in the natural world around him. The candidate's power place on Mother Earth will serve as both a womb and a tomb, a place of birth for the man and a place of death for the boy, in the mystery of the natural world. There he will learn the challenge of being a man, a son of the Mother, and a brother to all the things on the earth. He will emerge from the split husk of his childhood with the goddess at his right shoulder. The ritual birth of a man must take place here, in the wilderworld of his true home. The boy must learn that his Mother cares for and rewards those who care for and respect her. He cannot learn this sitting in an enclosed room. He leaves the comfortable placenta of boyhood and enters the all-powerful world of the goddess. She visits with him in the winds; she shakes him in her fist of thunder. She blinds him with her lightening eyes. But mostly she blesses him with the birth of herself within him as his own eternal, internal guide.

Taboo And Trial – A rite of passage always includes one or more ordeals or trials. The boy's experience of the trial is the formal confirmation of his readiness to take on the role of manhood. Though threshold trial models are many and diverse, certain taboos or means of being tried are common to most. One is the trial of aloneness or solitude. The boy is denied the support and comfort of others and is left alone in a wild place for extended periods of time. With no one to go to, he is forced to deal with outward circumstances by discovering inner resources of strength and resolve. Without other human eyes to judge him, the candidate will watch himself "be." Apart from the accoutrements of his boyhood life, he learns what is essential to him and what is not. The closed door of his heart opens to the beauty and mystery of the natural world around him. He becomes aware of, and communicates with, his natural relations – the other creature children of his Mother. Another restriction almost universally practiced is the prohibition of food. Among ceremonial tools, fasting is one of the oldest and finest. The candidate's psyche is opened to orchestration by the elements and rhythms of the natural world. Sunrise is his meat and noon is his wine. The dark wind sets a banquet for him. Although his physical strength wanes, another kind of strength gathers within him: the silent, immovable strength of the great mountains. Without ballast in his belly, he orients himself to the harmony and proportion of his Mother, compensating for loss of strength by applying the muscle of spirit. The goddess rushes into the breach and teaches him about surrender. A man who does not know the power of surrender does not possess true power.

Male Midwives – One of the most important components in any model of an adequate rite of male passage is the presence of older men, or elders, who supervise and enrich the progress of the young men through the ceremonial birth canal. The older men help the younger men to bring themselves forth. They are not there to answer questions, but to ask them. They work to enable their charges to give birth to answers of their own, to know themselves. The midwives are exclusively male, because the time has come for the boys to become men, to live in, to respect, and to accept the men's world. A father must not be the principal midwife to his son, as the past often shadows them with too many habits for the father to be an effective teacher or the son an attentive learner.

Discipline And Work – The classic male archetype is unaccustomed to self-indulgence. He has learned to accept hardship as his lot. He does not brag of his harsh life nor does he secretly hope this woman will pity him. Any passage rite for men must include components of hard work and self-discipline. The candidates must be expected to be part of the crew, to pull their own weight. Hence, the young men facing adulthood must be gathered together within a communal order where each has his work, and does it, as part of the preparation for the passage. They must be expected to accept the discipline that communal living brings and to seek the joy that comes with the exercising of self-control and the intimate knowledge of the meaning of work.

Sexual Instruction – Sexual instruction and advice on marriage is traditionally a part of ceremonies of passage into manhood. The importance of a young man coming to understand and accept the power of his own sexuality cannot be underestimated. Any ceremony of passage into adulthood must take into account the young man's sexual growth and relationships with women (or men, if he is gay or bisexual). Open, honest, adult sexual education would seem necessary and appropriate. Supervised by wise, qualified male elders, such education might also include older women who can present the issue from the feminine point of view. Without the woman's input, the candidate's sexual education would only be half complete.

Giving Birth To The Goddess – All young men require an official introduction to the intuitive, psychic, and mysterious darkness of their inner beings. They need to learn how to surrender, how to listen closely to an inner voice, how to clarify their values, how to pray, how to seek vision, and how to prophesy. All young men must ask themselves such questions as: "To whom do I pray?" "Who are my sacred ancestors?" "What is my life story?" "Why was I born?" "Why will I die?" "Who are the true heroes and teachers of my life?" "What gifts have I been blessed with?" "Who are my people?" Above all, young men must confront and ponder the meaning of death. Time spent with death will make an inward space in them, and the goddess will be born and live within this death space. Her presence will enrich his appreciation of life and enable him to face the justice of his own death.

A Model For A Rite Of Passage

Applying these elements and more, I have created a model for a modern male rite of passage. What follows is a somewhat detailed description of that model.

The boys who are candidates for passage into manhood formally begin the severance phase one week after their graduation from high school. They will leave their childhood homes and family behind and assemble with older elders and midwives of the community at a retreat in a secluded, natural place. There they will remain for nearly one month, or one cycle of the moon, during which time they will enact the rite of passage into manhood. During this month they are gathered, the young men will not be allowed to leave. The area will be sealed off and consecrated for the purpose of the rite. No drugs, alcohol, or non-participants will be allowed.

Severance: The End Of Boyhood – The severance phase will last approximately 20 days. It ends when each initiate crosses the threshold and undertakes the ordeal of the second phase. During the time of preparation, the candidates and the older men will live together in large tents or yurts in groups of 25 (20 candidates, 5 midwives). All work and cooking will be shared on a communal basis among the men. Each group is led through a disciplined routine of daily activities and classes by the five elders appointed for that purpose.

Throughout the ceremony, from end to beginning, each midwife will be responsible for the welfare of four candidates. His role is to facilitate their passage through the three phases of the ceremony, to personify the Mentor function to them, to aid them in giving birth to the goddess. He acts as surrogate uncle, teacher, counselor, wilderness guide, vocational guidance counselor, personal friend, or superior officer, according to what is needed at the moment.

The curriculum for each group includes the following:

*Activities related to the natural environment and self-orientation within it: solo or group medicine walks, night hikes, environmental awareness studies, "survival" activities, and individual seclusion in a natural place at least once a day.

*Activities related to the use of the intuitive or "feeling" facilities: Instruction in self-hypnosis, meditation, communication with other species, listening to the "inner voice," praying, and other "goddess" processes.

*Physical education, with emphasis on cooperation, leadership, self-discipline, concensus democracy; ropes and obstacle courses, relay races, and other activities involving group problem solving.

*Sexual education, from the mechanics of "how to" and contraception to broader issues of relationship, including marriage and fatherhood; films, other audiovisual aids, frank discussions of ethics and manners involving women elders as co-facilitators.

*Spiritual education, with emphasis on individual religious expression: personal values, ethics, and morality, storytelling, myths, discussions regarding death, afterlife, life destiny, and personal ancestry.

*Preparation on an individual basis for incorporation as a man: the setting of goals and priorities, vocational counseling, clarification of personal ambitions regarding profession, and other concrete particulars involving life on the physical plane as a man.

*Ceremonies of togetherness and preparation: saunas, sweatlodges, communal bathing, or other activities involving self-purification.

*Activities related to preparation for the threshold trial itself.

On the eve of the threshold trial, all the candidates and midwives will assemble together, and a celebration of the end of boyhood will be held. At that time, each candidate will be given an opportunity to symbolically enact his severance from childhood. Then the individual groups of 20 will reassemble with their midwives and embark on their several journeys to remote, secluded areas where the threshold trial will be enacted. The following morning, the trial begins.

Threshold: Passage Through The Goddess – Each candidate is removed from human contact. With just the barest essentials requisite to his survival, he will live alone in a wild, natural place for four days and nights. Though water will be provided during this time, he will otherwise ingest neither food nor any other kind of sustenance, relying instead on the beneficence of Mother Earth to protect, nurture and teach him. Depending on the advice of midwives, he may or may not undertake certain ceremonial activities during his time alone to heighten his receptivity to nature, the goddess, and the spirits or deities he worships. But the basic elements of trial – aloneness, fasting, and exposure – must be preserved in as pure a state as possible.

The threshold trial must be designed with an eye to harmony and balance. The idea is not to make the candidate suffer unduly for the sake of a "vision." What really matters is whether or not each candidate stands ready, with a pure heart, to receive impressions from his experience. Within the limitation of his fast and his environment, each candidate should feel free to express himself as he desires, to investigate the many dimensions of his image as reflected by the natural setting. He may spend his time walking, sitting, meditating, sleeping, dreaming, praying, crying for a vision, writing in a journal, talking with the stones or the wind. Regardless of what he does, he will learn to yield, to be patient, to watch himself, to look within, and to listen to the voice of the goddess.

The allegorical nature of the trial must be clear to each candidate. He is enacting a "story" with a mortal/immortal meaning whose main protagonist is both human and divine. The protagonist lives out the plot of the story in an environment having two levels of meaning. The goddess is both nature and his own anima. Fear is both a monster and an opportunity. A dream is both dream and divine visitation. Absence from the company of others is also presence with their spirits. Signs or messages appear in this natural/sacred world, carrying the same double meanings. An animal is both an animal and a spirit. A mountain is both a mountain and a god. A star is both a star and an angel. A mosquito is both a nuisance and a messenger. A sunrise is both a sunrise and a birth.

The midwives should employ effective means to insure the safety of their charges while they are alone. A system of daily checks called the "buddy system," whereby their safety is ascertained (without their solitude being intruded upon) can be effectively used. Provisions must also be made for the early return of candidates to basecamp should they become ill, suffer accident, or otherwise be unable to continue their lonely vigils. The early return of a candidate, for whatever reasons, must not be accounted shameful or a failure. Rather, he should be encouraged to come to an understanding of why he returned and what he learned from such an action. He must then be given another opportunity the following year to confirm his readiness by completing the passage.

Incorporation: The Birth Of A Man – The incorporation of a boy into manhood is not without its difficulties. Birthing is accompanied by powerful contractions and much inner conflict. The new man meets, and takes on, the consequences of his boyhood life; he finds out whether or not he learned his lessons well. His return from the threshold is a delicate matter not to be treated lightly by the male elders. Now he is back in the "secular world" of his everyday body, and his life as a man stretches before him.

The confusion and bewilderment of the incorporation phase (especially in its initial stages) can be mitigated by the preparedness of the elders and their careful, ceremonial attention to the re-entry process. Each candidate's spirit must be brought back into his body and aided to reside there solidly. Each candidate must be debriefed and helped to see the meaning of his threshold experience. Each must be formally welcomed and recognized as a man, brought into the group of men, and given a symbolic gift by his midwives. Then a sauna, sweatlodge, or bathing ceremony can be held, at which time the dust of the threshold world can be flushed from the new men's bodies and prayers said in thanksgiving for their well-being. After the ablutions might come new clothes befitting a man, a feast of thanksgiving, and a time of giving. Afterwards, a council of elders may be convened, and the young men brought in one by one to answer the elder's questions regarding their threshold experience. The elders can offer comments and suggestions regarding the young man's future course, personal gifts, life story, etc., in a positive, supportive manner. Within the first two days of their re-entry, the young men must also be given a good deal of time to be alone, to rest, and to reflect on their encounter with the goddess.

On the third day after their return, the separate groups will reassemble at the place where the severance phase was basecamped, for a mutual celebration of their brotherhood, to formally mark the conclusion of the rite of passage. Soon after, the gathering will pack up and return to the community. There, a final celebration of commencement into manhood will be held for the new men and all those who had a hand in their childhood growth. The parents can be singled out for special honors for their untiring efforts on behalf of their sons and the community at large.

Beginning A New Life

When the ceremonies and congratulations are over, the new men will enter the mainstream of adult male life. They live apart, independent from home, working for their bread, attending college, enlisting in the armed services, getting married, etc. They do not return to their boyhood living situation unless, for unusual reasons, they cannot do otherwise. If they must return to their old home, they must henceforth be treated as adults, and adult behavior and attitudes must be expected from them. As the new men grow older and themselves become fathers, they will return to participate as midwives in the births of other men.

Within a week or two of the rite's conclusion, most of the candidates will experience a predictable depression, a period of integration when the enormity of the step taken becomes apparent. The new man may feel like forgetting about all this manhood nonsense and wish fervently he could be back home in his childhood nest. Such feelings should not be seen as a setback, but as a challenge. For most new men, this depression strengthens their ability and resolve to live as men. Within a few weeks of their return, each group of candidates might plan a reunion meeting with their midwives to discuss their progress in their new lives. Further support meetings might be scheduled by those in the group who feel a further need for them. The emphasis on such meetings would not be on problem solving, but on sharing, friendship and brotherhood. As time passes, the new men should be weaned away from the glory and hoop-la of the rite of passage ceremony and cleave to the goddess and to their "people," those who, as men, they are committed to serve with the give-away of their lives:

> *Now you belong to your greater mother. And you return to her womb to emerge once again, as a man who knows himself not as an individual but a unit of his tribe and a part of all life which ever surrounds him.*

Frank Waters, *The Man Who Killed The Deer* **[64]**

Becoming-Man
Colin Ingram

The spot on which he sat, a spot that he himself had chosen, was at the edge of a small plateau, surrounded on three sides by towering granite peaks and, on a fourth, by a long downward slope that ended in a valley 4,000 feet below. The night in the high desert was cold and dry and brilliantly clear. This was his third night.

Michael had hiked on high mountain trails before and when he was younger he had been to several scout camps. But he had never been alone before, certainly not alone in the wilderness. Michael had recently turned sixteen and, like his young peers, his life prior to this quest had consisted of a constant search for stimulation. Now, deeply isolated in the Ventana Wilderness near the California coastal area known as Big Sur, he had nothing but himself. Nothing to do but feel the pangs from his empty belly, listen to his thoughts and to witness the excruciatingly slow passage of time through the night.

Michael was one of four teenage boys on this week-long quest. They were accompanied by four "uncles" – highly regarded men who had assumed the responsibility for guiding the boys through their rite of passage into manhood. Now, on the third night of his vigil, Michael had ample time to reflect on the words of the uncles.

The purpose of the quest, the uncles had said, was for each boy to become acquainted with his own inner self. They suggested that from that experience a lasting confidence would be gained, based on self-control and self-mastery. Words like "self-control" and "inner self" hadn't meant much to him then, Michael recalled. They were grownups' words, and he had lots of other, more important things on his mind. Like baseball and his girlfriend, Nikki, and the stupid pimples on his face and finding the money to replace the burnt valve in his 1984 Camaro. And the very important fact that now he was alone and hungry in the wilderness, his only supplies some drinking water and an insulated blanket.

First it had been stiffness and sore joints. Worse than that was the itching. It seemed to Michael as though he had spent the first three days and two nights scratching. Then there was hunger – real hunger. This was a new experience for him. Before this week, Michael's desire for food had always been just that – a desire for food that could either be satisfied or temporarily overlooked while he played another game of basketball. But on the second day of his vigil, Michael's body began sending him clear signals that it wanted sustenance, and it was a continuing struggle not to leap up and hike the four-mile trail back to camp and a hot dinner. A dozen times he almost quit. All that day he visualized giant platters of french fries, smothered with ketchup and followed by rows of hot fudge sundaes.

Other thoughts began to intrude upon his awareness. Unpleasant scenes, replaying over and over. Like when he missed his foul shot in the semi-finals when the game was tied 76-76, and the whole crowd booed him off the floor. And, oh geez, that day Nikki's family had invited him for a day of sailing and he had gotten sick and barfed on the polished teak deck in front of them all.

By the third day of the vigil, Michael thought he had relived every embarrassing moment of his life, and every stupid and every cruel thing he had ever done. These painful scenes finally seemed to diminish and, on the afternoon of the third day, he began experiencing something different. It was a strange kind of lightheadedness – followed by . . . how could he put it . . . a feeling that began as calmness but increased in intensity until all of his thoughts – his jumbled, racing thoughts – slowed and then ceased. In this quiet space a window opened. Michael peered through it.

On the other side was a view that was a feeling rather than a scene. The feeling was like sitting in a pool of deliciously warm water, and the water was alive with knowledge and benevolence.

In that quietness, in that glow of communion, a sixteen-year-old boy understood, for the first time, that the world was a friend and not an adversary.

At long, long last, the vigil ended, and the Michael who returned to the camp was not the same Michael who had left it. There was a serenity in his eyes, and a confidence in his step and in his voice. The uncles saw it and, in the discussions that followed, they said he had stepped across an invisible boundary . . . a boundary of knowing that could never be undone.

There were hours of lively discussions with the uncles and the other boys. Michael could not even recall all the topics, but they were things like: How important are possessions? What does it mean to be a real friend? How valuable are the traits of loyalty, of tolerance and of forgiveness, and should they have limits? Are there universal ethics? What are the important goals in life, and how did each boy's past behavior compare with his professed values? In a remote and beautiful wilderness, four teenage boys and four men wrestled with concepts that have frustrated and, at the same time, enlivened the human race since its inception.

As the week unfolded, the boys alternately cracked up with laughter, or were elated or embarrassed. During the discussions on sexuality, like most adolescents they covered their embarrassment and ignorance with wisecracks – or at least they did so until it became obvious to everyone how much they didn't know. The uncles were great. They could tell and enjoy the raunchiest of jokes and at the same time, they were capable of the most delicate tact in dealing with the boys' tender feelings. The boys felt safe with them. During one talk, Michael admitted to being a virgin and that he was scared he didn't know how to "do it" properly. There was no derision. His honesty was respected and his fear was addressed. The uncles told Michael that the most important aspect of the act of love is the intent to give as well as receive. They instilled in him the sense that his urge and his strength and his seed are necessary male components of a beautiful sacrament. A sacrament to be thoughtfully entered, respected and relished.

Michael especially liked the last days of the quest, which were devoted to a celebration of maleness. It was like a decathlon except that there were dozens of events and no losers. Feats of strength and agility were balanced by challenges of precision and delicacy, like when the boys, as a team, had to thread one hundred sewing needles within five minutes. Finesse, grace, balance and careful judgement were shown to be an integral part of masculinity. And the uncles demonstrated, through their own prowess, that male strength and determination were magnificent characteristics, not something to be repressed.

For boys there is a time of life when their growing souls must be nourished by challenges and adventure, just as their growing bodies must be nourished by food. Near the end of the week, Michael had a chance to prove his mettle. The whole group had hiked a series of switchbacks through a narrow canyon and it was now near dusk, with two miles remaining on the trail back to camp. They were hiking along a fast-moving river and had come to a place where the river narrowed and deepened. A waterfall, cascading from above, doused all of them with a fine spray. Michael's sharp eyes spotted a possible river crossing that would save them half of their trek. He knew he could do it, and without a word, Michael jumped from the river bank and landed precariously on a rock under the plunging water. He wavered against the onrushing water and the slippery, algae-coated surface of the rock and, for a moment, it was close. But he kept his balance and braced himself with one arm against a sheer rock wall. With icy water pouring down on him, Michael held out his other arm and shouted, "Come on!". One by one, he helped each of the others leap safely across. One of the uncles was last to cross, and when he had reached the other side he held out his arm to provide a handhold for Michael. Michael jumped, grabbed his arm and slithered up the opposite bank to safety. No one scolded him for a reckless act. He had calculated and he had been right, and they all recognized that. It was reward enough when one of the uncles said to him, "That was really something, Michael. I couldn't have done it myself."

The boys' guides called themselves uncles deliberately. This was meant to foster close bonds and, at the same time, bring necessary objectivity to their teaching that fathers do not have with their own sons. The uncles weren't father-surrogates – no one can take the place of a dad – but for the boys, they were the personification of strong and effective manhood. Part of their purpose was to demonstrate that male strength does not mean brutishness. And so they took pains to demonstrate empathy and compassion, grace and beauty, and tolerance and patience. The stronger among them helped the weaker, and the faster aided the slower. Everyone contributed to the success of the endeavor and there was simply no need to keep score.

The ruggedness and beauty of the Ventana Wilderness Area made a profound impression on the boys. On the last day there was a solemn ritual, welcoming each boy to the brotherhood of men. It included prayer, each boy in his own way, and was meant to instill a sense of wonder of the Creation and a respect for all of its creatures. And it further cemented the bonds of friendship between them.

Of the four boys who took part in the rite of passage, Michael and Josh were sixteen, Jaime was fifteen and Kurt was seventeen. Each of them had asked for the privilege of participating. They had done this when they felt ready – there was no pressure on them or any other boy to do so, and no boy was ever thought less of if he did not come at all. None of these boys failed this rite of passage, nor do any other boys who undertake it. A rite of passage is more a celebration than a test, and no one, neither the boys themselves or the uncles, know for sure how far any individual has come and how far he has yet to go.

The quest that Michael completed was not the only rite of passage he had experienced. Previously, he had been confirmed, he had graduated from junior high and he had received honors at a scouting ceremony. But Michael's glowing face and newfound confidence suggested that something very special had occurred during his week in the wilderness – something he had never experienced before. Perhaps it was trials he had successfully undergone, and the new feeling of self-mastery that resulted. Maybe it was the bond he had formed with the earth. And a part of it must have been the male friendships and mutual trust that evolved.

Michael was lucky. Not all boys have such an opportunity, but all boys need a chance to set their male spirits free. At the end of the week, when Michael departed for home, he felt that freedom, and it cried out within him, "I am a man!". And he felt the exultance of his great strength. Who among us men has not rejoiced in that strength, or longed for it when we did not have it? And who among us has always used it well? Michael felt his new strength, and with it came the sobering knowledge that he would spend the rest of his life learning to use it wisely.

Spiritual Warrior
Joseph Jastrab

Creating connections to positive masculinity

"The world needs a man's heart . . ." The words echoed down through the desert canyon walls, dropping like so many pebbles into the quiet pools of my evening's meditation. I was fully engaged that Summer Solstice eve with a group of datura in full bloom. Their trumpeting, ghostly white blossoms seemed to be enjoying a secret courtship with the moon rising in her fullness. I had come to these plants, to the moon, to seek counsel, intent on learning more of the ways of Earth Mother. I had come with a wounded heart disguised in the question, "How might I better serve the planet?" Again and again, just the echoing words, "The world needs a man's heart." My first reaction was to try to whisk the words away as I would attempt to blow out a burning ember. Of course, the harder one blows, the brighter the ember. At the time, such counsel seemed out of place, as I was expecting an initiation of another sort. Like many wounded and searching men of my generation, I believed that my personal and planetary salvation lay entirely within the cultivation of the inner feminine. The Earth, in her compassionate wisdom, threw me back on myself that night. "If you wish to serve me, forgive . . . forgive your heart to me . . . your *man's* heart. It all starts with forgiveness."

(from Joseph's journal)

Wingspan: Joseph, can you give us some of the context of this experience? Were you questing alone, or with a group?

Joseph: I was a member of a group of about 35 men and women who responded to a call put out by Elizabeth Cogburn. Elizabeth is the chief choreographer, shaman, and vision-keeper of the New Song Ceremonial Community. We had come together in the canyon lands of Utah for two weeks during the Summer Solstice of 1981 to participate in the New Song Sun Dance Ceremonial. Part of our time together was devoted to separate men's and women's lodges, where we worked to understand and embody male energy and female energy and sought to create life-affirming ways to bring these energies together in balance. I honor Elizabeth for creating a context which encouraged a radically new look at what it means to be a man, what it means to be a woman, and what it means to be in a relationship with a fully-empowered "other."

The experience from the journal excerpt happened one night when I left our camp to sit alone. It was such a set-up! I was surrounded by images of the feminine: the full moon, night-blooming datura, the womb-like canyon, a powerful woman as our community leader.

Wingspan: It almost sounds like your deeper masculine side was evoked to meet the feminine energies present.

Joseph: It was either that or choose to remain a little boy in relation to a powerful mommy – a relatively secure position, but very boring after a while, for both parties. Basically, I was put on notice that it was time for me to grow up. I use the term "Earth Mother" advisedly in that description. That's who I was seeking at the time, and for an early phase of development, that's fine. Now I heard the Earth saying, "Please, haven't we had enough of this 'mother' business?"

If I relate to the Earth as "Mother Earth," then the highest relationship I can have is to be a "good little boy," and I am blind to the possibilities of relating to the Goddess. As Goddess energy is awakened in a man, the deeper aspects of his masculine side, or God nature, are likewise stimulated.

Wingspan: I am aware that you credit that canyon experience with being the origin of the Men's Quest. How did you bring this experience home, and how did it relate to the work you do now with men?

Joseph: Well, walking in the everyday, business-as-usual world with the seed of a new vision is rarely easy. And this certainly was a case in point. I returned home with great enthusiasm but few words. My trying to rationally understand or verbally communicate the experience always seemed to trivialize it. I brought the vision to the personal therapy I was engaged in. There was an initial stirring of energy that promised germination, but that soon fizzled, and once again I was left carrying just a seed of possibility.

I spoke with individual friends most receptive to processing the inner life – mostly women at the time. I received much encouragement from each of them but still felt incomplete. I kept asking myself the question, "How do I nurture this seed?" It seems so obvious to me now, but at the time, I was a man blind to the most natural source of support for my quest. It eventually dawned within me that the encouragement of the potential of my canyon experience required a larger context, a group context. But not just any group: a group of men. And I thought, "God help me!"

At that time, I had little regard for men as co-travelers, except in the realm of sports and idea polishing. Women seemed to be the ones who could draw the best out of me. I was involved, along with many of my brothers, in trying to open my heart by cutting off my balls (or at least pretending they weren't there).

But what a revelation, to consider for the first time the possibility that men, indeed the masculine principle, might carry a healing, nurturing aspect of its own! I opened to the possibility that my search for wholeness as a man had led me into a box canyon which allowed only the narrow vision that all of the evil in the world was due to masculine qualities of perception and action. You know, the all-too-familiar notion that "Men create war, men create poverty, men create pollution, etc." and the distorted indictment of the entire masculine principle that grows from that. I realized that, while many men and women were looking to the Great Mother for salvation, nobody I knew was seeking to embody the Great Father. In fact, at the time, I hadn't heard of such a thing as the Great Father. Imagine what it means to be a 31-year-old man in our culture. We all seemed to be reacting against the "terrible father," the one who fathers reason cut off from love, truth hardened into static form, law and order void of compassion.

Wingspan: Wasn't it the role of the elder males in traditional cultures to introduce the younger males to the positive ways of manhood?

Joseph: It certainly was, and still is in some parts of the world. Yet, for most men in our culture and generation, such initiation is haphazard at best. The father is away from the home much of the time; the mother is the predominant force in our lives. Men can't get very far by using their mothers as role models, except to attempt to be not like them. It's difficult to grow up with a positive self-image when all you have to go on is a sense of who you can't be like. That's like trying to get somewhere by backing away from what you don't want. No wonder we stumble!

Occasionally we turn around, face forward, and in the absence of positive male role models, we face nothing; that's scary. Every so often, into that vacuum comes crashing a figure like Rambo. The young boys of today are so hungry for a male model. With dad gone, you can't blame them for latching onto figures like Rambo.

Wingspan: Getting back to the process of creating the Men's Quest, after you opened to the value of being together with men, what moved you to act on that?

Joseph: The most important single event was Keith Thompson's *New Age* magazine interview with Robert Bly, entitled "What Men Really Want," in the Spring of 1982. I read it and the world stopped for a moment. It was more than just reading an article; Bly put words to the instinctual call to a truly heroic and vital manhood that was seeded in me the summer before. It was as if Bly had written a personal letter to me. But this, of course, is the gift of the poet: to give voice to the pulsebeat of creation in such a way that we hear our own voice speaking as we read the poem. Something came through Bly's words that provided the act of confirmation for my vision seed. It was if all the elder males of my tribe encircled me, gave their blood for me to drink, and said "Go for it!" And feeling the ground confirmed beneath my feet, I was encouraged to take my next step in growing my vision.

Wingspan: Which was . . .?

Joseph: At the time, I was guiding Vision Quests for mixed groups of men and women. It was a natural step to then put out the call for an all-male Quest. I remember the mix of enthusiasm and terror that accompanied that act. It was clear that the only way I could "guide" a men's Vision Quest would be as a full participant. I would be coming with as much ignorance about what it meant to be a man as anyone else. And none of us had any idea where this thing was headed. We all stood pretty naked, gawking at each other. Yet, I trusted that there was fertile soil for our questions and stories that longed to take root.

Wingspan: What happened in those early Men's Quests that you now remember as significant?

Joseph: I remember an early perception that each man came to the Quest as a "seed", a seed carrying medicine that could heal both itself and the planet. And I remember being shocked at the depth of suffering within men. The most censored, most ignored story of our times is the story of men's suffering. Until that story is fully told by men and heard by both men and women, the medicine contained within a man's "seed" will be forever impotent. But it is precisely the tears released as the story is told and witnessed that moisten the hard seed coat, initiating that rooting into the Earth; that is an act of love, an act of courage.

We began to open our hearts to both our joy and our suffering, and further, to the beauty and suffering of our planet. And through this we began to understand what courage was really about. Gaia (the Earth) is calling for her spiritual warriors now, perhaps more than ever. She is calling for warriors who are courageous lovers as well as courageous hunters. I find that men who are open to their suffering make better warriors. And better lovers. That is where the counsel on forgiveness from my canyon vision comes in.

I noticed during the early Quests that most men were attracted to the warrior image and came with an inner list of criteria for being a warrior. These lists generally included such qualities as commitment, courage, strength, discipline, etc. The warrior archtype awakens me to a more fully embodied life of service and action. It helps me focus strong, primal male energy towards service to one's people. And one thing is for certain: to follow the warrior's path necessarily means that one will repeatedly fall flat on one's face, short of the ideal.

For me, the warrior's way is about doing whatever it takes to live life at the highest level of integrity. There has always been risk involved in that, and likely there always will be. Without forgiveness, the highest ideals of the warrior's way remain ideals at best and severe reminders of one's inadequacies at worst. We men must come to forgive those aspects of ourselves, our brothers, fathers, grandfathers, generations of grandfathers that have fearfully denied life. This forgiving is the give-away of renewed life. And this renewal must begin at home before it can expand to embrace the Earth. I see this beginning to happen.

Wingspan: Tell us about your use of the term "warrior."

Joseph: I use the term "warrior," or even "spiritual warrior," and I know many men feel both a strong "Yes!" reponse and a strong "No!" response. Some feel there is something regressive and barbaric about the image of the warrior that might keep us stuck in an old story that isn't working. Well, there certainly have been men who have called themselves "warriors" whom I would consider barbaric. But let's explore those two responses. Where does that strong "Yes" come from? Perhaps it's the excitement, the adventure of the warrior that we're drawn to, that part of us that feels fully alive when we have a mission in life, a sense of purpose and commitment.

And what in us says "No" to identification with the warrior? Perhaps we react to images of destruction, blood-lust, war, and violence that arise. We fear that the term "warrior" might somehow tend to validate these images.

Let me say at the outset I am not encouraging wholesale acceptance of the warrior identification for men of service and action. I use the term "warrior" because it is a transformer for me, now. It reveals to me those aspects of myself that are destructive and war-like. So this play with the "spiritual warrior" image has catalyzed an awareness of the war that goes on inside of me between, let's say, sub-personalities engaged in a win/lose conflict. For example, I have a couple of inner characters I call "Striver" and "Layback." Striver says "Go, go, go!" and Layback's motto is "*Manana*, tomorrow." Needless to say, these two are often at odds with each other. They each feel that their freedom can be met by wiping out the other. They create a win/lose game built around fear and distrust, which is essentially war. I find close parallels in the tensions between the U.S. and the U.S.S.R. I don't think war would be the most popular world game if it were not the most popular inner game as well.

So, I can personally relate to anyone's yes/no reaction to the warrior image, knowing that both sides live within me. It's helped me come clean with myself to acknowledge that war is not just somebody else's problem.

Wingspan: What would you say is the difference between what you call the "new warrior" or the "spiritual warrior" and the warrior of the past?

Joseph: I would say both share qualities of aliveness, courage, and committed action, but they are dedicated to different purposes. The old warrior still believes in the win/lose game, and he dedicates himself to protecting the life and values of a particular ideology or nation. The new warrior's allegiance is to the whole planet and to the whole self. And I imagine that the battleground of the self is a well-traveled territory for the new warrior. I think another important aspect in our imaging the new warrior is this: the new warrior has a very inclusive definition of his or her "people." This warrior's people include, as the Lakota would say, "the flying people, swimming people, tall-standing tree people, four-leggeds" and the rest of creation, as well as the "two-leggeds."

There is a world war going on at this present moment that rarely gets recognized as such. It's the imperialistic violence of us two-leggeds against the other people of the Earth. I see the new warrior as one whose heart grieves for this loss of life and takes inward and outward action to show a way to peace. The spiritual warrior, I would say, is one who is not willing to substitute the kind of action that simply buffers one's heart against the suffering of the planet.

I'm thinking now of my many political protest acts during the 60's. On the surface, they appeared, at least to me, to be acts of healing service. But not far below the surface there was desperation, and now I see that many of those acts were done to resolve the tension and discomfort I felt when I really opened up to the suffering of Viet Nam. My grief tolerance was very low then, so many of my acts were a defense against feeling. And I think men generally have a more difficult time than women with simply being with suffering. When I hear "The world needs a man's heart," I sense that there is a healing that takes place for both men and the Earth simply by keeping our hearts open to the grief that pervades our planet now – just that. And our tendency to do, do, do all the time cuts us off, and the Earth off, from the nurturing presence of the male heart. Of course, it's not that doing is wrong. Yet, if action covers up or denies feeling, then the action has little potency.

I love the image Chogyam Trungpa offers to the warrior in his book *Shambhala*. He speaks of the "sad and tender heart of the warrior." You cannot be a warrior without a sad and tender heart, he says. That's beautiful; there's strength in that. Trungpa says that without the sad and tender heart, one's bravery is brittle like a china cup. You drop it and it shatters.

We're to call on the tenderness, the courage, that allows us to hold the Earth in our hearts – the whole Earth, not just the "nice" parts. Can you can feel the compassion that arises from carrying the whole Earth in your heart? It's a compassion that is enduring enough to inform all our actions, so that everything we do becomes "Earth-healing work." **[65]**

The Horned God

In closing, I leave you with an exquisite passage from Starhawk. For me, it serves as a beacon of the man I yearn and strive to be:

> *The image of the Horned God is radically different from any other image of masculinity in our culture. He is difficult to understand because he does not fit into any of the expected stereotypes. He is not the 'macho' male nor the reverse image of those who deliberately seek effeminacy. He is gentle, tender, and comforting, but He is also the Hunter. He is the Dying God, but his death is always in the service of the life force. He is untamed sexuality, but sexuality as a deep, holy, connecting power. He is the power of feeling and the image of what men could be if they were liberated from the constraints of patriarchal culture. The Horned God represents powerful male qualities that derive from deeper sources than the stereotypes and the violence and emotional crippling of men in our society. If Man would follow the*

Horned God's image, he would be free to be wild without being cruel, angry without being violent, sexual without being coercive, spiritual without being un-sexed, and able to truly love. For men, this God is the image of an inner power and of a potency that is more than merely sexual. He is the undivided Self in which mind is not split from body nor spirit from flesh. United, both can function at the peak of creative and emotional power. [66]

❈   ❈   ❈

One of the most meaningful things I've ever heard went something like this:

> *When it's all said and done,*
> *when you're lying upon your death bed*
> *looking back upon your life,*
> *the single most important question*
> *you'll ever ask yourself is;*
>
> *did I love well?*

I truly hope the journey we have shared through these many words, feelings and stories from the hearts of men have brought value to your life . . . and assisted you to receive and love well.

With love,
Yevrah Ornstein

For more information about
The Men's Journal
write:
PO Box 545
Woodacre, CA 94973

Out beyond ideas of
wrongdoing and rightdoing,
there is a field, I'll
meet you there . . .

Rumi

Footnotes

1. The Grief of Parenting, Maxwell Reif, *The Men's Journal*, Spring 1987.

2. *The Prophet*, Kahlil Gibran, Alfred A. Knopf, New York, 1923.

3. The Wimp Conspiracy or Where's The Beef?, Yevrah Ornstein, *The Men's Journal*, Winter 1984/85.

4. *You Can't Have Everything,* Letter To A Dead Dad, University of Pittsburgh Press, 127 North Bellefield Avenue, Pittsburgh, PA 15260, 1975.

5. Letter to a 16-Year-Old, William Harrison, *The Men's Journal*, Summer 1985.

6. Mine Died, Warner Jepson, *The Men's Journal*, Summer 1985.

7. *Selected Poems of Rainer Maria Rilke – A Translation from the German & Commentary*, Robert Bly, Harper & Row, NY, 1981.

8. *The Prince of Tides*, Pat Conroy, Houghton Mifflin, Boston, 1986, page 421.

9. Men's Bodies – An Intimate View, Patrick Reilly, *The Men's Journal*, Spring 1985.

10. Face To Face, Frank D. Cardelle, *The Men's Journal*, Winter 1985/86.

11. Lessons My Father Taught Me, Stephen Barlas, *The Men's Journal*, Fall 1986.

12. Locker Room Memories, Andrew Hidas, *The Men's Journal*, Winter 1985/86.

13. The Way of the Lodge, Keith Thompson, *The Men's Journal*, Spring 1987.

14. Beyond The Place Where There Is Time, Yevrah Ornstein, *The Men's Journal*, August 1984.

15. No One Told Me, Robert F. Anderson, *The Men's Journal*, Summer 1985.

16. *Journey To Brotherhood – Awakening and Healing Men's Hearts*, Frank D. Cardelle, Gardner Press, NY, 1988.

17. Your Fathers, Maxwell Reif, *The Men's Journal*, Summer 1986.

18. Fathers and Sons, Shepherd Bliss, *The Men's Journal*, Spring 1985.

19. Why Men Are So "Crazy," Stan Dale, *The Men's Journal*, Winter 1984/85.

20. On Manhood, Yevrah Ornstein, *The Men's Journal*, Winter 1984/85.

21. *The Individual and the Nature of Mass Events*, Jane Roberts, Prentice Hall, NJ, 1981.

22. *The Nature of the Psyche: It's Human Expression*, Jane Roberts, Prentice Hall, NJ, 1979, page 77.

23. Ibid, page 58.

24. *Seth Speaks*, Jane Roberts, Prentice Hall, NJ, 1972, page 350.

25. Ibid, page 352.

26. *Unknown Reality, Volume II*, Jane Roberts, Prentice Hall, NJ, 1979, pages 316-319.

27. Ibid, pages 681-682.

28. *Baby In A Pouch*, Leah Wallach, Omni Publications International, July 1986, 1965 Broadway, NY, 10023-5965.

29. Alex Marshall, *The Men's Journal*, Winter 1986/87.

30. *Love*, Leo Buscaglia, Ballantine, NY, 1972.

31. Men and Massage, Dave Mueller, *The Men's Journal*, Summer 1987.

32. The Myth of the Dangerous Dad, Jed Diamond, 22 Salvador Way, San Rafael, CA 94903, 1988.

33. Masturbation: Touching One's Self Anew, David Goff, *The Men's Journal*, Fall 1985.

34. *Beneath This Calm Exterior*, David Steinberg, Red Alder Books, PO Box 2992, Santa Cruz, CA 95063 1982.

35. My First Condoms, Eric Small, *The Men's Journal*, Fall 1987.

36. *The Nature of the Psyche: Its Human Expression*, Jane Roberts, Prentice Hall, NJ, 1979.

37. *The Man In The Black Coat Turns*, Robert Bly, Penguin Books, NY, 1981.

38. The New Man: Limits and Possibilities, Jim Conlon, *The Men's Journal*, Winter 1986/87.

39. Pencil Stubs, Bill Roberson, *The Men's Journal*, Summer 1986.

40. *The Prince of Tides*, Pat Conroy, Houghton Mifflin, Boston, 1986, page 539.

41. Understanding Men, Sherman Burns, *The Men's Journal*, Spring 1985.

42. *He*, Robert Johnson, Harper and Row, NY, 1974, pages 26-27.

43. *What Men Really Want*, Keith Thompson & Robert Bly, Keith Thompson, PO Box 104, Aptos, CA 95003, 1982.

44. *The Bridge Across Forever*, Richard Bach, William Morrow & Co., NY, 1984.

45. Fathers and Sons, Shepherd Bliss, *The Men's Journal*, Summer 1985.

46. Fathers and Sons, Shepherd Bliss, *The Men's Journal*, Spring 1985.

47. Impotent Rage and the Myth of Attis, Jim Moyers, *The Men's Journal*, Summer 1986.

48. Encountering Rape: Not For Women Only, *The Men's Journal*, Winter 1985/86.

49. Tarzan Must Weep, Robert Masters, *The Men's Journal*, Summer 1985.

50. The Roots of Male Violence, Ian M. Harris, *The Men's Journal*, Fall 1987.

51. *The Prince of Tides*, Pat Conroy, Houghton Mifflin, Boston, 1986.

52. The New Man: Limits and Possibilities, Jim Conlon, *The Men's Journal*, Winter 1986/87.

53. Love Comes Quietly, Robert Creely, from *The Collected Poems of Robert Creely 1945-1975*, University of California Press, Berkeley and Los Angeles. © 1982 by The Regents of the University of California. p. 249.

54. *Journey To Brotherhood — Awakening and Healing Men's Hearts*, Frank D. Cardelle, Gardner Press, NY, 1988.

55. One Bullet Too Many, Mike Felker, *The Men's Journal*, Winter 1986/87.

56. Emotional Scars of War, John Macchietto, *The Men's Journal*, Winter 1985/86.

57. Fathers and Sons, Shepherd Bliss, *The Men's Journal*, Summer 1985.

58. Where Are The Fathers?, Robert Nixon, *The Men's Journal*, Fall 1985.

59. My Child's Heart, Steve Grubman, *The Men's Journal*, Winter 1985/86.

60. *The Birth of a Father*, Martin Greenberg, Avon, NY, 1985.

61. Hints and Guesses, Kent Hoffman, *The Men's Journal*, Fall 1985.

62. *Fathering, It's Not The Same*, Robert Sayers, 374 West Baltimore, Larkspur, CA 94939.

63. *Momo*, Michael Ende, Doubleday, Garden City, NY, 1984.

64. Toward An Adequate Rite of Passage Into Manhood, Steven Foster, Box 55, Big Pine, CA 93513.

65. Spiritual Warrior, Joseph Jastrab, *Wingspan*, Summer and Fall 1986, 405 Main Street, Wakefield, MA 01880.

66. *The Spiral Dance*, Starhawk, Harper & Row, NY, 1979.